ALLEN

A FIREFIGHTER'S JOURNEY THROUGH PTSD AND HEALING

KEITH HANKS

FOREWORD BY
ADAM DAVIS

PRAISE FOR "ALLEN"

"Keith has an incredible story and tells it in compelling fashion in Allen. With *First Responders in Crisis*, we were only able to tell part of what Keith's gone through, so it's gratifying that the rest of his story can be told."

COREY MOSS - PRODUCER/DIRECTOR
BOLD SOUL STUDIOS

"Brutally honest depiction of a man who endures repeated trauma from childhood, throughout his lifespan. As you read Keith's story, you walk with him on his life's journey of abuse, self-discovery and ultimately healing. As a first responder advocate, Keith's story, his strength, and hope, acts as a guide for other first responders who have experienced similar traumas and can find traumatic strength through shared experience."

LIZ WALKER - VP BUSINESS DEVELOPMENT
FORGE HEALTH

"I found Keith Hank's book both a combination of heartfelt pain and a journey of hope to overcome childhood trauma. His ability, within the words that come from his heart, capture the reader to experience a tidal wave of emotions. I recommend his book to gain insight for those who might be dealing with their own personal issues."

JEFF DILL - FOUNDER, FIREFIGHTER
BEHAVIORAL HEALTH ALLIANCE

"Keith's narrative embodies the essence of vulnerability, offering readers a poignant exploration of the intricate relationship between family history and mental health challenges. His deliberate attention to familial background serves as a crucial reminder of the profound impact our early experiences can have on our adult lives—a perspective often obscured by our own perceptions. Keith's unflinching honesty serves as a beacon of solidarity, reassuring others grappling with similar struggles that they are not alone. In graciously sharing his personal journey, he not only fosters empathy but also paves the way for collective healing. This book is a testament to the transformative power of open dialogue and shared experiences. Thank you, Keith, for courageously illuminating the path toward understanding and resilience."

DEANA BROWN MITCHELL - FOUNDER THE REALIZE FOUNDATION

"This is a raw, wrenching, and captivating memoir of persevering through family tragedies and the horrors that come with being a firefighter and EMT. Keith vividly captures the toll that PTSD and dissociative identity disorder takes on both a person and their loved ones. He shows the importance of tearing down the stiff upper lip culture that failed too many first responders after they witnessed the awful devastation of fires, natural disasters, health events, and human cruelty. Since almost every person will require the services of a first responder during their lifetime, we owe it to them to learn about their sacrifices. We then have an obligation to support these heroes and heroines. This book is a good way to start."

NATHANIEL ERSKINE, MD PHD UNC CHAPEL HILL PREVENTIVE MEDICINE

"My wife and I both read Keith's book. Myself as a 21 year Fire Lieutenant and her as a schoolteacher. It truly gave her a deep understanding of where we can go in this profession and the work it takes to come back from a major mental wellness setback! This book is riveting, transparent and raw from beginning to end. I can honestly say, you do not want it to end but you also want to gain the knowledge from a man that has been to the depths of low, to help save your own life. I wish I had this book in my hands in 2013 when I experienced the very worst of what life can throw at you as a First Responder. In my humble and personal opinion, this book needs to be placed in the hands of each and every recruit and their families as their loved one starts a career in emergency services."

RET. FIRE LIEUTENANT KENNY MITCHELL JR FOUNDER OF OPERATION YELLOW TAPE

Keith bares his soul with a raw vulnerability that will give anyone who is struggling with trauma the strength to carry on and know they are not alone. Keith's ability to overcome the staggering depth of trauma and shame that he carried for so long will inspire others to choose life and healing. Allen is a testament to what the human spirit can endure and overcome. If you are struggling with trauma or secrets causing you shame, this is a must-read.

CHRISTY WARREN AUTHOR OF *FLASH POINT: A FIREFIGHTER'S JOURNEY THROUGH PTSD*

"Mr. Hanks book tells a story that is too often experienced and too rarely discussed among our country's first responders. His poignant story should serve as a call to action to consider and enact the preventative and interventive efforts needed to help those who help us."

"There are no words. No words to convey a life of inescapable trauma and loss from the beginning. A life of resilience and strength. Overcoming what would, individually, break most. This rare story is an in depth description of a traumatic journey from a first-hand perspective to a remarkable ending of hope and fullness. Realistic, detailed, and relatable explanations of a how a child, a boy, and then a man dealt with the psychological processes most would describe as their worst nightmare. You will not receive insight like this from any university."

"I applaud Keith for being brave to tell his story from childhood trauma to becoming a firefighter and then an advocate for first responders mental health awareness. His bravery will inspire other first responders to know that sometimes rescuers need rescuing too!"

"I found the writing to be raw and thought provoking. It is not often we are pulled into the "closet" to witness frame by frame, the childhood trauma that forms the literal building blocks of the adults we become. I found myself committed to read chapter after chapter and feeling deep empathy for the child who needed to be shown love. This is a story of using years of pain, confusion, sadness and trying to survive, and turning it all into healing, strength and thriving. I found myself invested right from the beginning of the book."

CHIEF (RETIRED) DEBORAH PENDERGAST, BA, EFO MENTAL HEALTH AND WELLNESS COORDINATOR NH FIRE ACADEMY AND EMS

"A compelling story that is raw, emotional and no holds barred. From chapter to chapter, you will have perspective on an individual's traumatic journey from youth to adulthood that most do not have the courage to share. Keith peels back the curtain on his traumas and the toll that a public safety profession takes on first responders. Keith is an inspiration and example of resilience and strength for others. As a veteran and thirty plus year fire service professional I believe this book will go a long way to ending the stigma surrounding behavioral health in the first responder community."

BRIAN L. BORNEMAN FIRE CHIEF, US NAVY VETERAN

Robert Moody Jr.
June 22, 1990 – April 27, 2018
This book is dedicated to "Robbie" and others who fought the battle with their demons until the very end. He died by suicide at only 27. He was a son, a brother, a firefighter, and a friend to so many who were blessed to have experienced his kind and sincere presence.
Godspeed brother.
May we create a world free of the stigma on mental health.

CONTENTS

FOREWORD

"I'M HERE."
ADAM DAVIS

I sat on the set of *Good Morning America* during an interview in June 2023 when the host asked, "How has it changed your life?" Referring to faith.

My response was simple, unplanned, and unscripted:

"I'm here."

And you are too. You're reading this, you're still here. No matter the hell you've faced, no matter the pain you've endured, and no matter how many times you've wanted to quit, ***you are still here.***

Throughout the past nine years or so, I've had the opportunity to meet people who have impacted my life in ways words cannot accurately describe.

This is one of those encounters, although not in person.

Before I go any further, I'd like to preface this foreword with something you may be aware of.

We're all connected.

Somehow, someway.

Most of the time, however, it's the fine threads of pain that interweave our lives, building rapport faster than a baseball team or other hobbies could.

As a result, we often hide the messy parts of our lives. Why?

Why do we hide the most painful parts of ourselves when they could possibly be the very thing that connects us to another person?

Shame.

Shame is a learned behavior.

But pain is real, no matter the source, and while we are all connected by pain, we all respond to it in our own ways.

As I have crisscrossed this beautiful land sharing a message of hope, including my own deep pain, I have shared just that: we're all connected by pain, but we're also connected by healing and hope.

Keith Hanks has an incredible (understatement) story fit for the cinematic screens. It's one that will have you feeling every emotion possible, from anger to grief, rage, and joy.

Your gut will sink at times.

It may even take your breath.

That's okay.

When I wrote *Unconquered: Ten Principles to Overcome Adversity and Live Above Defeat* in 2022, I was asked to "dumb down" some of the stories I shared for fear that others would be offended by my pain.

Here's what I can offer you, the reader before you dive into *Allen*.

This book is a true story based on a real human experience by Keith Hanks.

It's messy. It's painful. But at the same time, it's all of our story. It's a pure reflection of what most of us try our hardest to hide from the rest of the world. You will read one page to the next, and the biggest hurdle you'll face is trying to find time to finish the book because you will not want to put it down.

Trauma is a word many want to ignore. Kind of like death or divorce.

Keith and I share some similarities; he was a firefighter, and I was a cop. But we both have been down the path of wanting and trying to end our lives. And we both are men who were victims of childhood sexual abuse.

When Keith asked me to write the foreword for his book, my first thought was whether I could do it justice. His book stands alone and needs no accolades from me. His life is one that, although riddled with deep pain, grief, trauma, and despair, reflects a beacon of hope for those who will seek it. It's like a literary version of the red lights flashing in the night and the sounds of the fire engine screaming as they run to your rescue. To get you from the fire, they must willingly walk into it. Keith is here. He's still here, and he's doing something with his pain, something that will have a positive impact on others.

There's not much I can guarantee in life, but I can guarantee you *Allen* will have a positive impact on lives. I am proud Keith Hanks is still here, through all the mess of his life, there is a shining beacon of hope, faith and love.

Adam Davis
www.TheAdamDavis.com

DISCLAIMER

This book addresses sensitive topics such as sexual abuse and suicidal thoughts. It's important to note that it is not a replacement for the advice of licensed therapists or physicians. For concerns related to your mental and physical health, it is recommended to regularly consult with a medical professional. In case you ever grapple with suicidal thoughts, reach out to the 988 Suicide and Crisis Lifeline for assistance.

CHAPTER 1
SMALL TOWN AMERICA

Every legacy has an origins story.

To truly tell an honest representation of my life you need to go back to World War 2. Long before myself or even my parents were a thought. A time before television, cell phones, Facebook, and other technological advances we take for granted and abuse these days. More importantly it's a time LONG before mental health was being addressed, especially the trauma component. Back then if you veered from the social norm with the way, you thought or how your brain functioned, you were wrapped up in a strait jacket, thrown in a "rubber room" and forgotten about.

And that's the mild version of how those with mental health issues were treated.

So, it's no surprise when Grampa Elliott and Grampa Hanks returned from service in the European and Pacific theaters, that they stayed tight lipped. None of what they or their brothers in arms saw was talked about and when the horrors of war and the atrocities of man caught up to them, it was termed "Shell Shock" or "Battle Fatigue". This would weigh heavy and eventually resurface in the form of anger, abuse, and alcoholism with both my grandfathers.

My father, Calvin Hanks, was the second born son in what would eventually be a group of three other brothers and a sister. Born just two years after the end of the Second World War, Cal, as he would later go by, was the black sheep of the family from the start. Born in Vermont, the family would move to Townsend Massachusetts while dear old dad was still a small child. A troublemaker and cast out by the rest of the tribe, my father would forge a fake license around age 15 and began driving tractor trailers for a living. A career that he continued for over 45 years. He had an average build and stood about five foot 11 inches and his hair apparently got scared of being on top of his head, as all he ever had was a ring just above ear level. Olive skin, of which on his face was almost always covered with either a thick beard or at least a mustache.

There are stories on both sides of the family tree of how my old man lived his early life into his twenties and most of them aren't the most flattering. With some of the activities he got wrapped up in as a truck driver, Cal would eventually find himself doing a bid in a state prison at a young age. During this two-year sentence, he "broke out" of prison for a short time only to be caught and served an extended stay. Or so the story goes.

My mother was the first born of four Elliott children and the only daughter. Nine years younger than my father, she was raised in Townsend as well, growing up in the West part of town. My grandmother hailed from Northern New York and had strong Native American roots along with French-Canadian. She and my grandfather eventually settled down in Townsend in the mid-fifties and started a family. My grandfather was a taller man at about six-foot with a slim build. With The War over a decade in the past, my mother's father carried a burden that likely started in his childhood, made worse by his time in the military. Drinking, domestic violence and abuse along with being an unreliable father and husband were some of his best traits. My mother herself was a taller woman at about five foot ten inches with a thicker build. Once the early 80's was a thing of the past, she always seemed to have her thin brown hair done in a perm which I always thought made her head look like a gumball machine.

My parents would end up meeting, the exact manner to which I've never been given the details to. It was always just said to be one of those older men love stories where my mother fell in love with the town badass. Given the tyrant my mother had grown up with as a father, it's not surprising that she fell for someone with Calvins resume. My mother's mother, my Nana, finally got sick of Grampa Elliott's shit, kicking him out of the family home a few years after my youngest uncle, Jack, was born in the late '60's. Before leaving my family a broken mess, riddled with years of trauma, self-doubt, and a new generation of angry individuals, my mother's father had served on the Townsend Fire Department. Something that many of his past relatives also did, dating back to around 1875.

Around 1977, my mother's oldest brother, Chucky joined the ranks of the same fire department. A year later, his 1-year younger brother, Eddie got on the department as well. The same year the blizzard of '78 hit New England with a force much like the finger of God. My parents stuck in the apartment with nowhere to go and nothing to do, I was conceived. A little over 9 months later, in early December I made my grand entrance into the world.

My birth is one riddled with rumors, manufactured feelings, and uncertainty. I'm told my actual due date was sometime in November but for "some reason" they forced my mother to carry me longer. The other story is that I was supposed to be twins. This part being based on a birth mark I carry on my chest. A traumatic birth that caused damage to my mother given my size as a newborn, another story. Regardless of what may be true or not, when I think back to some of my initial feelings and interpretations of the world, cold and emotionless run rampant. The part of the story that always remains the same is that almost immediately, my parents began having marital problems. The attraction and thrill that was rooted in a forbidden love, started to fall apart with me now around. Again, happy, and healthy relationships were not a strong trait of either side of my family, so this likely was already a doomed pairing.

A few years after my birth, my uncle Chucky would have an event in his life that many tried their hardest to keep a secret while he was working as a firefighter. Whatever horrors he had faced both at home and from the job, would eventually catch up to him and lead him down a dark path. Chucky's attempt at ending his life via hanging by a rope in one of the fire stations, became not only one of my family's deepest, darkest secrets, but that of the Townsend Fire Department's. Nothing was ever spoken of this, beyond little murmurings from time to time that would be quickly put to rest with the old "people never have anything nice to say" line.

Shortly after this suicide attempt, Chucky would meet a woman, and move to an area of upstate New York not far from his mother's birthplace. He would become disowned by my Nana for a long time, not showing his face till I was older. Chucky would end up having two children, a boy, and a girl, with this woman while living in New York. Not long into their lives, he would leave the situation for reasons that to this day, aren't 100% clear with no one really knowing the truth.

While all this was happening with Chucky, my parents were slowly becoming more and more distant with their love for one another. In my mother's case, she also began to disregard her ability to show her only child the love and affection he needed as a small child. By age four, my father wasn't around much and short of a bunch of pictures depicting the truth that he would spend time with me, I don't have many memories of him doing so. My mother would job hop from one entry level position to another, typically in manufacturing, to keep a roof over our heads and food on the table. While she was working as a nanny of sorts, for a wealthy family in a nearby town, she had put me in a private preschool down the road from this family's large house.

And this is where my story begins. One fateful afternoon while playing on a playground across the street from the preschool, I fell off the monkey bars, landing on my face. This event wouldn't likely register as abnormal had it not been for the almost two-inch nail that punctured my skull, immediately next to my right eye. Barely missing my eyeball, it also came within a centimeter of my brain, according to doctors. Within a few months I would have another fall while running around a brick fireplace at the family's house, splitting the back of my head open. Again, these situations are fairly common when you have kids as they take spills all the time. What set these moments aside for me was the cold and even callous way my mother handled them. My memory never registered any images or sensations of her being upset because she was scared for my well-being as most parents typically respond when their child gets hurt.

No. In fact there was a sense of inconvenience more than concern. I felt alone during these two early episodes of getting injured in a pretty serious manner as a very young child. A faint snapshot of me asking for daddy was answered with "Your daddy don't care that you're hurt." Of course, my father would come and go from our lives until I was a little over five years old. A night here, maybe a few hours on a Saturday there, me and his time was as infrequent and irregular as the love, affection, and compassion I was receiving from my mother. Once I was in kindergarten, Cal took off for the last time, leaving me with the angry and bitter other parent who then took it upon herself to remind me every chance she had, that my father left me. This was made worse by the comments that he never loved me, and never wanted me to be born, along with the blame for him leaving.

When you're five, an only child, poor, and already have a fractured family dynamic, having the responsibility placed on you for one parent leaving destroys several growing parts of your brain. The first is your sense of responsibility and the impact you can have on the world around you. The second, and possibly more important, is trust.

Now, it wasn't all doom and gloom, hate and discontent. My mother and the rest of the family that stuck around, did in fact try to raise me the best they could. Given the known family history of bad stuff, along with a whole bunch of unknown variables, my mother's side of the family tree made sure I went to school, had clothes, a roof over my head and food to eat. There just wasn't a lot of love and support in the way I would later discover from those in school, was customary in families at that time in the 1980's. I always felt a longing for more from my family. More hugs. More compassion. More caring. And a better sense of safety and security.

With my father gone, I spent most of my childhood days at Nana's house only a half mile from the apartment my mother and I lived in. We often didn't have enough money to have all three meals in our house, so to ensure that I ate, I was sent to my grandmother's house. The house where my mother and her three brothers were raised in what I was told was at times a 24/7 hell of uncertainty, anger, and drunken melees aimed at my grandmother, and all her children.

The house, that already held so many dark and horrible secrets, became more of a home than my actual one. I would go there for most dinners, every Sunday, after school along with most days off.

At this time in my life, my circle was small with regards to friends, and most if not all of them were girls. For whatever reason, I just didn't have any close males in my life that weren't relatives. I was awkward, scared, and unsure of not only myself but the world beyond that of my family and they were most definitely put on a pedestal in order of importance to others in my life. We kept to ourselves in these early years, short of occasional visits from Nana's two older sisters or a fellow firefighter or member of their family. There weren't a lot of smiles but at the same time, there wasn't a lot of yelling and screaming either.

It just always felt empty.

Growing up with a detached mother, two uncles who seldom showed emotion, and an old school grandmother that had lived with a nightmare of a husband, my childhood was odd to say the least. And I knew it was. In my own way, as kids often do, I made do with the lack of empathy and at times compassion that defined my family and grew to not expect it. What I was struggling with was an overwhelming sense of not feeling safe. Almost as if something really bad was lurking around the next corner, just waiting for me.

My Uncle Jack was just over ten years older than me and an "oopsie" baby according to the family lore. He grew up from around age 3 without his father in the picture, and looking back, Jack definitely had the occasional issues with anger. He was about six foot four inches in height with a slender build. Thick black hair, a lighter tone in his voice with an almost childish face, made Jack a more approachable person than his two older brothers. Not surprisingly, we grew up with a sort of brotherly relationship that centered around how we treated each other. This included learning how to piss off the other one quite well. But at the same time there was a love between us, that was unrivaled by any other male in my life. If I had to put a word to it, I'd say he was the first male I gave my trust to as a child not really sure what that meant given my father running out a few years earlier. Jack would be the first to break my trust and began what became a series of unwanted events that molded me into what I was destined to be as a man.

Before we get into that, let's get to know why Townsend was such a perfect postcard town in New England.

Located in Northern Middlesex County along the New Hampshire border, Townsend is a larger town, area-wise, at over 33 square miles. A population of around 7500 back when I was a kid with a moderate amount of commerce and retail throughout the center and eastern parts of the town. The town is divided into three sections, geographically. There's the center, or downtown portion that build off the intersections of route's 119 and 13. The eastern side of town is affectionately known as The Harbor, with the Harbor Pond being front and center off the intersections of route 119, South and Spaulding streets. The harbor boasted the larger percentage of the town's population with several residential developments come the late 70's into the 80's. The last part is the west side of town that is officially West Townsend. With its own zip code and at one-point separate post office, the west is the least populated and has almost no business or retail. There are two state forests and lots of woods with the Squannicook River running west to east through geographic center of town.

The one thing Townsend has a lot of is churches. Which is ironic given the amount of bad juju that runs rampant within its borders. My mother's family were all West Townsend natives, with my Nana's house being conveniently located diagonally from the fire station. Across the street from the fire station was the First Baptist Church. The fire station would become another home of sorts throughout my life as my uncles would spend a lot of time there and given its walking distance from Nana's, it was an easy hangout.

Shortly after my father left, around age five or six, my mother would take me to the Baptist church at the end of my grandmother's road for Sunday School. We were not a religious family in the traditional sense; however, we were God fearing, and using the lords name in vain typically got you a smack. Even at a very young age I could tell my family liked to pass off that they were religious and always did the right thing, acting in good faith towards others. Being a consistent attendee of church was short lived and I've retained no real memories of my time learning the children's version of the Good Book. My grandmother's house was adorned with a few God themed decorations included ivory light switch covers. These switch plates were handcrafted into the image of Jesus standing in the center, with his arms around two children to either side. They evoked a protective and love sort of image which at times my family would insist were their strongest qualities.

My grandmother's house, when I was a young child, was a very simple design. The ground floor had an entry way off the driveway which opened into what was once a three-season porch, now serving as an unofficial extension to the living room beyond.

Nana's bedroom was off the back corner of the living room and was extremely small. So small that the twin size bed, and two bureaus left little room for anything else, including a closet. An open area or walkway led from the living room and acted as a place for storage of various items over the years, including the toys, puzzles, and books that I would use while there. At the end of this walkway was the larger bedroom my uncles would sleep in, which was also just big enough for two full-size beds, two bureaus, a radio tower and nightstand. Outside of this bedroom was a short hall that had the basement stairs situated diagonally from my uncle's bedroom. At the bottom of these stairs was the kitchen and only bathroom. At this time around age 6, there was no operating shower in the house. Everyone took sponge baths via the kitchen sink. Off the backside of the kitchen was the field stone and dirt basement.

Plaster and lathe walls were hidden by outdated wallpaper with faded and cigarette-stained paint and draperies. During this time, my Nana, Uncle Eddie, and Jack all lived in the house they called home since the early 1960's. My grandmother and Eddie both smoked cigarettes, so there was an almost constant haze and an odor in the house. The house itself sat on about an acre of land with an old, unmaintained garage or shed, in the back left corner of the property. Truth be told, it was the worse looking house in the entire neighborhood back then. Later on, an addition would be put on with a kitchen and bathroom. Complete with a working shower!

My uncle's bedroom would become a place of secrets, pain, and even horror while at the same time, housing a sense of belonging and affection. I remember watching certain movies on the living room tv, that these days would likely be deemed inappropriate given my age, and wondering why I was being shown these things. Images of intimacy, naked women, lude acts between adults were a common occurrence when I was in the attendance of just my uncles and their friends. Interactions with Jack would later take place in this back bedroom, that I felt obligated to take part in. I had no say, I was helpless and unable to avoid the situations when they came up. Having seen certain acts being played out on the tv down the hall, and now being put in the position to partake in similar behaviors was as confusing and horrifying as it was an almost welcome form of affection.

My family had failed to show me the love and attention every child deserves up to that point, so when the opportunity arose to receive a form of this, I took it. Repeatedly I took it. Not knowing it was so wrong and destroying me inside as I just wanted to be loved. Time after time I would put myself in a position that led to being molested, abused, and eventually raped by not only Jack, but his brother and others in that cold, dark, back bedroom that served as my gateway to Hell. As unwanted and violating as it always was, there was a peace to being manipulated into acts of intimacy with the men in my life. I felt like I belonged to an exclusive club and the acts being committed upon me were just my dues. The others in this club seemed to enjoy the part I played in these events, but I was often warned not to speak of what we were doing.

When you're a young child, the way you develop a sense of right and wrong is obtained from the adults in your life. This is typically the role of the parents, however, with my father gone and my mother not doing a great job, the line was already blurred. These heinous acts I was being led into skewed my view of the world, and where what was right and wrong fell on the everyday. At times I was being physically hurt with what was being done to me, at the same time the attention and "love" I was receiving made it seem as if that was what was supposed to happen. Then to be told I couldn't tell anyone, especially mommy, about what was going on made differentiating right and wrong a handicap for years to come.

Then there are the frequent occurrences of my mother being in the bathroom at the same time as me. This was far past the time of potty training, and often included her being naked. My memory banks are plagued with images of my mother walking in on me whiling I was going to the bathroom or taking a bath or shower with no clothes on. What made matters worse is this freelance nudity also took place when I was brushing my teeth. The behavior would combine with my other abuse in the forms of nightmares I couldn't escape.

This destruction of my innocence in the form of performing sexual acts for those meant to keep me safe and protected did more than derange my concept of right and wrong. It established a stranglehold on how I experienced guilt and shame, often confusing the two not knowing any better. It created a form of loyalty to my family and the secret I was now cursed with. In a messed up and likely intentional side effect, I began to feel as if my family was the only thing that mattered in life and that because some of them were showing me love the way they were, I owed it to them to stick by their side. I even felt fortunate to be the "apple in their eye" and that every kid must experience what I was as the concept of this being evil and wrong, I could not grasp. Between the sexual abuse, rape, and mental warfare my mother was spewing, my awkwardness and inability to make friends took hold. This was only made worse by my constant fear of the thought of someone finding out.

I knew I was different, and not like the other kids in a lot of ways. My initial thought that most kids must be receiving the same kind of "love" from their family was quickly put to rest by the 1980's campaign to rid the world of child exploitation and sexual abuse. Be it a cartoon version of Spider-Man, or a group of characters from McDonald's, an effort to bring some attention to an apparent epidemic level problem was being pushed through different media. Whether it was on tv, in comic books, or material and conversations from teachers and staff at schools, the message of it "not being ok" for someone else to touch your body was beginning to be had.

This confused me further and led to an almost constant state of fear. It was at this point around early 1986 at age 7 that my mind began to bounce between fight or flight in a severely irregular manner. I perceived even the most minor event as a possible threat. Any chance or hint at a potential loss in my life was made into the end of the world. I would cling to those around as if my life depended on it while remaining completely unattached emotionally. I was at a pivotal age regarding the development of my brain and all it did, I could not handle the thought of what was being done to me as being so wrong. I internalized it, and kept it buried as deep as I possibly could. The problem was that the damage was already done, and the abuse wasn't over.

Around this same time, my mother felt I needed to start seeing a child therapist because of certain behavior I was exhibiting. This so-called rebellious and angry behavior was, in my mother's words, because her and my father had separated, and I was feeling the typical child guilt over the matter. Dr. Shout came into my life at a time in society when we were still sending mentally ill people to a locked hospital to be committed. The conversations we began having and the questions he was asking me, were a new experience that put me on high alert. Asking if I was safe at home, or if anyone in the family hurt me got a response rooted in lies and cover-ups.

The fact of the matter was that the entirety of the abuse, manipulation, and brainwashing that I was experiencing had me convinced that I didn't want to tell anyone the truth. Not saying I was fooling Dr. Shout with what I was giving him for answers, as I can look back on it all and know that I showed signs of abuse. There was an almost denial in my head that anything wrong was happening to me. It was too much to bear to think of what would happen to those around me if someone found out they were hurting me the way they were. If they were to be removed from my life then all forms of love, support and affection would be removed with them. Along with this came the conviction that if I told someone what was happening to me, it would be my fault.

Driving this last point even closer to what would be the truth was how often my mother made it apparent that my father leaving was because he didn't love me. Not being loved translated to not being loveable which to me then meant I had to take whatever form of love was being given. No matter how hurtful and damaging it may be.

My mother would have the occasional suitor that would result in a strange man sitting at our kitchen table typically after dinner time. Most of these gentlemen paid me no attention other than the small talk one exchanges with a kid that's not yours and means nothing to you other than a possible roadblock to intimacy with the woman you're there to see. In my own indirect way, I was trying to vet these guys in an effort to sniff out the next father figure. None of that happened of course and I was usually left lying in bed with a pillow over my head to not hear whatever was going on outside my room.

Late 1986, my uncle Jack would join the family tradition of firefighting when he turned 18. Our brotherly relationship with all its ups and downs had begun to morph in different and even unwanted ways as we both grew older. He had become increasingly angry and at times a bit of a bully towards me, especially when the occasional friend would be near. I had grown more confused about how relationships were supposed to work and had begun to lose hope that another man would step into the role of father. I also was starting to explore my body trying to understand what some of the sensations and feelings I was experiencing meant. At the same time, the activities at the secret club were changing. While most of the initial forms of sexual abuse were still taking place, I was also being put in a position of watching these acts take place.

This next period is where my brain gets mushy and full of holes.

In what can only be explained as an extremely dark time, the full details of the actual events are still unavailable to my conscious mind. My Uncle Eddie had busted his leg at work by falling out of an excavator and tearing all the ligaments in his knee. He was working as a heavy equipment operator with one of his close friends who also happened to be named Jack. We will refer to this Jack as Jack M.

Jack M ended up moving in with my mother in I after some sort of altercation got him kicked out of his living situation. At first having a man in my life that wasn't a relative seemed to provide some semblance of hope that maybe someone would step into the vacated spot of father. Very quickly though, him living with us was just awkward and even uncomfortable at times. His presence brought a smile to my mother's face seeing as Jack M was a good-looking guy in great shape. What was uncomfortable for me was that we didn't really have room for him in our apartment, and at no point was he putting any effort to establish a relationship with me. If anything, I felt ignored by him apart from the handful of times he made dinner. Overall, most of my memories involve him coming home late, usually after drinking, or working out with the small set of weights he had.

Shortly after Jack M moved in and while Eddie was out of work with an injured leg, further damage was done to what was left of my innocence. My brain has blocked out most of the horrible details that likely would have completely crippled my ability to exist in any socially acceptable way. Around the time of school vacation in February 1987, I was violated and raped repeatedly by several different men, my Uncle Eddie included. I have images of shadows, angry faces, and an overall sensation of being penetrated in such an evil and violent manner. Because of the previous molestation that I had endured, I told myself not to fight back, not to try and get away and that no one must ever find out. This last part was largely due to how much trouble I knew I would get into if I told someone my family was hurting me.

There were outward signs of my sexual abuse, that I was displaying. Some were subtle, while others were textbook abuse victim behavior. I became withdrawn and turned completely inward. My ability to make eye contact ceased to exist and I developed a speech impairment. I had angry outbursts followed by crying fits. I had frequent bed wetting incidents, which at 8 years old, is not normal. I wouldn't leave my family's side, and even felt an obligation to spend more time at my grandmother's house including sleeping there at night. I had nightmares every single time I closed my eyes. When it came to going to the bathroom, I would hold it to the absolute last minute, often wetting my pants.

Bowel movements were even worse as I would sit on the floor, typically by myself, and just not go.

None of this, my mother or others in my family seemed to care about or ever ask if I was ok.

So, I pushed on.

The nightmare: Playing with my toys, acting as a normal child would, I begin to feel as if a danger is quickly approaching from a direction I can't figure out. Panic sets in, with the fear and sensation of impending doom right behind it. As I stand up to try and locate this hidden danger, suddenly everything around me grows larger than life and I feel small and insignificant. My hands feel inflated, I'm unable to grip any of my toys that still surround me on a larger scale than before. Male voices, loud and deep echo in from every corner resulting in more panic as I scream for them to stop. PLEASE STOP repeats from my mouth until I feel the walls of life closing in on me, with the light starting to fade to black. I begin to curl into a ball, crying, begging whatever is yelling and now trying to grab me to stop. Suddenly, I feel warmth, an almost awkward and inviting sensation all at once. The voices begin to fade, but it gets darker, and I fall into a hole of some sort. As I fall, I feel myself shaking violently, from side to side, trying to break my downward spiral. One final shake, and I startle myself to the point of my eyes opening and reality setting in. I'm panting, covered in sweat, and sitting in a puddle of urine.

My birthday in December 1987 ended up being one of the darkest days in Townsend history. A girl I went to school with, Abigail, who rode the same bus as me, was murdered along with her little brother and pregnant mother. This took place immediately after Abigail got off the school bus and walked into her home which was a half mile from my grandmother's. The murderer lived a street over in the same neighborhood as Nana and my two uncles. This whole event hit about as close to home as it possibly could. I remember not being able to conceptualize what a murder was, and why someone would do that to a child. It was at this point the residents of Townsend began locking their doors. Up to that point, most people, my family included, left the keys in the ignition of their cars, doors unlocked on the homes, and the kids were free to run around as they pleased.

The Gustafson murder on December 1st, 1987, changed all of that.

Not that my birthdays were ever made a big deal before, but after that year I never looked forward to the day. Shortly after Abigail had been killed, I begun the unhealthy process of trying to wrap my head around why so many bad things had happened to me. My view on the world at not even ten years old was skewed to say the least. I felt as though this was how my life was going to be, which was hard to grasp.

Meeting my estranged Uncle Chucky for the first time came on the heels of all these bad situations. Given the fact that I had no prior memory of meeting the man that was supposedly cast out by the family for some reason, I was anxious to say the least. My mother dropped this information on me shortly after the usual Saturday morning cartoon lineup had finished and I was engaged in an all-out battle with my He-Man figures on the kitchen floor. The thought of having another of my mother's brothers in my life left me questioning the future of the family dynamic. What was an uncle supposed to be like, was a question I had struggled with my entire life. Would this uncle hurt me like the other two? Would he show up and be part of our lives then just disappear like my old man? Would he cause the hurt I was receiving to cease to exist? All possibilities had to be considered, in my mind.

My eldest uncle walked into our apartment at six foot three inches, wearing his best flannel shirt, a ball cap, smoking a Marlboro cigarette. A bit more menacing of a stature than Eddie, with a weathered face that had been on the receiving end of a few bar room fists. His voice was often goofy with a matching laugh, a stark contrast to his physical appearance. He greeted me with an outstretched hand, a "Hey Buddy, I'm your Uncle Chuck!" that was said in a matter-of-fact way, as if I was an adult. Immediately he and my mother sat at our kitchen table that was something out of an early 70's Sears Robuck catalog, complete with the plastic cushioned, metal framed chairs that adorned this outdated piece of furniture. As he drew the last of the nicotine from the cigarette in his mouth, I watched as Chucky put another cigarette up to the cherry to ignite what would be a continuous line of lung darts.

Smoking. It was something that had become an almost soothing aspect of the family make-up with both Nana and my Uncle Eddie partaking in the custom. This nasty habit was never withheld in my presence or anyone else's for that matter, nor was consideration given to when they lit up. It was a known occurrence that when they were done eating, whether everyone else was or not, a butt had to be lit and enjoyed. Others around them could be sick, coughing and hacking, and in would go that disgusting personal chimney. My grandmother's house had a permanent odor and even a slight twenty-four seven haze that left no doubt that smokers inhabited the four walls that felt more like an ash tray than a house at times. Now sitting on the floor at my own house, looking up at this strange man I was being told was family as he partook in the habit shared by kin, I almost felt at ease with his presence.

The amount of planning and coordination that went into getting Chucky and Nana back into each other's life that day in a time before the internet, cellphones, and texting must have been impressive. The meeting place was set for a local Chinese food establishment that had become the one restaurant my family visited on a semi-regular basis and held a sort of sentimental value. Eating out was a huge deal for me back then considering how little money anyone in the family had. That night, not only did I see atypical smiles on the faces of people that almost never showed emotion, but I also felt what I interpreted as love between the most stoic humans in my life.

A heartfelt and genuine embrace between mother and son that was demonstrated by Nana and my Uncle Chucky, was something I longed for, most of my life. My mother, not known for her reassuring hugs, had yet to convince me that I was suitable for the love and affection our relationship deserved. Now seeing this take place between one of my favorite people in existence, and this newly introduced stranger, I felt what could be considered a form of hope develop deep inside my heart. I was convinced one day I would be enough to receive the same from my mother.

As a family with two uncles that could be called away at a moment's notice to run off to some unknown emergency, we lived a flexible life regarding events. Especially meals and the bigger events like birthdays and holidays. With one police scanner always operating at home, and another two at my grandmother's, we were always aware of Townsend and the surrounding areas 911 activity. We were submerged in it, with the scanners always powered on. Because of the long-standing tradition of service to the fire department, my family had grown accustomed to the possibility that on any one of these incidents, we could receive a phone call that someone may not come home. Or even more likely, was the chance that a fire department vehicle would pull up out front of my grandmothers with the task of telling us one of my uncle's died saving someone.

With the emotional disconnect in my family and everything else I was dealing with daily, the added stress of losing an uncle to a fire came at me in an interesting way. Now having Chucky back in the picture, albeit the first time for me, I had yet another person who lived and breathed the world of firefighting from a fascination standpoint. Often when he was over my grandmother's, and Eddie and Jack were called out to a fire, Chucky would take me to the scene to watch my two other uncles at work. Describing the scene, tactics, and strategies, along with the danger associated with it became a common occurrence that filled me with a knowledge most didn't obtain even in their initial training. Certainly, none of the kids I went to school with were *blessed* to know this stuff.

For some reason the thought of Eddie or Jack dying didn't hit me the way I'm told most would take the death of a family member. Now being ten years old, I was beginning to see the world through a filtered lens that often left me confused regarding death. The knee jerk would be that because these individuals were responsible for so much pain and anguish in my life, that I wouldn't be bothered and maybe even rejoice in their doom. For me, the opposite was the case. I feared losing them but not because of the death component. There was a fear that I would somehow be blamed. It didn't seem irrational given how much guilt was thrown at me when Dad left that if either of my uncles bought the farm, certain fingers would point my way. My concept and view on the end of life, was within view of changing drastically.

By this time, I was being watched by the wife of one of the Lieutenants on the fire department, George Collins' wife Charlene. After years of being dumped at a house that belonged to one of my mother's friends, or a member or relative of someone on the fire department, Charlene became the most consistent "babysitter" I would have. At first it began with getting on and off the school bus at Collins' with the occasional full day stay when there were no classes. Soon after I was going on full day trips and even weekend getaways with Charlene and her adopted daughter, Marie. About four years younger than I, Marie was technically the daughter of Nora, George Collins daughter from a previous marriage. Given certain circumstances, it was deemed necessary for Charlene and George to take over care for Marie when she was still a toddler.

One of our frequented spots was the beaches of New Hampshire and Southern Maine. Up to that time I had never seen the ocean and had only been to a few smaller lakes or ponds. Because of this I was also never taught how to swim more than a quick lesson or two here and there. I loved going to the beach with Charlene and Marie especially when it involved a prolonged stay. We would often stay at the Black Bear Campground right outside Hampton Beach, sleeping in a tent enjoying the warm summer nights with the occasional campfire. While on one of our stays, Charlene did in fact try teaching me how to swim in her own special way. After a few stern attempts at getting me to get into the deep end of the campground pool, she had enough. Grabbing me under my arms, I was thrown into the chlorinated blue liquid, not having enough time to take a breath in.

After a few nerve-rattling moments at the bottom of the pool, I managed to resurface, frantically trying to find the side. Catching my breath, trying to slow my heart rate, while feeling my eyes swell up with tears, I heard Charlene utter her approval of my newfound abilities.

"See. Now you had your first swimming lesson!" casually ran from her mouth as she turned and walked away.

One time, we found ourselves up at Ogunquit beach which was in Maine just south of Kennebunkport. The beaches here were known to be cleaner with seemingly nicer folks sunbathing and swimming in the cooler clearer waters. Beyond less trash in the sand and far fewer vagrants than its southern New Hampshire beaches, this area was also known for an incredible rip tide, or undertow depending what part of the country you're from. This being my first summer even seeing the ocean, never mind knowing anything about it, I was oblivious and just happy to be in the sun acting like a kid.

By this day at Ogunquit, I could at least keep myself above water with a half-assed version of the doggy paddle as my lifeline. Wading in the ocean waist deep having a good old time as I watched Marie walk up the beach leaving me by myself. I started noticing I was getting deeper and deeper in the salty cool water, going from just below my waist to my nipple line. I didn't think much of it and tried to start walking closer to the beach, to which I found myself getting further and further from my intended destination. Before I knew it, I was up to my neck, and that's when the panic started to set in. I found myself trying to tread water and getting nowhere fast. Then shit got real and my feet couldn't touch the bottom anymore. I was way out above my head with each wave crashing over me, pushing mouthful after salty mouthful down my throat. I tried yelling for someone, but the closest person I could see was at least 20 feet away and with a mouth full of water, your voice doesn't carry too well.

I was sure I was dead, which I couldn't quite wrap my head around. I took a deep breath just before a big wave hit my head, certain this would be the last time I enjoyed the beach. As I looked up at the sky through the blur of the water, an almost peaceful feeling overcame me. All the past years of pain, abuse and even neglect, began to float away. I began to lose my grasp on reality as I became more and more lightheaded from holding my breath for what seemed an eternity. I felt my mind drift in and out of consciousness, almost feeling like I had slipped into a weird form of daydream. I started to not feel my hands or feet, soon followed by my legs and arms. Soon, it would be all over, I remember thinking to myself.

I was ok with that thought. I was no longer afraid.

Then suddenly a big hand reached down and grabbed my shoulder, lifting me out of what I was convinced was going to be my watery grave. I came out gasping for air and started to cry. Then I saw the guy who saved my life grab me again, putting me on his surfboard and telling me it would all be okay. He paddled me back towards the safety of the clean golden sand and asked where my parents were. I told him who I was there with and pointed Charlene's location out to him. Letting me off the board and telling me in a genuinely caring way to be more cautious, he took off back into the water. I was scared shitless but thankful to be breathing on my own. Walking up to Charlene and Marie, I told them what just took place. With a quick once over making sure I had all my parts and was ok, Charlene flipped onto her stomach to finish her tanning without saying more than a few words.

Tough love, I guess.

Back at Charlene's house in West Townsend, where most of my time was spent when under her "care", things were pretty run of the mill. The house was a ranch style with what used to be a one car attached garage, converted into Charlene's office for her various endeavors including selling Avon beauty products. The yard was average size, situated against the L shaped property line of the cow farm next door. Most of the time spent there, especially first thing in the morning, you were overpowered by the smell of manure then by afternoon, at least in warmer weather, attacked by armies of black flies. The house itself was on a small hill compared to Elm Street that lay below and ran north to the geographic center of West Townsend. The Collins were about ¾ of a mile from my grandmother's house, with their street being one over from Nana's.

It being the 80's, abductions were a popular topic in the media, be it the evening news or local newspapers. Much like the child abuse ads that ran using cartoon and comic book characters, the campaign to find missing and abducted children got represented in much the same way. Being kidnapped was always a fear, often reinforced by my mother's comments that she was convinced that my estranged father would try to take me from her. Though my father removing me from the grips of my mother and her deranged family wasn't exactly my worst fear at that point in life.

Marie and I would spend most of the nicer weather outdoors, running around the yard, at times with some of the other kids Charlene would be watching. One early afternoon while the light smell of cow shit was still adrift, and the flies that were drawn to it hovering, I would learn firsthand just how fast a situation involving a stranger could take place. As we played a modified form of hide and seek, I was walking along the roadside of the house when a dark van came screeching to a halt at the bottom of the Elm Street driveway. Immediately following this, a man wearing jeans, a brown jacket and sunglasses came running up the hillside with one of the most menacing looks I had seen on an adult's face. We locked eyes briefly before I realized I was in danger and took off running to the back yard.

"Get back here!!" Could be heard, in an older, raspy voice in the distance as I ran, heart pounding, tears swelling up, primal fear coursing through my body. Making it to the rear deck and door that led to Charlene's kitchen, I bolted in, panting with sweat dripping from my forehead. Obviously startled by my entrance, my adult caregiver shot me a look of utter disgust and demanded to know what the reason was for my behavior. Explaining the situation, she blew me off with a hand gesture and turned her attention back to her previous task.

Now remembering I had no idea where Marie was during this whole situation, I ventured back outside onto the rear deck, then slowly walked down each step whispering my friend's name as I did. She appeared from the far corner of the property, over by the farm, as I made the corner towards the driveway. As I peered around the side of the house, down the hill towards the street, I couldn't believe what I was seeing. Police cars were now parked in front and back of the dark van with the terrifying man nowhere to be found. Convinced I was safe, I leaned against the house, head back looking up at the sky, when Marie ran up and screamed "Gotchya!"

I never did tell her what had happened not even ten minutes earlier. After the response I received from Charlene, I was convinced no matter what happened to me, no one would believe it. This situation reinforced what I was already feeling regarding my abuse from my uncles. I had to keep all the bad stuff to myself. I could not allow another adult to know what I had gone through. So, I bottled it up, deep inside me, never to leave the dark caverns of my soul.

It was around this same time I also started hanging around with who would become my first real male friend. Andres. Going to school together and at one point having the same teacher, he and I grew close over our love of toys, using our imagination and even video games. We would hang out on the occasional Saturday, always at his house which was located off the center of town behind the elementary school. We became great friends, however, I never shared with him any of what my home life was like. As a matter of fact, Andres only came over to my house on rare occasion, and never once stepped foot on my grandmother's property. His parents were going through a separation which often caused his older brother and sister to act as additional tormentors in my life. Although it was a welcome situation based on the alternative.

My sexual abuse with Jack changed forms again around this same time. Being between 10 and 11, I began to explore my body due to the, at times, overwhelming thoughts and images racing around my head regarding sex and intimacy. At first, exploring my genitals felt extremely inappropriate, almost as if I needed permission to do so. Then I worried if I ever got caught that I would get in trouble. The latter happened one day at my grandmother's, while she and my mother were doing their normal Sunday afternoon routine of playing cards in the kitchen. I was in the living room by myself under the impression that my two uncles were out back enjoying the summer sun.

That was until Jack came around the corner and saw what I was doing.

With my shorts and underwear down around my ankles, I froze as my youngest uncle entered the room just staring at me. He didn't look mad or upset. He didn't look happy or sad. He just stared at me, as he came closer. My heart raced, my fists clenched as I felt a bead of sweat form on my brow and lower back. I feared the absolute worst given my vulnerable position as Jack sat on the couch across from where I was standing. What happened next, in some ways, had longer lasting effects than his initial molestation. As I braced for some form of physical interaction, Jack pulled his own pants down, exposing himself, telling me to keep doing what I was doing when he came into the room.

Fear and panic gripped my entire body, as my stomach began twisting and turning making me sweat even more. I didn't know what to do as Jack just stared at me with a satisfied look across his face, while he began touching himself. Not wanting to be hurt physically, I began to do the same to myself as I fought back tears and the instinct to run away screaming. It was almost as if he had me in an invisible tractor beam and he knew it.

This situation played out several more times over the next few months switching from him masturbating in front of me, to him having me do so in front of him. It was during this time that I realized I wasn't as aware of what was going on around me as I normally was. I felt distant, almost as if I was in the back seat of a car being driven by someone else, watching what was happening from an almost third person perspective. As I concentrated on this sensation and mindset, I also realized that it had been taking place ever since my sexual abuse began years ago.

Even though it was only a few years prior, I could not call up actual images of my rape. Not that I wanted to, but there were times where I felt as if maybe I imagined the whole series of ordeals. Maybe because of everything else going on, the physical violation of my innocence was just a terrifying sensation. As I sat with the realization that I was checking out whenever I was molested, I started to feel a new fear grip the deep parts of my being. I began to wonder not so much whether any of this was true, but more about how much I had blocked out. That thought alone scared me more than thinking about the parts I knew and remembered in somewhat detail.

What could I not remember?

Time drudged on and eventually my mother began dating a guy she worked with at the picture frame manufacturing plant in town. In the beginning she would mention that she had been talking to a guy at work, and that they were getting closer. She kept hinting at bringing him by the apartment for the two of us to meet which started to give me hope from two different angles. One, I've been longing for a dude to come into my mother's life, that would be decent enough to play Dad and to fill that void we had since my old man took off years prior. The second was the hope that with a fatherly figure in the picture again, that was not a blood relative, some if not all my abuse would stop or at least lessen.

Little did I know that the damage was done, and eventually it was going to catch up to me in a monumental way.

CHAPTER 2
ONE HAPPY TEENAGER

've never really liked chicken noodle soup. Back when I was working my way through age 11, if you got sick, you got served this atrocity with the expectation that it would heal what ails you. It was the winter of 5th grade, and I was battling stomach issues weekly. There was always a thought of me being allergic to milk since I was an infant, however, this never stopped my mother from making sure I had a glass of it or a bowl of cereal every morning. I recall most mornings starting my school day having to run to the bathroom in order to release the intestinal evil that was building up inside. Added to this was my constant state of high anxiety due to several old and even a few new factors.

With my mother dating this new guy, Donald, I had both fears and hopes for what might become a new life for all of us. With him being a male, there was the obvious fears that he would hurt me the way two of my uncles had. In contrast, him not being related gave me hope that wouldn't be the case. There was the fear and almost expectation that he wouldn't stick around long enough to leave much of an impression, while the hope of his presence would right my family dynamic. Either way, I was getting to know Don in a relatively expedited manner.

One thing that had tapered off since his arrival in our lives was my uncle's abuse. Neither of them had put a hand or anything else on me in months. I was always thinking about it even though no new damage was being inflicted. I was still having awful nightmares; however, I didn't seem to have wet the bed in a few years. I was still holding my bowel movements, unless of course it was morning time in which I had no choice. I often fought off what felt like very irrational thoughts about sex and intimacy, especially while in school.

School was a whole other animal.

I had a bullseye on me every day with the typical hallway and playground tough guys seeking me out daily to be sure I knew just how different I was. For the most part, it was name calling and poking likely due to my physical awkwardness. Being the age I was, my body was beginning to morph into its adolescent form but hadn't yet decided what part was going to be what size. I had larger ears which protruded from my irregular shaped melon, which was only made worse by the constantly out of style hair cut I seemed to maintain. Smaller shoulders, a bit of a belly and wider hips made no matter what I wore for clothes just not fit right. In a nutshell, I was goofy looking. To boot I had a lighter voice and a bit of a speech impediment which added all together made me a target for a lot of the other kids.

Even the girls would get in on the heckling from time to time.

All this began to rear its ugly head in the form of massive stomach pain, diarrhea mixed in with times of constipation. After seeing my pediatrician, who was also doctor for my entire family, it was determined I needed to see a gastrointestinal specialist. Being in a doctor's office was an issue in itself due to it usually involving just me and the provider with the door closed and no other way out. I had grown comfortable with my primary doc, however the thought of having to be examined by another strange male, set my nerves ablaze.

During the visit with this stomach specialist, the routine questions were asked while my mother was in the room. These included asking if I was safe at home and if anyone was or ever hurt me or touched me inappropriately. Back then they didn't separate children from the parents when this type of interrogation took place. So obviously I answered in the form of lies in order to avoid upsetting my mother and possibly facing backlash. They determined I needed to have what they told me was called a barium enema. The doctor then described the procedure, stating he was going to need to stick a tube in my bum to pump liquid in to then take an x-ray in order to diagnose the problem. The look of terror must of have dropped over my face as both my mother and the doctor stared at me asking if I was ok.

Before having this nightmarish procedure, I was going to need to endure a different ordeal. Per the doctor, I needed to go two full days only taking in water and chicken broth in order to clean out my system. I already despised chicken noodle soup, but now I was being forced to only take in the broth part which as a kid seemed completely unnecessary. Because my mother had to work, and it was during the school week, I spent the two days before the procedure at my grandmother's, not eating a thing. Punishment is the only frame of mind I was in during this time, seeing as though I wasn't being allowed to eat, and was forced to stay at the house responsible for so much of the stress I was under. The procedure being what it was weighed heavy on me as well.

My two-day liquid diet came and went, and the day of the enema arrived. My mother took me up to Burbank Hospital in the city next door, early the third day. I was brought to a room with my mother, handed a hospital gown and told to change into it taking ALL of my clothes off. This included my underwear. Already I was feeling the overwhelming pressure of being extremely vulnerable. Once in the procedure room, the reality of what was about to take place hit me full on as the staff started going over the equipment they were going to use. Showing me a wand with a penis shaped tip, telling me where they were planning on putting it, I checked out.

All I could do was cry. I tried to run out of the room, but they

stopped me, my mother leading the charge. I began screaming as they grabbed me and held me face down on the cold table. The tan and white walls suddenly turned brown, like wood, and darkness surrounded me making it hard to see anyone's face. The doctor's voice became deep and unrecognizable as everything in the room grew in size and intimidation. A hundred hands were all over my body grabbing and pulling at my bum, trying to penetrate me with their wand. As I felt the cold plastic enter my body, I stopped fighting. I stopped screaming. I just laid there, crying, letting them do what they wanted as I had in the past.

Not a lot remains in the form of memories from that day, or much of the time surrounding it. My "rear seat" perspective seemed to be happening more and more often as grew older. Don was now a staple in our lives and brought with him a positive vibe. He was eight years younger than my mother, making him only 14 older than me. He soon moved in with my mother and I and with our age difference we started to develop a sort of friendship. As much as Don was clearly entering a parental role, his demeanor and personality made it easy for me to become more of a friend at first.

Eventually Don moved his German shepherd, Kira, in with us. Don was just a cool guy. Laid back, good talking, but reserved in other ways and he liked to make funny voices and sounds. He also had a nice collection of vehicles and a few motorcycles that were again, kept up at his mother's. One car in particular I took an immediate liking to. That was his 1984 Mustang GT. It was blue with black racing stripes with the stereotypical Mustang rumble. Before Don, I had never seen and certainly never ridden in a muscle car. The closest thing was when I rode in Andres' father's Pontiac Fiero when I hung out over his house.

My friendship with Andres began to grow even further. Now being almost a teenager, some of our interests had shifted with age, and Andres began to pique my interest with his talk of comic books. I was always able to use my imagination, especially considering I was an only child and often had no one to play with.

This new hobby of collection, reading, and following the storylines of superheroes and their antagonists filled me with a satisfaction I had not yet experienced. Many a Saturday afternoon was spent sprawled out on the living room or bedroom floor of Andres' house reading book after book. Conversations of how we felt the next issue was going to play out occupied much of our time. We still occasionally used action figures in an effort to play out what we felt our conversations would look like in real time.

This sort of behavior was frowned upon by almost everyone in my family as they felt I needed to just grow up. Sports card collecting, in particular baseball, was the pushed hobby that began back with Jack. My imagination was never encouraged nor was reading for that matter. Comics brought both together in a way that often got me ridiculed by my mother and her brothers. For me, the colorful drawings and outlandish stories provided an escape from the prison my own head had become.

Shortly after Don moved in with us, we ended up moving to a different apartment, still in West Townsend. This new place was set up more like a house with the bedrooms upstairs on the second floor. The Canal Street address actually made our location only a quarter of a mile from Nana's and just down the hill from the intersection with Main Street. Shortly after moving in, I would meet one of the neighborhood families who had three children. Their son Jonathon was the oldest and just a year and half younger than me. Immediately we started hanging out, playing together, and getting to know each other. He would come over to my house as often as I would go to his. I got to know his entire family, and together we began to gather other neighborhood kids to our newly formed posse.

My mother and Don now married, and me halfway through age 13 my life was beginning to come together in some ways. In other ways I was convinced I was falling apart, and that given the thoughts I was having I was also a deranged human.

My heightened sexuality and inability to not touch myself whenever I was alone reached a peak during this time. I was still losing chunks of time whenever my stress levels reached higher levels and the bad dreams I was having at night seemed to be occurring while I was awake now.

Because of Andres having an older brother, I had access to pornographic videos fairly easily and at a rather young age. Even before I had started hanging out with Jonathon, I would end up in the audience in Andres' bedroom watching men and women engage in varying types of sexual acts. Much like the scenes I witnessed years prior in my grandmother's living room, I was unsure of everything I was witnessing. One thing I was sure of was I liked some of how it made me feel.

Combined with all this was the attraction I was beginning to feel towards some of the other boys I went to school with. This was especially true of Jonathon and often we would end up wrestling on the ground doing more than just trying to pin the other for a three count. One time in particular I had borrowed a sex tape from Andres, Jonathon and I watched after school while my mother and Don were at work. The intensity of the acting and the behaviors being shown, combined with our own curiosity turned out to be too much for Jonathon and me. We chased each other upstairs, to the closet in my parents' bedroom that I used for my clothes. Before either of us knew it, we were in a full embrace, trying to do our best version of kissing each other on the face and neck. Kissing led to rubbing our bodies together and grabbing each other's groins. We were both still fully clothed and the moment was filled with such a high level of adrenaline, lust, and intimacy that almost as quickly as we started we pushed each other away.

Now staring at Jonathon, not really sure either of us were at all ok with what happened, I watched as my friend's face sank into his chest. Sobbing with tears running over his now red cheeks, he pushed his way past me walking towards the bedroom door, nearly knocking over my parents' bottle of Absolute Vodka that stood center stage on one of their bureaus.

"We CANNOT tell anyone about what just happened! Ok?" Was all Jonathon said as I nodded to him in agreement.

This event created a permanent tension between Jonathon and I and caused me to think even deeper about how I felt about intimacy and my own sexuality. Up to this point I assumed the feelings I had towards some of the other boys at school were rooted in my abuse by men. After the event with Jonathon, I realized that I was not only intimately attracted and aroused by females but males as well. It wasn't merely a trauma brain reaction. The more I sat with this state of mind I found myself realizing that the thought of just being around a boy in a romantic way felt the same as it did when I thought of it with a girl.

This self-realization scared the shit out of me. More in the way of what my family would do to me if they found out I was the "faggot" they always talked about in the most hateful of ways. Racism and bigotry fueled by an unbridled hatred towards certain groups of people was no secret within the confines of my family. It was long preached that white is right, straight is the only way and there was only one God and He was unforgiving towards any deviation from the norm. So, I shut it down, locked it away, trying to forget it happened. Most of the time putting on my oversized headphones and allowing the extreme ends of the musical spectrum take me away from the daily stress of being me.

Music has always been a source of comfort and even escape from reality from an early age. My mother being the age she was, 80's music was pushed on me during the decade known for its colors, clothing, big hair and unique bands. Once I was approaching teenager years I developed my own taste, mainly hard rock and heavy metal which I used as a way to connect with others via my headphones with the volume up as high as it would go. Even while still acting as a child, the heavy riffs from bands like Metallica, Megadeth, and Anthrax soothed my inner pain I kept hidden. Often while drifting off into daydreams, I pictured myself being taken away from all the horrors I had endured.

One Saturday shortly after this took place I would reexperience a previous situation while playing in the driveway of our Canal Street apartment.

As I had just finished lunch, I was following the Saturday afternoon tradition of running around the yard, in particular up and down the driveway with my toy guns. At one point, while halfway to the house, something behind me caught my attention. I turned to see a black pickup come to an abrupt stop on the side of the road right by our mailbox. Immediately an older man stepped out of the driver's seat, followed by a younger guy racing around the back of the truck straight towards me! In a panic I screamed and ran to the side door of the house which led to the kitchen, where Don was finishing his bologna sandwich.

Seeing me enter the house the way I did, he immediately knew something was wrong and asked what happened. Hesitant to tell him based on past situations, I began crying pointing to the driveway to which Don made for the same door I just came through. Not finding anything and coming back in, I was eventually able to tell him the story. Surprisingly he gave me a hug and told me everything was going to be ok.

When told, my mother didn't seem overly impressed.

This was the straw that broke the camel's back. I had enough with the constant fight to exist and be accepted for who I was. Sure, my homelife had simmered way down regarding the amount of abuse. My mother still threw her occasional verbal punches at me and there was an overall sensation that she didn't love me the way a mother should. My sexual abuse had ended but after what had just transpired with Jonathon, and the emotional aftermath that followed. I couldn't mentally handle it anymore.

I was having bad dreams every single night. It seemed every time my eyes closed I saw bad shit. My self-esteem was at an all-time low due to the combination of the aforementioned, with the onslaught of ridicule I received from classmates, the icing on the cake. I felt gross all the time with how I appeared when I looked in the mirror. I was, at times, physically sick with headaches, growing pains, or the still remaining stomach issues that never actually resolved. My family didn't seem to want me, but total strangers kept trying to take me. Don now being in the position of stepfather, and doing well with his role, gave me a recess from some of this. But it wasn't enough, and I felt like it was too little too late. I needed it all to be over.

I had learned what suicide was through health class in school that year. The end of one's life by one's own hands, I remember the teacher saying. Being on the cusp of junior high we were beginning to learn all sorts of new things and death, in an age-appropriate way, was one of them. I just had to figure out how I was going to do it, and when.

I figured this out with the help of a fellow student who had the ability to procure certain commodities. This young lad was known around middle school for being able to get everything from candy and soda, cigarettes, and porn, all the way to alcohol and drugs. Going to him was a risk as he was also one of the many who would occasionally shout insults at me or launch my body into the lockers in the hallway. With a "what do YOU want?" response I told him I wanted a bunch of pills to fall asleep. After a 5 second stare down, he told me how much it would cost and when he would have the desired items.

To pay for this, I had to save up some lunch money for a few days, but ultimately purchased half a dozen white and pink tablets from this pillar of society. My plan was to take the pills with some booze knowing that if you mixed certain medications with alcohol, it would have a fatal effect. A Saturday night soon after this, my parents went out for a date night at one of their favorite places in Leominster. This small city was about 25 minutes away and they usually didn't come back home till around 10pm. I was now old enough to be home alone, in their eyes, so the stage was set.

On their way out the door, I didn't even move my eyes off whatever tv show I was watching. I simply stared straight ahead, telling them I loved them and would "see them later". About an hour after they left I went upstairs to my bedroom and took out the small bag of pills I had stowed underneath my bedframe and made my way to my parents' room.

The lone bottle of Absolute Vodka stood staring back at me, as I sat on the edge of my parents' bed. I contemplated for a few minutes whether I really wanted to do this. As I was about to walk out, my eyes caught the closet off to my left, where only a few weeks prior I had committed a sin with Jonathon. That was all it took to bring everything else back to the forefront of my brain and convince me of what had to be done.

I didn't really want to die, but I really wanted the hurt to. And with that last thought, I put all six white and pink pills in my mouth and took a large swig of the nasty clear liquor. It took all of me to swallow the vodka that felt like it was burning a hole straight through my cheek.

I put the bottle back, walked into my room, and laid down on my bed for one last time. As I stared at the ceiling waiting to fall into eternal sleep, I began to think about the peace that awaited me. No more ridicule, pain, love lost, or horrifying images and dreams for me. Just peace. I began to feel myself drifting off when panic hit me.

I HAD FORGOTEEN TO FILL THE BOTTLE BACK UP WITH WATER!!

Part of the plan was to make sure my folks didn't notice there was any booze missing from their bottle just in case this didn't work. Resolving that small detail, placing the bottle back at its home, and now having a hard time keeping my eyes open, I crawled back into my bed.

I had no dreams that night. Not one.

At first, I thought it had worked as I began to feel very peaceful with a bright light shining in my eyes. I couldn't feel anything physically and it was as if I was floating. I knew soon I would be in the protective arms of my creator and all would be ok. Suddenly I began to feel my arm. Then my chest and head followed by voices and the light growing brighter. I was startled to then wake up in my bed with my mother saying my name.

"Wow. Someone was tired. I've been calling you for three minutes." She said as she left the doorway of my bedroom and walked back downstairs.

I failed. It didn't work and now I was worried that my parents, more so my mother would find out I tried to kill myself. It being a Sunday, I was ordered to get ready to head to my grandmothers, which I did. The rest of that day I sat quietly not speaking to anyone in my family. I was let down in a monumental way and now how to deal with life.

Only now it was with a pounding headache.

CHAPTER 3
THE HEAT OF THE MOMENT

Townsend being the size it was, had three separate schools when I was a teenager. Two other towns, Pepperell to the east, and Ashby to the west, joined my hometown in making the North Middlesex Regional School District. Ashby is a smaller town of around 2500 people with more farms and open fields than anything. They began sending their kids to my middle school at seventh grade and this continues until graduation from high school. Pepperell is a town a little larger than mine with about 10,000 people. They had their own elementary and middle schools, sending students for high school only.

My middle school, Hawthorne Brook, hosted grades four through eight at the time. Junior high for me was an interesting experience. We began a rotating schedule of daily classes, still had recess to run around and meet with friends, and most of the students were going through massive physical and mental changes.

The bullying hadn't really stopped, but it did shift. No more were kids pushing me or trying to bounce my head off a wall. Name calling and finger pointing at my physical appearance had tapered off come the eighth year of public schooling. Because we were still very poor, I wore a combination of hand me downs, thrift store purchases, or simply very cheap clothing. It was always clean and beyond my occasional pubescent body odor from not enough deodorant, I never smelled. Certain kids, AKA the popular bunch, found it their obligation to constantly point out the lack of Saks Fifth Avenue in my wardrobe.

My time spent with Andres occasionally involved hanging out on a Wednesday afternoon. This so happened to be the same day his father, with his parents now divorced, had visitation with Andres and his older brother. Many a Wednesday was spent driving around with my friend and his father going to comic book stores and usually grabbing a bite to eat. I almost never had cash to buy anything when we went out, so Andres' father typically gave me a few bucks so I could at least get a few comics. This act of kindness to a kid not his, always meant the world to me. Especially the fact that he was always ok with me joining in on his time with his kids, spoke volumes of how this man differed from my own kin.

My family had really taken a liking to Don, and it was as if he had always been there by this time. He himself took a particular interest in the family firefighting tradition and all it entailed. With Eddie and Jack running out the door for fires, and Chucky going to these scenes to watch the boys at work, Don began to tag along. From time to time, he would take some pictures and quickly had gotten fairly good at doing so. Soon after Don started going to fires all around the area, with his portable police scanner in hand, and often me in tow. This I loved, and it created a bonding time that brought together the good parts of my family with what Don symbolized in our lives. He would also find use this time to share some of his own struggles, while in school, with me.

Don was average height, around five foot eight inches, with thin, wavy blonde hair. What set him aside, that apparently led to quite a bit of ridicule when he was younger, was his physical appearance. Don, his older brother Jason, and their father all were born with a rare physical deformity closely related to dwarfism. It created an odd, elongated head, clubbed finger, thin chest with protruding stomach and thin arms and legs with very limited range of motion. He wasn't handicapped or even limited in his physical mobility; however, he could not turn his arms and hands beyond a certain degree.

None of this mattered to me as I never judged Don, but it did create a mutual understanding with regards to our dickhead classmates. It also helped that Don was the one that took me and my mother on our first vacation of sorts as a family. We went up to York Maine and spent three or four days in a hotel on the beach. Short of an overnight in a tent with Charlene and Marie, my mother and I had never gone on a trip together.

It was during this time, around age 14, that the push for me to continue the family tradition in the fire service really accelerated. Whether it was subtle hints over family dinner, or the lack of encouragement in any of my other interests, I began to realize what was coming. I did in fact love some of what firefighting brought into my life, be it the get-togethers, added "family" members, or even just the thrill of fire itself. The issue was that I did in fact have other career aspirations that I knew wouldn't be supported, therefore I never tried to bring them up in my family. I definitely felt pressure from all this, which when added to teenage life and the associated stressors made me feel trapped.

Eighth grade was definitely a weird experience for me all around. My body was doing funky things, my voice kept changing at the most inappropriate times, and the confusion in my head was at an all-time high. For some reason I had become accepted by some of the "popular" kids at school, most of them being involved in sports. A lot of them were also sexually active by this point as well. Conversations with the guys surrounding what they were engaged in with their girlfriends, often left me longing for what was absent in my life.

Companionship and closeness.

It wasn't even the need for sex or the opportunity to get to whatever "base" with a girl. I just wanted someone, anyone, that I could grow close with, hold and have hold me. Sometimes, even just hearing some of the guys talk about having actual sex, I would be extremely uncomfortable on the inside, but played it off like I loved it all on the outside. None of them knew that I had already been engaged in some of the same acts, years ago, in very horrific ways. Ways that left me not wanting to experience any form of affection or intimacy ever again. Ways, whose origins, were about to be brought back into my life in an interesting way.

My mother's father, who had been estranged for almost 20 years, was in the hospital and the prognosis was not good for him. Me, my mother, grandmother, and all three uncles ended up going to the hospital he was admitted to. It would be the first time since Jack was about three that my grandfather would see his youngest son. It was also the last time. He died later that night after we had left. I was not allowed to see my grandfather before he passed, and I was later told he never even knew I existed.

After his death, there seemed to be a shift in how some of the family members carried themselves and even how I was treated. It was as if a weight had been lifted on some of those I was related to. Unfortunately, the period of celebration was cut short by the seemingly vicious cycle of bad circumstances that plagues my family.

Shortly thereafter my parents fell into some hard times financially that caused us to have to move around a few times. The first move being up to Don's mother's house in Ashby. This took place as I was finishing up eighth grade. The house was nice, and well maintained on a larger plot of land, with enough bedrooms for me and my folks. Besides Don's mother, Lucy, his older brother Jason also lived in the house that had been the family homestead for about 20 years.

Located where it was, about a half mile outside of the center of Ashby, I would often hop on the ten-speed bike Don had given me that was his, and ride around. Most of my trips took me to the market right in the center, where I would typically buy myself some candy before heading back. On one of these rides, I was feeling pretty low. My mother was very sick, often confined to her bed and at times needing to be seen at the hospital. She was having some sort of stomach issue that ended up requiring surgery. I was told on a few occasions it was a serious condition that could possibly kill her. As much as my mother had played verbal nuclear war with me over the years, I never wished her death.

As I left on my ten speed fully equipped with a speedometer, I was determined to break a land speed record going down the hill into the center of town. I rode down the sidewalk and crested the hill, where it made its decline just before the Main Street cemetery and began to pick up more speed. Wind in my face, with an ear-to-ear smile, my mother's misfortunes seemed to drift away as I coasted down the pavement feeling as if I was floating through the air. Just as I made it to the cemetery entrance, a car turned directly into my path. Striking the front driver's side, I was launched off the bike, my body slamming across the hood and windshield of this metal and glass adversary. As I rolled off the other side of the car, my hands, elbows, knees, and head smacked the sidewalk with an unforgiving force, blurring my vision and causing a moment where everything seemed to be narrowing in view and reality.

I heard someone yelling so I began to push myself up from the heap I was in on the ground. I wasn't sure where I was but knew it must be somewhere near Don's mother's house. As I looked around I found a bent and twisted bicycle lying on the other side of a car that had an old lady standing next to it. She was screaming at me and pointing her finger. I felt warm sensations all over my body, and a dull roar was echoing through my head. Looking down I saw blood covering my legs, arms, and hands. The shirt I was wearing was ripped, and more blood was dripping on it from somewhere on my face. I felt no physical pain, and my walking seemed to be ok. Looking over at the old lady, unable to understand what she was yelling, I saw a familiar red Ford pickup slow down and pull to the side of the road.

Don's brother Jason stepped out of his pickup, running over to me asking if I was ok. Reality finally came back at me in the form of chirping birds, passing traffic, an old lady's anger, and an overwhelming full body pain. I doubled over, grabbing my arms, and starting sobbing uncontrollably. With this the old lady hopped back into her car and drove away. "Uncle" Jason picked the busted ten-speed up and placed it into the bed of his truck and then opened the passenger door where I sat defeated, for the quick ½ mile ride home.

Not being able to remember every detail at that moment, Jason kept asking what happened, even as we pulled into the dirt driveway of his mother's house. As much as I didn't want to, fearing the backlash, the only person I wanted at that point was my mother. Getting to her closed bedroom door, I gave it a light knock as I whimpered, staring at my feet trying to figure out what I was going to tell her. Her tired, drained voice beckoned me to come in, to which I was already turning the knob not planning on waiting for her permission. As I entered, she turned her head to look at me, as the head of their bed was against the same wall as the door. The shades were pulled, and the midday sun was doing its best to infiltrate this cold, boring cave of a bedroom.

"WHAT THE HELL DID YOU DO!?" Rang from her weakened vocal cords, still packing the same uncaring, how dare you disturb me, power it always had.

She never even got out of bed. Jason helped me get cleaned up, as I sat on the edge of the bathtub watching the faint red water make its way down the drain. I kept telling myself how great it would be to float away with all the blood, soap, and dirt to be carried off to a place where things didn't keep happening to me and a mother that cared. The pain now setting in, I focused on it, almost enjoying its presence at it provided a release from the reality of the current situation.

I was hit by a car, bruised, and bloodied, not sure if I had any broken bones and my mother didn't even shift positions in her bed. I was never brought to the doctors, never mind the emergency room to be given a once over. When Don finally got home from his job I didn't even acknowledge the compassion he was trying to throw my direction. I thought back on my failed suicide attempt, and everything that led to it. I felt cold, hollow, and void of hope. I sat in my room staring at the walls, that were covered with pages from rock magazines of some of my favorite musicians. I closed my eyes and prayed for God to take me from this heartless world that nobody wanted me in anyway.

Pushing on, I turned my attention to the small group of Ashby kids I had already begun to make friends with. One in particular, Alex, had shown a greater interest in friendship than most. The occasional visit to Andres' broken home with his older brother, who by this point had become more of a bully, pushed me closer and closer to Alex and his much healthier family. Now that my bike was beyond repair, he had expressed interest in the speedometer that somehow survived the collision earlier. In what became known as the key moment in the beginning of our friendship, we made a historic trade. He received the speedometer that would never make it to another bicycle and in return I was given his Castlevania video game. In contrast to the unused speed tracker that likely still sits on the garage floor of his parent's garage, that vampire hunting themed video game cartridge saw so much play that it stopped working within a year.

Alex, a chubby, and rather quiet kid of about five foot seven, with blonde hair and strong Finnish roots, was the youngest of four siblings. Two older brothers and a sister all grew up in his Turnpike Road home that was just through the woods from Don's mothers' home, which made hanging out even easier. His father a long-time staple of the town's fire department, made for mutual family respect between the two of us. Alex was about nine months younger than me but in the same classes with the two of us meeting back in seventh grade. Overall, he was laid back and at times even a bit lazy.

My life living with my parents at Don's mothers was less than perfect. Soon after moving in, his mother, who I began to refer to as Grammy Lucy, moved her younger sister Natalie in with the five of us. Natalie, born with Down's syndrome and significant cognitive delays, had numerous tics and behaviors that made life with her challenging at best. I had never experienced a person with mental delays up close, and given my families prejudices, they often made these people out to be a burden to society and referred to as simply "retards". I began to find myself having a better understanding and appreciation of Natalie. I was able to exhibit more patience with her than most others that might be considered "normal". Part of me could relate to her disposition.

The part about being an outcast.

Up to this point in school I was an "A" student. I didn't like going to school because of how I was treated, but junior high ended with a positive change in that. My grades reflected how much time and effort I put into learning all my subjects, often craving more than my teachers could provide. When I began walking the halls of the high school, things took a rather drastic downward turn. Again, I was part of the newer, younger students and for the most part, no longer one of the tallest. The ridicule started almost immediately in a manner more aggressive than years past. I began to act sick to avoid going, and if I made it in, I would go to the nurse's office to be sent home.

Things in Ashby came to a head, and we moved back to the first apartment that I grew up in on Main Street in Townsend. I was struggling in school both with my grades and attendance. My attitude was horrible, self-esteem non-existent, and my circle of friends relatively small. Luckily, before exiting middle school, I had received enough speech therapy to rid me of the impairment that had brought with it years of harassment. So, I had that going for me. But the degree in which the bullying was coming at me was relentless and at times violent. Random smacks to the face, shoves into lockers turned into being cornered and sucker punched in the stomach at an alarming rate. Girls even got in on the fun, often standing on the side lines pointing and laughing at my torture.

I began to hate life even more than before. I felt myself beginning to question God often asking if I was being punished. As much as I was numb to certain emotions and not able to experience joy like other teenagers, I tried my hardest not to wear my inner torment on my sleeve. With all that was going on, my slipping grades, and unusual behavior, my teachers relayed concern back home. My mother took my teacher's advice and brought me to a therapist who tossed a diagnosis at me.

I was labeled as having attention deficit disorder or ADD, along with hyperactivity. With this came a daily medication regimen not dissimilar to the one I was on briefly back in middle school. Almost immediately I began to gain weight which added to the low self-esteem I had already. It being high school, it was required to change clothes for gym class. This came with a high price tag as taking my clothes off around other people wasn't my favorite thing to do. Making it worse was the almost constant adult eyes, that seemed to peer in from the coach's office on one side of the boy's locker room. Without fail, as most of us were down to our underwear, you could find a coach leaning against the open doorway supposedly making sure nothing happened.

At one point during one of my attempts to flee the school day, Nana had come to pick me up from the nurse's office. She had recently been forced into early retirement from her last job, and became my savior, showing up on an average of once a week. This time while she was walking in the front door, she tripped, fell, and dislocated her shoulder. It so happened to be right before a holiday, and her inability to cook and cater to the family was deemed my fault. I was even shamed by my mother and Eddie for not being able to just stay in school.

The summer of '94 between my freshman and sophomore years, I began working for the same farm Eddie was over in Groton. They grew mainly herbs like basil, oregano, thyme, along with some fancy plants. They also had a very large Christmas tree field. I took an almost immediate liking to having a job, with its structure, discipline, hard work and being mostly outdoor work. I used tools I never had, worked in greenhouses, and ran tractors both to move land and mow the fields of trees. I also learned how to drive as I was almost 16 by this point.

At home things had leveled out with my parents doing their thing, and me doing mine. Sundays were reserved for the usual family dinner at my grandmothers with me occasionally needing a ride over to the farm for a few hours of watering the plants. School had gotten slightly better, and I was being left alone by the upper classmen and had even befriended a few of the members of the football team who "kept an eye" on me. I also made a close friendship with another kid from Ashby, Scott.

Scott was six months older than me and had his driver's license by December of my sophomore year at the same time I got my learner's permit. A thin muscular build, with short black hair, goofy face with narrow eyes and large front teeth, Scott was the second youngest of four siblings. We met in science class and hit it off while dissecting an ill-fated frog. He had a car, and began driving me into school every morning, which my mother did not approve of. She dealt with it most likely because Scott driving me in meant I was at least going to school every day. I was also managing to stay all day and had gotten my grades up.

Being from the same town, Scott and Alex knew each other, and at times we would all hang out. Dave came into the picture about the same time and shared a close birthday to Scott, so he also had his license that year. Dave was shorter than everyone, thick black hair, with a chubby face, complete with rosy cheeks and an attitude likely rooted in his Italian heritage. My posse was growing, and it wasn't showing any signs of letting up as other boys kept joining in on our shenanigans.

I was finally getting accepted by some of my peers.

Junior year arrived and I was starting to see the light at the end of the tunnel of my public-school career. Me, Dave, and a few other friends had joined a new curriculum at our school that was being "beta tested". This new course schedule that ran the final two years of our high school career was focused on technical applications for the core classes of math, science, and English. The short term was placement at one of the state community colleges for a two-year degree then transition into a science program at a four-year school. I was approached by my guidance counselor towards the end of my sophomore year, as he felt it would be a good fit for me now that I had begun to excel again with my grades.

It was a smaller group of us in this pilot program, about 16, and from across all parts of the student population. Nerds, jocks, band geeks, pot heads, popular kids and the self-termed rednecks all stuffed into at least three of the same classes and teachers every day. It was actually kind of nice and for the most part we all grew pretty close, learning more about how the others were pretty much the same as we were. At the same time, however, I began feeling my inner confusion and awkwardness bubble to the surface and often in the form of rebellious anger. A short-lived round of defiant interactions with one of the drafting teachers over my choice of "offensive" clothing, finally woke me up to what I was doing, and I stopped mid-way through 11th grade. This was after about a dozen times being sent home for my behavior, which now having my license and own vehicle, I gladly did and may have taken advantage of.

A few years prior, a Walmart had opened in Lunenburg, the town to the immediate south of Townsend, and Don had gotten a job there. His position changed from overnight shifts, to eventually the department manager of hardware. Once he was in this role, it was suggested that I come work with him as Walmart offered better pay, flexible work schedule, and a more consistent environment.

Now 16 with my own vehicle and working an afternoon and weekend job at the local Walmart, I was beginning to come into my own and my family's treatment shifted greatly. I was driving a 1979 Pontiac Firebird that was a bright yellow and had previously belonged to Jack. After purchasing it for a dollar, the "fire chicken" became a bit of a staple of the student parking at the high school, with many of a fellow classmate marveling at its glory. I was still facing the stereotypical heckling from certain kids, but overall, I was doing better, and my self-esteem was at a level unlike it ever had been with regard to my friends, family, school, and work. I was "checking out" far less and wasn't losing chunks of time as I had been. My nightmares had tapered off, with only the once-a-week bad dream causing me to not be able to forget my past. I was even paying some bills and had a bank account so I could buy my own shit when I wanted.

Girls and dating were another story.

They scared me to some degree and for the most part, short of the required interaction at Walmart, I would steer clear every chance I had. Come spring of 1996, I had not even gone on a date with a girl, and not for lack of a few attempts that resulted in laughter in my direction. A few of my female co-workers had taken an interest in me, sending winks in my direction with the daily embraces telling me how much they loved seeing me at work. My lack of confidence was obvious, and in one case, this girl Jessica, basically sat herself in my car after our shift demanding I take her home knowing I wasn't going to offer it. Parked in her driveway, we engaged in what would be my first of many, failed make out sessions that left me feeling both thrilled, turned on, and terrified and unsure of what would happen next.

Another short-lived kissing and body exploration experience with a different girl would be it for a while. Every time one of these girls touched me whether it was hugs, kisses, and touching each other's body intimately, I felt an uneasiness blanket my entire body. I would get a churning stomach, the walls would close in, things would go dark, and a few times I even pulled back with a look of sheer terror across my face. With none of these individuals being understanding or compassionate of what was happening, I put my attention elsewhere.

A night of smashing mailboxes with Dave and Matt, who was another Ashby kid, proved to be the beginning of a journey for the three of us that would set the stage for massive maturity. Long story short, we got caught. I was the only one not actively smashing the "letter garages" or driving the vehicle responsible for it. I got a verbal beating from both my parents and the town cops. Dave and Matt received a court date and eventual gift of community service. Dave ended up getting tasked with painting the Harbor Fire Station as part of his community service. This allowed fate to shine it's never shifting light into our lives.

Until this point, Dave never expressed an interest in the fire service and at times scoffed at me when I spoke about what I was destined to do as a career. His time being surrounded by some of the men I had known for years, shifted his gears in a monumental way. My Uncle Eddie had said that the fire department was putting together a recruit class for on-call firefighters, that was going to start that September and for me to put in for it even though I would not be 18 before it started. The age requirement, Dave would be of age and put in an application the same day as me one warm June day as we were wrapping up Junior year.

That summer was filled with incredible firsts, parties, new versions of bullying and an overall coming of age that helped pave the way for what the future would hold. Me and Scott's friendship had gotten to the point where I was spending the occasional Friday or Saturday night over his house in Ashby on a dead-end road occupied by only him and his grandparents' homes. Ironically named Elliot Road, though spelled differently, I spent more time there than any other friends. What began with going out to eat, seeing a movie then crashing in a spare bedroom in Scott's basement grew into nights filled with uncontrolled teenage laughter and eventually drinking.

My mother didn't like that I was living a life not under her thumb and whenever possible would be sure to remind me of it. Even though by this time I had all but stopped hanging around with Andres, which should have pleased her, it was as if because I was further away she felt even less control over me. It wasn't just the Spanish Inquisition regarding whether I was drinking when I was with my friends. There was almost a "how dare you do not spend more time with your family" undertone in what was often said to me. At times, I even questioned whether I was allowed to spend the time I was with my friends. There was always a thought of concern for my mother floating around somewhere in my head. Short of my journey into the fire service, she never encouraged any of my other activities. Especially ones that involved people outside the family.

At the beginning of my senior year, Dave and I began our initial training with the Townsend Fire Department. Two weekday nights and a Saturday full of putting the book work into practice filled the rest of my teenage schedule between school and my shifts at Walmart. Men who had been merely family friends or figures at the scene of the fires I was watching from the sideline, became influential instructors in what would be my first taste of structured discipline. Phrases like "Train till you can't get it wrong" and "Get comfortable being uncomfortable" became frequently spoken passages as we worked our way through fire training.

The written tests were hard, the PT on Saturday, grueling and unforgiving, but I found it all to be a welcoming change. I immersed myself into my studies especially the more scientific parts like fire behavior and pump hydraulics. The early Saturday mornings filled with exercise, drilling and putting what we had read during the week to work simulating all the physical activities on a fire scene filled me with determination. I aced the tests and was one of the best recruits in the class of 10.

Dave and I were the youngest, followed by Hannah Smith who was the daughter of one of the Lieutenants stationed at Engine 3 in the Harbor. Nick was around Hannah's age and had no family associated within the fire service. Tom also graduated from North Middlesex and was around Nick and Hannah's age. Hannah, Nick, and Tom were all two to three years older than Dave and I and the five of us grouped together more than anyone in the class. The rest was a mix of ages, with two gentlemen in particular being in their mid-40's.

I realized that I was hyper-focused during this period in the fall of 1996, even my high school studies, tasks at work, and parts of my family life were benefiting in different ways. Part of me was beginning to put the brutal images from my early childhood in a deep closet within my brain, and it felt good not to be tormented by them on a daily basis. I was holding on to the hope that maybe what I went through as a young child would simply fade to black and leave me alone for the rest of my days as I quickly approached adulthood.

During this time, a few classmates from the 11th grade got into a horrific car accident on a road known for reckless teenage speeding. The resulting death rocked the entire student body as well as the first responders that were called yet again to pull the lifeless body of a high schooler from the mangled wreckage. The student that died, Nathaniel, was known to everyone. His circle of friends, some of which were also in the accident, including the driver normally sat at the same long lunch table as me and mine in the cafeteria. Following this incident, the kid driving always seemed to be off in a different place, never present, often found walking the halls staring at his feet. He would get ridiculed by others, pushed, and shoved with various sounds mimicking that of a car crash, often shouted at him. Even when my voice joined the chorus of laughter, I often wondered what he was going through.

Late November brought with it my favorite holiday, Thanksgiving, and the final tests of our fire school. A two-hour-long written test, followed by a skills session involving ropes and knots, tools and equipment knowledge and first aid station rounded out a very mentally taxing weekday night. The live fire practical the following Saturday put to work all the reading, testing, long nights, and longer weekend drills into one singular event.

I was still 17 with my birthday not for another week, so, I wasn't supposed to participate in this activity because of the dangers due to real fire being used. All the other drill days where we simulated a fire situation, a smoke machine was used. Being under 18 brought with it the need for my parents' permission to engage in the final day of testing. With the signature of my mother, and Eddie agreeing to run one of the fire engines at the drill yard, I was a go to have my day of play.

It was a pivotal day of finally experiencing "real" fire, thermal layering, and taking in an unexpected lung full of real smoke. At one point, while working on a rooftop operation, Hannah misjudged where a hole was, falling through and landing on a pile of straw and pallets, which is what we used to create our fires. Panic filled the radios, including that of the one strapped to chest of her father, Steve, my officer on a hose line that we were pushing deep inside the other side of the building. Being half led, half dragged through the concrete "Burn Building" to get to his daughter's side, was an adventure to say the least and she was uninjured. All in all, the day went great, with the remaining eight of us officially graduating from recruit to probationary firefighters.

Two days after my 18th birthday, on December 3rd, 1996, I was officially sworn in as a firefighter for the Town of Townsend Massachusetts. With a pinning ceremony held at town hall, being given my badge by the selectmen with the rest of the recruits along with some of the fire department present was one of my proudest moments. My family couldn't be bothered to be there, as they felt it was "no big deal". Being a Tuesday, meant it was department training night as well, so I was able to attend as an actual member. I was so caught up in my pride that I honestly don't even remember what the training was. What really made that night was what happened about 10 minutes after I walked back in my house.

We lived across from the town common, downtown, and were only about two blocks from the central fire station that I was initially assigned to. Walking into my parents' living room, high on pride, and riding on the energy the night had already given me, I was greeted by two different ends of the spectrum by my mother and Don. Not surprisingly my mother barely acknowledged me as I entered the room carrying all my firefighting turnout gear. My stepfather, wearing his always goofy smile, standing up off the couch next to his wife, came right over to me asking how everything went. As sore as I was at them both for not being at town hall earlier, I was almost more let down with Don. Approaching me, all inquisitive with an ear-to-ear grin, came across as an act that he was putting on trying to make up for not having the balls to get himself to the earlier ceremony. After a few words, I put my gear by the front door and began walking to my bedroom in the rear of the apartment.

With the fire department pager on my hip, to alert us to emergencies, like a personal police scanner, I walked into the kitchen looking to do what I had always done best. Use food as a coping mechanism for a moment of letdown. Before I could, the dispatcher opened the radio waves, announcing what would be my first emergency response.

"KBR 231 to the Townsend Fire Department, reported building fire, 2 Railroad Street….." the female dispatcher cool and calmly relayed not only across my pager, but the two other scanners in my house.

Before she was done making the initial dispatch, I was in full sprint from the back of the house. Running through the living room with the biggest smile either of my parents had ever seen on my face, I stopped at the front door to grab my gear. Off like a bolt a lightning, I decided in the heat of the moment running to the fire house was my best option. I hurdled the rot-iron fence of the town common like a veteran Olympian, all while wearing my bunker pants, sliding my arms into the coat, and balancing the helmet precariously on my head.

Making it to the station before anyone else, I paused to catch my breath as I lifted the cover on the garage door keypad. Within moments, another firefighter was by my side, and good thing as in all my excitement I had forgotten the passcode. The giant garage door rumbled skyward, revealing with every foot, more and more of the bright red chariot, we would soon ride into battle. The diesel motor roared to life; its eyes gleamed yellow as its driver inched it from its shoehorn fit within its cave. Hopping in the rear of the cab on the CF Mack pumper truck, that was open to the night air, I took my seat behind the officer. That night, one of my recruit training officers, Mark Gaines, was in charge of the crew. With another firefighter getting in the seat across from me, behind the driver, our horseless chariot lit up like a Christmas tree. The song of our people trumpeting from its mouth with a plume of black exhaust leaving its tail end, we rode off into the cold, dark, December night to fight the red dragon.

The fire was on the street right behind the fire station we just pulled out 15 seconds earlier. Once at a stop, I stepped off looking up at the second floor of the small home, where thin wisps of black smoke made their way from the only window and eaves of the roof. I was ordered to stretch a hose line to the front door, as Mark entered the home to find where the fire actually was. As I walked up the front steps, he motioned for me to continue in, flaking off lengths of hose as I made my way. Stopping at the bottom of a set of stairs inside, I put the nozzle on the floor, got down to one knee as I began the process of putting my face piece in place. The rest of the hose stretched out by the other crew members, I stood air tank turned on, ready to mount the first step. Notifying the pump operator, we were ready for water via radio, the hose line jerked to life.

With a grab of my shoulder, Mark leaned in to tell me the fire was at the top of the staircase to the right in a small bedroom. Bleeding off the excess air from the hose line and looking behind me to see the other firefighter, I made my accent up into the darkness of the unknown. Once within the staircase, I could begin to feel the heat, with every step growing in intensity. At the top of the stairs, I banked right, adjusted my grip on the nozzle to make my way to the faint orange glow a few feet away. With a whoosh, water was forced at the seat of the fire, knocking out the only light in the room. Instantly a deeper black engulfed the two of us, followed by a higher heat. A few moments later two more firefighters made entry into the room, and a window was smashed open to release the toxic and extremely hot smoke and gases trapped behind it. Within a minute or so we could see each other with the smoke lifting. A moment later we were able to get back to our feet as the heat began to lower.

I was a bit overly excited and had to be told to calm down in a rather direct, but appropriate way, eventually to be relieved of my position in the now burned-out bedroom. I walked out of the house, ripping my air tank face piece off as I made the front steps, looks of respect and approval upon the faces of my brethren. Big smiles, pats to the back and "atta boys" filled the next several minutes as I began the process of taking off my air pack and getting a drink of water. Apparently I had an ear-to-ear grin, and was glowing, as Lieutenant Collins had to walk over to me.

"Try and hide your satisfaction Hanks. The homeowners are right over there." Jack said as he gave me a reassuring shoulder grab and a look that confirmed a job well done.

Walking out to the street to suck in some of the fresh, cold night air, I saw my Uncle Eddie standing by his truck, Engine 2, feeding the big hose line that came down from the driveway previously laid out by the truck I was on. More members greeted me with impressed smiles. Eddie's face was stoic as he simply tapped me on the shoulder, told me I had "done good" and walked past me.

His reaction didn't even phase me, as I was on cloud nine. That night gave me something I wasn't fully aware of at the time, but I definitely felt the gears had shifted. I felt respect from those around me which in turn gave me a level of self-confidence unlike anything up to that point in my life. I looked up at the clear fall sky, peppered in faint twinkling stars, and took it all in. Convinced my life had hit a turning point, I felt a subtle smile come across my face as the past horrors seemed non-existent. I truly believed with all that had taken place that evening there was nothing I couldn't face and overcome. The badge I received earlier became my new identity, and I embraced it with all that I was.

The next day in school, I held my chin high for the first time, as I walked the halls and attended my classes. Stories of me running into a burning building had reached both the students and teachers alike. I received smiles from kids that hadn't previously acknowledged my existence, teachers who could have cared less but suddenly found respect as they offered handshakes. It felt good. I held onto it and used it as motivation in my life.

Except girls. I still wouldn't approach girls.

The next few months were filled with light schoolwork, running emergencies with the fire department, and my afternoon and weekend shifts at Walmart. It seemed like at least once a week we were going to a fire either in our town, or one of the neighboring communities. This combined with a slew of car accidents, and other mundane "emergencies", I began to get more and more confidence and cocky. I often felt invincible and even better than my fellow classmates, seeing as me and Dave were the only kids in the high school now working as firefighters. Sure, there were those insecure few that tossed insults in my direction, but this new "power" brought with it an ability for me to pay them no attention.

I began the process of applying for a college in Northern New Hampshire near Lake Winnipesaukee that specialized in Fire Science. My guidance counselor was less than impressed with this decision as he was convinced robots would replace firefighters within ten years. My family seemed to appreciate this show of strength and my commitment to the firefighting tradition. I was also going to be the first in the Elliott bloodline to attend college, which to me was a huge deal.

I noticed with some people, mainly other kids, I was becoming a bit brash and maybe in some forms a bully towards. I was aware of this and given my years of being tormented by hallway bullies myself, I felt as though I was now on the giving instead of receiving end. However, I made no change in my behavior. Leading into late winter and early spring, I felt unstoppable and on top of the world often looking down upon others. Little was I aware of what was waiting for me just around the corner, hidden behind a newfound sense of self-confidence and arrogance.

I was about to be served a slice of humble pie.

CHAPTER 4
COMING OF AGE

New England is a unique place to live. As one of the oldest parts of America, it's littered with colonial age buildings, historic landmarks, postcard perfect small towns and nature scenes and the childhood homes of those that created the nation. It's also home to an unpredictable weather system. We still have four seasons, but the months these fall across leaves even the best meteorologists baffled. Brutal winters with subzero temperatures to summers in the triple digits, 75-degree Halloweens to a foot of snow on the ground second week of May. We have a saying here that's fitting not only for the weather but speaks of the true New Englander attitude.

"If you don't like the weather, give it 15 minutes."

This unpredictability in the weather often hampered our efforts as firefighters not only at fires, but any emergency. Hurricanes, varying temperatures, blizzards, and floods didn't mean we had a day off from dealing with a 911 call for help, it typically brought even more work, just making it more difficult. You had to be a slightly hardened person in order to deal with the stress of a chaotic scene and also the weather you often worked in.

The winter of 1996 into 97, brought with it a larger amount of snowfall to my part of Massachusetts. Almost weekly a fresh layer of snow fell from the sky, blanketing everything in a beautiful, picture-perfect scene. The beginning of March, the fire department was hosting a series of trainings on the incident command system put on by the Massachusetts Fire Academy. The final of these was scheduled for Sunday the 9th with an 8am start time. A foot and a half of snow covered the entire area from a "small" storm a few days prior. The region looked serene with even the roadside snow still remaining relatively clean in appearance.

It evoked a sense of peace and tranquility.

Laying in my bed, trying to get every last wink before my alarm inevitably woke me a little after 7am, I began to toss and turn. My fire department pager sat dormant in its charger on the bedside table, as my giant feet poked their way out of the sheets at the end of the twin-sized bed. My end of the house was always a bit colder than the rest, as it was located above a series of open garage stalls. Feeling the cold hit my body, I retracted to my linen cocoon. I turned my head, squinting to see the time on the clock across the room, my pager awoke from its slumber, jolting me upright.

"KBR 231 to the Townsend Fire Department and EMTs, reported building fire with people trapped, 72 Bayberry Hill Road.." The dispatcher trailed off as I sprang upward and into the bunker pants conveniently positioned bedside.

Securing my feet into the boots, pulling the pants up, placing each red suspender over my shoulders, I raced out of my rear bedroom making haste through the kitchen. As I got to the front door I was met by Don, camera in hand, who was heading to his truck to go take pictures of the possible blaze. Helmet and coat in my arms, I made my way across the town common in usual fashion, taking big strides only stopping to navigate the few cars at the traffic lights. I made it 50 yards from the familiar two-story brick fire station, Engine 1's door was already open. The distinct rumble from within was immediately followed by the front of the ole red hose wagon rolling out onto the asphalt apron. Hopping behind the driver, with Mark Gaines, now officially a Lieutenant, again in the officer's seat, I saw Nick from my recruit class take the seat across from me.

The fire chief had signed on the air, stating he was responding to the fire as I was making my way to the station. As we pulled out onto Elm Street to make our way south, he then signed out confirming a working fire.

"30-C to 231. I'm out with heavy fire showing and a confirmed person trapped. I'm going in to do search." The Chief stated in a calm and collected voice.

This transmission would be the last we heard as we made haste now climbing Bayberry Hill Road towards the same scene. The fire dispatcher several times trying to hail the chief over the radio received no communication back. The rear sliding window opened between the cab and where Nick and I were now staring at each other in disbelief. Mark yelling back our orders and the update that the chief may be now trapped in the building as well.

My vision narrowed, and I could feel my pulse climbing as the rpms from the motor housed next to me grew in intensity. Looking across the cab, I saw what I was feeling plastered across my brother firefighters face.

Fear.

Pulling up to the scene and turning into the driveway, I hopped off the truck making my way to the rear of the hose bed. My orders were to pull the big supply line off, so we could drop the big yellow four-inch hose up the length of the hundred-foot dirt driveway. As I motioned for the driver to pull ahead, I looked through the barren trees to see 50-foot flames racing skyward from the small wooden home below. Yelling and panic fill the air, with the sound of crackling wood as I made my way up. Losing my traction and falling more than once.

Still no word on the fire chief.

Coming up to the house, I stand in awe of the scene playing out in front of me. Flames pour out of almost every window, the front door and roofline with thick, menacing black smoke rising high into the winter air. The acrid smell of burning wood and building materials is strong as my concentration is broken by the image of a piling of brown blankets being carried towards me by sprinting EMT's. As these blankets go past me the smell of cooked human flesh and hair fill my nostrils, as I realize it's a body. Focusing forward again, my attention is drawn over to the right, towards the small garage. An elderly man about 80, stands with burns to his arms and hands, bleeding from his wrists, next to a police officer. In a daze from all the images, my ears start to pick up a familiar sound.

"Hanks! Get up here now!" is screamed from Lieutenant Gaine's strained vocal cords, as he stands by a smoking window on the front left corner of the engulfed home. His arms motioning for me to hurry.

As I step up the hill to the front lawn, following my officer's orders, a body covered in white turnout gear dives through the heavy black smoke pushing out the window. As the fire chief lands on Mark and another firefighter, all three fall to the ground, and flames chase the chugging, black smoke to the now brightened morning sky.

Relief and even disbelief flowed over me. Taking in the entire scene that just unfolded in front of me in 30 seconds time, I began to feel both at ease and in shock all at once. Realizing the fire chief was in fact alive, I found myself trying to make sense of everything that I witnessed.

The rest of the morning was spent putting the fire out, while trying to conserve the scene as an investigation was sure to follow. The fire chief received minor burns to his head, face, and hands. The elderly woman he rescued succumbed to her massive burn and smoke injuries in what ended up being a murder/suicide attempt. She was reportedly tormented by daily pain and didn't want to live the way she was. Her loving husband of over 40 years, heeding his suffering wife's pleas for help, set their family home a blaze. When he went to enter the house to die alongside her, he couldn't, due to the intense heat, instead cutting both his wrists in an attempt to end his own life.

All of these details raced through my head filling me with a confusing assortment of emotions. On one hand, I questioned how someone could willingly end another's life. On the other hand, I completely understood being in the mindset to end your own life. This combined with the physical toll of working for hours at a fire, weighed heavy on me.

I was relieved of duty in the early afternoon and was exhausted both physically and mentally. The horrible images from earlier raced around my head accompanied by the nauseating smell of burnt flesh. Walking into my parents' living room I was greeted by the concerned eyes of my stepfather while my mother didn't even turn in my direction.

"How ya doing kid? I got some really good pictures." Don went on to explain his perspective along with describing what ended up being the only initial pictures of the fire. These were used in both the investigation and distributed throughout all the requested newspaper and media outlets.

Less than impressed and uncaring, my mother uttered something like "How was that?". My answer was long winded, and I'm pretty sure Don was the only one that actually heard the words I said as he stood from the couch to meet me by the bathroom door.

As I shut the door and turned towards the tub, I was overwhelmed with a feeling of nausea. Dry heaving into the toilet, I gathered myself and prepared to take a long hot shower. Stepping into the scalding water, I lay down on the bottom of the porcelain basin, allowing the water to pour over me. I reach up along the shelf above and grabbed the Pert Plus shampoo. Driving handful after handful of the green slime into my nose attempting to relieve the overwhelming smell seared into the inner walls of my nose from earlier. Succeeding only in making myself vomit green, sticky goo.

The next day in school, less than 24 hours after all this transpired, I sat feeling hollow and distant. Growing up with my family being part of the fire service, I was not naïve to the knowledge that someday I would see chaotic and terrifying events.

The fact that this ended up being a murder with a suicide attempt upped the traumatic ante in my mind. Throughout the day I carried a blank affect, showing little to no emotional response to the situations around me. Teachers concerned over my well-being, finally sent me to the nurses' office, alerting the principal to meet me there. Sitting in the same room that was my safe haven almost daily, three years prior, I told the principal and the elderly nurse about my Sunday morning.

Jaws hit the floor, and a lack of comprehension filled the air as the two stared at me in disbelief. Needless to say, I was allowed to lay down on one of the familiar cots to rest for a few hours.

The nightmare: Running through long hallways with doors that were all locked, a growing darkness chased me, swallowing all that it passed. The walls grew high, I feel small, insignificant and without a voice. I try yelling but no words come out. I focus forward, running towards a now green light, that seems to be pulsating around the outline of the last door. Bursting through I land on my bedroom floor with a bunch of pink and white pills all around me. I start crying, attempting to back away from the small capsules, I put my hand into green slime with an almost pleasant smell. Laughter breaks out as dark faces surround me up high, looking down on me. Shear panic grips me as I look around for a way out. As all feels lost, my mother's voice comes in like a high-speed locomotive emerging from a tunnel.

I awaken, sitting bolt upright covered in sweat with the nurse rounding the corner into the room. Asking if I was ok, I assured her I was, giving her some line about the day before and the shit I saw bothering me.

About mid-week, the police department held what is termed a Critical Incident Stress Debriefing/Meeting (CISM) for the fire a few days prior. All officers, EMT's, firefighters and the dispatcher who was on duty, were invited to attend. Intended to allow space to share experiences, perspectives and even feelings, these meetings are classically misrun. Sitting in the far back of the room with about 20 of my fellow first responders, the feeling was part dismal, part opportunity to catch up with those we work with.

A shorter man in his mid-40's approached the front of the room with an almost bothered look on his face. What he said next set the tone for the evening.

"So, you guys were at a fire where someone died, you almost lost your fire chief. Anyone wanna share some feelings?" The last part came across in the most sarcastic way.

As I remember it, nobody said a word and we were quickly given a recap of the event then dismissed to enjoy some coffee and donuts in the back of the room. I realized right there that night, surrounded by men I looked to as roles models that we were not allowed to be bothered by this job. I had to "suck it up buttercup" as it was often heard around the fire stations even before I got on the department. I sat thinking to myself of all that I was feeling until another of my brethren approached me, motioning to the spread of "fat pills" and java on the table. I poured a cup and grabbed one of the circular pastries. Keeping my mouth shut only to take a bite and chew.

Time pressed on and I kept responding to a number of emergencies heading into the spring. At a brush fire in the southeastern part of town one April day, I found myself staring at the lifeless body of the homeowner with the assistant fire chief. The charred roles of flesh, bursting in some areas, with his jeans being the only remaining clothing not decimated by the flames. An unfortunate casualty in what began as a controlled burning of yard waste, this poor guy apparently had a heart attack, falling into the path of the fire that destroyed 2 acres of the now ownerless property.

I felt myself running through a gauntlet of emotions and sensations as these calls added up. My young mind was struggling to process the intricate and delicate details of seeing these horrible parts of life. Often getting overwhelmed by this, I turned to my circle for distraction.

Nicer weather brought with it Friday or Saturday night parties at Scotts in Ashby. His father had his own business, and he and his wife would disappear north camping every weekend after Easter leaving their house to our disposal. One time in particular we gathered around the unopened pool to barbeque burgers and enjoy some adult beverages. As Scott and I awaited Dave, Alex, and some others, one of our less frequent guests, Bobby, showed up. Having been drinking for a few hours by this point, the level of ball busting that ensued when he showed up was monumental. In the end I was dared to put an ill-fated frog, that had found his way to the cooking surface, onto a burger and feed it to our unsuspecting "friend". With Scott and I doubled over laughing, and a frog leg hanging out of his mouth, Bobby gave chase and the three of us fell to the ground in hysterics.

A pleasant break from the stressors of school, being a teenager, and what at least I was seeing with the fire department.

Car accidents, fire alarm activations, and assisting the ambulance seemed to be an everyday occurrence when I wasn't working at Walmart. The fire chief and school administrators even reached an agreement where Dave and I were allowed to leave our classes if certain calls occurred during the day. I was plowing through the remaining days of my senior year, looking forward to ridding myself of the memories of years of being pushed around and laughed at. By this point, most of our classmates left Dave and I alone and at times even gave the impression they looked up to us for what we did with the fire department. The fatal fire back in March had hit me deep and brought my ego down a few pegs.

I went up for my orientation for New Hampshire Tech Community College in Laconia shortly before graduation and was looking forward to attending. Ken Crenshaw, whom I previously worked with at the farm in Groton, was working as a firefighter in Laconia at the time. One day, we went around the surrounding towns, trying to secure me a spot in one of the "live-in" programs.

The college having the fire science program they did, several of the Lakes Region fire departments offered students an option to live at their stations in exchange for running on calls and maintenance to the trucks and fire house. A situation I had already basically been living since I was a kid. It felt like it was meant to be.

Graduating in the middle of May was a breath of relief. I had a small get together after with just my parents, grandmother, and three uncles present. I didn't really care, as most of my friends barely knew my family, short of Dave's interaction with Eddie and Jack through the fire department. The weekend after me and my circle had one of our rock star level parties. One for the history books as they say.

Ending my shift at Walmart a few hours earlier than normal, I met my posse over at what had become our restaurant, Applebee's, in Leominster. The full crowd was in attendance that night as about ten of us crammed into the corner booth in the back of the bar and grill. We had gotten to know most of the staff and often not asked for ID and were allowed to buy a few rounds of beers, so long as we left a good tip. After indulging in the typically spread a group of teenage boys would consume, we made for the woods of Ashby and Scotts. On the way we learned of his grandparents also being out of town for the night. Living in the only other house on his road and now not being home meant we could party up at their farm. With about six of us remaining to hang out, we decided we needed a hay bale fueled fire as we drank our Bud Lights and Cider Jacks. After an alcohol-induced drive through the farmland in the blue Ford Tempo I had as a winter beater, Alex and I rejoined our friend's fireside just as Bobby arrived.

The normal ball busting ensued, as the familiar bullseye appeared on Bobby's back. We were pretty unrelenting and for the first time he was giving some of it back to us. At one point when the skinny, blonde-haired victim walked off to urinate, I was handed his unprotected bottle of half drank beer. With the heavy eyes of peer pressure upon me, I was once again dared. Unzipping my pants, I relieved myself, filling Bobby's beer back up, while my conscious filled with shame. Handing the bottle over to Alex just in time for unknowing owner to reappear, I lowered my head, aware of what was about to happen.

"Here ya go bud! Have another cold one!" A smirk came across Alex's face as he handed Bobby the beer.

At first, his face was that of relief, acceptance, with the thought likely being that he was finally one of the guys. Then Bobby took a giant swig of the contents within, and the expression dropped. He didn't even chase anyone. Throwing the beer back in Alex's direction, Bobby simply disappeared into the night. A while later as our fire needed another bale of hay, Scott began walking towards the barn only to come to a sudden and panic filled halt. As headlights began to crest the hill, heading straight towards us we knew his grandparents just came home.

Half-drunk teenagers took off in multiple directions, as the silhouette of an elderly man stepped in front of the yellow headlights. About 10 minutes later, as I hid in the waist high field of grass, fifty yards from the house I heard the voice of one the cops. Yelling for us to come back to the house, stating he had one of our "buddies" and our night was over. With that, I took off sprinting through the dew laden fields in the pitch blackness of the midnight. Suddenly I felt the ground disappear below me as I fell ten feet into what was once the foundation for a barn. After making my way out, and regaining my direction, I finally made it back to Scott's basement to find Alex and Scott sitting covered in sweat and fear.

A knock on the upstairs door told all of us the gig was up. Scotts grandmother greeted him on the other side when he opened it, yelling and pointing her finger in his chest. Returning to join me and Alex with a serious look of knowing what was coming when his parents eventually got home, we all looked at each other. Within seconds laughter rang out across the room as my hand fell to my waist. In instant panic I realized something was missing.

My fire department pager was gone.

That ended up being the last real party event held at Scott's. I spent the rest of the summer working extra at Walmart and the fire department in an attempt to bank up extra money for college at the end of August. I did not get one of the "live-in" programs at any of the area fire departments, so my parents had to get me a place to live. This rental ended up being across the road from one of the bays off Lake Winnipesaukee and was not cheap. My mother and Don assured me they'd make it work as, at first, I wouldn't be able to hold down much of a part-time job.

Between my six hours of classes, Monday through Friday, and an eight-hour day of practical training on Saturday, I was the busiest I had ever been with my studies. I had gained a bit of extra weight since graduating back in May, which did not bode well with the military style morning PT we were engaged in every Saturday. I drew the attention of many instructors because of this and my inability to keep up with the required number of push-ups. A heavy boot could often be felt on the middle of my back followed with some spoken version of "Let's go pork chop!". I was actually more upset with myself than the "drill instructors" as I just wanted to prove to everyone that I could do this.

My grades on the other hand were phenomenal and with Dave joining me at the same school, we realized we could help each other. He had no issues on the physical part, but his grades weren't as strong. So, I helped him study, he tried to get me to eat better and exercise. This process continued into early October, when I began to grow tired of hearing how hard my mother was working to keep me in school. As much as I appreciated being given the opportunity to go to college, the first in my family, I didn't appreciate being made to feel I was putting my parents out every time we spoke. It was as if my being away at college was a burden I needed reinforced any chance that came up.

At this point, I was sleeping in this cabin style rental by myself, only coming home every other weekend. My bad dreams had amped up again, leaving me in a constant state of fear along with looking over my shoulder. This resulted in me never feeling rested. I began to doubt myself like I used to as a younger teenager. I felt between my weight and inability to perform in the top of the class physically, and the problems I was apparently causing for my parents that I had to quit school.

So, I dropped out in the middle of Saturday morning PT.

Disappointment was directed my way by more than family. Even prior to social media or cell phones, it seemed somehow everyone knew I had failed at college before I even moved back home. Now facing a different sense of low self-esteem, I began to question my existence and the purpose of it all. By this time, we had moved down the street from Nana, into a house that long ago was a chicken coop. The biggest of all our living situations to that point, this giant cinder block home had been a gymnastics studio before being converted into a rental property. It had three bedrooms, a big kitchen, and a huge living room with floor to ceiling mirrors on one wall where one could imagine past gymnasts stretching in front of it. The most adorable part of this house was the location of the shower which was not in the bathroom. Situated dead center on the back wall, the stand-up shower stall split the kitchen into two halves. Looking like something out of a local gym, it was always a great experience to be eating breakfast, to then have a half-naked parent wrapped in a towel stroll into your line of vision.

Before this move, I had taken a job as a phone sales associate at the same place my mother was working over in Groton, called NEBS. Planning on going back to school in the spring at one of the community colleges, I began working 40 hours a week for the first time in my life right before my 19th birthday. I was also working in a 95% female work environment, and of the men there I was definitely the youngest and one of the "better looking". I had started working out, beginning to shed some of the excess weight and sprouted up to my full height of six foot five. Being a clean cut, and relatively well-dressed young man caught the eyes of *a lot* of the opposite sex working not only in the same department as me, but companywide. For the first time since I was a child, I began having regular conversations with women, old and young, about everything from meals to school, movies to sex. My mind began to come in tune with the possibility that I may actually find someone willing to get romantic with me. However, that still wasn't my priority as fighting fires and responding to others worst days had become a pleasant escape.

As the fires continued to come in at high rates, I was getting more and more experience in fighting them. Be it smaller "room and contents" or multi alarm building fires, I was responding to, at times, two to three fires a week along with a mixture of other smells, bells, and medicals. I was loving it all and even got blessed with the rare opportunity to ride true rear step on the back of our old R model Mack fire engine. A bragging right not many firefighters these days can boast, standing on the rear bumper of a fire truck, flying down the road at 45 miles an hour is as thrilling as it is a great memory. At my height, my head was always a beacon above the canvas covered hose bed as we made our way across town to what always became false alarms. At least in my case.

Now living down the street from my grandmother's and Station 2, I was assigned to the same engine as Eddie and Jack. I had gotten the *Fire Chicken* painted black along with adding some of the typical Trans Am parts to the body to beef up the look. I was able to get rid of the old Tempo, when I purchased an earlier model Ford Explorer around December of 97. I was making good money for being barely 19 years old and still living at home. I only worked days leaving me all my evenings and weekends, short of the occasional Saturday overtime that I would pick up answering the phone. Mainly I did this due to the peer pressure I was receiving from my female co-workers that insisted I spend a Saturday morning with them at work.

When I did respond to fire calls from home, I did so, knowing I was going to be working on a truck with at least one uncle. Several times over the last year I had in fact been on their truck simply because I spent more time at their station than the downtown one I was technically assigned to. I almost felt compelled to work on my uncle's engine in the firehouse I was raised in. Some of it was the part about carrying on the family tradition and honestly it was an extremely proud moment when our truck pulled up to a scene and two brothers and their nephew stepped off it.

But there was another part. A darker piece that I often tried not to pay attention to. I felt drawn to them in ways that seemed completely out of my control and at times, not to my liking. I couldn't put my finger on it exactly, but our past was definitely involved in ways that weren't 100 percent clear to me. Jack and I had grown close. It wasn't uncommon for us to just hang out from time to time during the week. He even joined the same gym in town that I belonged to and made every effort to workout at the same time. Eddie's role hadn't really changed much and beyond seeing him at family dinner on Sunday's or the occasional fire call, we didn't bother with each other. Which was fine as he had begun to turn into a pain in my ass. Always being overcritical and questioning anything he found out I did. Often telling me I needed to concentrate on getting a full-time fire job and stop playing with girls.

I started taking various fire tests in Massachusetts and New Hampshire in an effort to land one of these full-time positions somewhere. Me, Jack, and a family friend, Grant, had started taking trips out to New York City to buff the fires. Grant was a Lieutenant for the city next door to Townsend and was around Eddie's age. About six feet tall, with thin to balding hair on his almost pointed head, complemented with the traditional firefighter mustache on his upper lip. Oddly shaped and very animated when he spoke, Grant had been going out to NYC for years to follow the fire trucks to fires and take pictures. More often than NYC, we would drive down to Boston to catch a good fire on an occasional Saturday night. It was usually a pretty good time involving drinking coffee, listening to the fire scanners, then racing across the city to see the big city brothers go to work.

Back at NEBS, I had caught the eye of Leslie. A skinny, red head about 5 years older than me that was part of the group of women I worked with in my section of the department. We used computers for the majority of our work, and they had an internal messaging system that allowed you to talk to co-workers. One day I received a message on my screen simply stating, "Hey big guy!" from Leslie. As I looked over my cubicle wall in her direction, I saw her thick locks of red hair peek over hers with that overcompensating smile she always seemed to have.

A few days later we went out for dinner and then back to her house, where she lived with her parents. As we walked in, her mother and father were heading out for a night on the town. After a quick meet and greet Leslie and I were alone in the dimly lit single story home. The kitchen located in the back, was across from her bedroom, which was in the front. Opening the fridge, she bent to look deeper at the lower shelves, at the same time making sure her back side was pointed in my direction. With a glimpse over her shoulder, she caught me staring at her and smiled.

"You wanna beer?" She said as she turned with two already in her hands.

Walking past me towards her bedroom, she handed over one of the bottles while twisting the cap off as I grabbed it. I stood, taking a large gulp of the pale lager as she stopped at her bedroom door, leaning against the frame. Her fingers motioning for me to come to her side, I obeyed and soon leaned against the wood frame across from her, staring back at each other as we sipped our beers.

"Wanna come in? My parents won't be home till after midnight and no one else is here." Words that had never been asked of me and I had been fantasizing about and dreading all at the same time.

Leslie took my hand and walked me into her large bedroom decorated in peach walls and white draperies over the two windows facing the front yard. A rather large bed was outfitted with extremely fluffy and inviting pillows and blankets. A nightstand on one side, and a bureau on the other against the wall, both had small lamps with pink shades. A giant bean bag sat opposite the bed next to a bookshelf with several sci-fi novels filling its structure. The whole room screamed girl and smelt of strawberries and jasmine. I never thought I would experience anything like it, at the same time, I could feel my insides starting to turn. As she sat on the edge of the bed, I came and stood in front, with her head level with my waist. With another smile, she put her beer down, grabbed me by my belt and pulled me down on top of her, my beer somehow landing right side up on the floor.

Now hip to hip, with my legs between hers, she began running her hands up along my back. With every inch I felt myself getting further and further distanced from the whole situation. Lifting her head, her lips met mine and I brought my chest on top of hers. Her arms wrapped around me with mine up under her back and head, we made out rolling back and forth on the bed. Everything seemed to turn black, and I could only feel sensations on my body. Her arms moved from my back to the front of my waist as she worked at undoing my belt.

I started to feel small, with the room growing larger and larger. The lamp next to me seemed to be a hundred feet tall. The peach walls faded into brown, like wood and darkness surrounded me making it hard to see Leslie's face. I felt moist, soft lips on my face, filling me with terror at the same time feeling oddly familiar. Suddenly a hundred hands were grabbing my entire body, with several on my bum. I tried to focus but felt myself getting aroused. I don't want this. Please stop. Ringing starts at a high pitch in my ears. I clench down on my back side as I felt a small hand grab my penis and a distant voice. The dark room begins to spin, and I feel a sudden jolt.

Looking up at Leslie from the floor, I see an unimpressed look. Covered in sweat and trying to catch my breath I stand and begin to make my way to the door. Apologizing for whatever I did, she follows me into the kitchen trying to reassure me I didn't need to leave. I can't even look her in the face as I tell her in a shaky voice that I just needed to go home. We would go on half a dozen more dates, with me even meeting her sister and other family before she grew tired of my lack of intimacy.

Over the next few months, I went on several dates with several different women all ending relatively the same way. That summer, shortly after enrolling in the fall semester at Mount Wachusett

Community College, a guy named Jim started working in my section. He was about 30 and married with a few young children. Jim was also openly bi-sexual. It being 1998, and in the part of Massachusetts it was, this was unheard of. It blew me away that he was so accepting and honest of his attraction towards other men, sharing a few stories from his past during a few lunch breaks.

Was this my problem?

Was I trying to date the wrong sex?

Too scared to explore this possibility for too many reasons, I started to tell myself it was just because of what happened to me as a kid. The only reason I felt attracted and at times aroused by another man was because I was molested and raped by them. So, I moved on, again.

A quick stint with a girl named Shelly got me invited over to my supervisor, Jessica's house one Friday night. Shelly and I had been messing around for a few weeks, with me getting tagged out between first and second base. She and my supervisor had been friends for a while. We met over Jessica's where I ended up way over my head. Shelly was 2 years older than me with Jessica being in her mid-30's. As we watched a VHS copy of Backdraft in her small apartment next door to the central fire station, I realized why I had been invited over. The groping of my body commenced around the same time as a shower scene played out on the tv. Feeling the pressure of now trying to impress two women, my insides began an all too familiar cycle. Stepping back, with both Jessica and Shelly standing in only their underwear and bras, everyone was immediately aware I wasn't up to the task.

With Jessica disappearing to her bedroom, Shelly and I laid on the floor with her wearing only a t-shirt. With a situation similar to the one with Leslie almost playing out, I finally rounded second base, sliding into third face first. Literally.

After that, I kept to myself. Word had gotten around regarding my sexscapade failures with over a dozen female co-workers even reaching my mother's part of the world. Less than impressed she made sure to tell me just how awful all those girls were, and how ashamed I should feel for making her look bad at work. Eventually I quit, not being able to look at my supervisor in the face anymore. I immersed myself into my studies and as many calls with the fire department as I could make.

I began losing large chunks of time again. Often sitting in my room, right next door to my parents, I would place the oversized headphones on, and turn the volume so high it drowned out even the loudest noises. I would drift into daydream after daydream of me just being comfortable with intimacy with somebody. When I wasn't listening to music, I deferred to my old past time of playing video games or watching porn. I stuck with going to the gym, getting myself back into shape. I still hung around with Dave and Alex, more often the latter as Dave had been dating Kristina now for almost two years. Kristina happened to be the fire chief's daughter and a childhood friend of mine. She was a few years younger than her boyfriend, with long blonde hair and an infectious smile.

Alex remaining single himself, not so much as dating a girl, we spent most of our free time together. We grew closer than ever, and it didn't matter if it were a movie, grabbing food, or talking on the phone, it seemed we interacted daily. My parent's always liked Alex, probably because when I was with him I wasn't getting myself in trouble with women. He had also recently joined his father on the fire department in Ashby. Still pretty lazy, most of our time was spent sitting somewhere talking nonsense about whatever floated into our mind. I always felt safe around Alex, and zero expectations from either side of our relationship. It just was what it was.

Early '99 brought with it a need for some changes for me. I was all in with my second full-time semester at college which when I was engaged in my studies was going well. My first series of fire service-based classes had begun and members from other area departments were in attendance which was comforting. When not studying or actively in classes my head seemed to be going its own direction filled with terrifying images, ear ringing, cold sweats, and periods of time I couldn't account for. I had given up on dating even though several female classmates were trying their hardest to grab my attention. Under pressure from my parents, because of my stand-offish attitude and frequent anger, I went to see a new therapist.

Walking into the second-floor office, plastered with décor out of the mid-80's, smelling of stale air and incense, I was greeted by this new "shrink". A round man, around 40 with curly hair thrown on a head that reminded me of Jabba the Hut, he wore square glasses and spoke with a high pitched nasally voice. I should have turned right around and walked out, but I decided to take a seat on the black leather sofa off to my right. As we got to know each other, he asked about my past, other therapist and if I was currently on any medications. I hadn't taken any prescriptions in almost three years by this time, to which hearing, Jabba's nose twitched, and he made a "ah-huh" under his breath. When the subject of my father came up, and I said how I wanted to piss on the man's grave when he died, the response I received closed the doors on this new relationship.

"You have no right to be upset with your father." Jabba said not even looking up from his little note pad.

With that I stood up, grabbed a ten dollar bill out of my pocket for the copay, and threw it in his direction as I stormed out of the office. I never returned to which I received backlash for until I told my mother what Jabba had said. After that she was more open to me looking into a different therapist.

Shortly after, I got myself a new part-time job delivering mattresses for a small store over in Leominster, which was a few towns over. The owner, Peter, was a jolly man in his mid-40's on the chubby side, with a round head, black hair, and glasses. He literally looked like Peter Griffin from Family guy which was ironic as the show had just aired around the same time. He had an awesome laugh, an approachable disposition, and absolutely loved that I was a firefighter. Almost immediately I shared stories with him regarding my other job, to which I found out he had moonlighted as a volunteer firefighter for a short stint somewhere in New Hampshire. This mutual respect came in handy when I would occasionally be late or miss a shift due to the fire department.

The first kid I began working with was a bit of a troublemaker, and your typically 20-year-old that liked to drink. Peter had another store up in Manchester New Hampshire that we would do deliveries for on Tuesday afternoons, and Saturdays. Three other afternoons were dedicated to the primary Leominster store. A normal work week ended up around 28 hours and fit in great with my school schedule. My head deep in the books and pushing my body at the gym in my spare time, I had almost no down time. So, when my co-worker would ask me to join him on his drunken after-hours escapades, I kindly declined. I barely had time for the few friends I had, and this kid just didn't impress me, although he tried every chance he got.

The pay wasn't great, but with the occasional tips we received from customers, we made out ok each week. Most of the cash we received on shift went right to meals, snacks or the "road sodas" we would enjoy towards the end of our day. Time pressed on and I had gotten used to my delivery partners behavior even the frequent shifts he was beginning to miss. When this happened I often had to do deliveries with one of the sales associates from the Manchester store, or worse, Peter himself.

At the end of March, the kid warned me on a Thursday afternoon that he wouldn't be in that Saturday. I shook my head with a smile that showed that I was trying to keep not being surprised inside me.

"Yeah, and you'll be working with Peter's daughter Heather too!" He said this as he stepped out from the driver's seat, knowing I wasn't impressed with this bit of information.

I knew my boss had three daughters, the oldest, Heather, being my age and in college down near Worcester. I had never met any of Peter's kids and only bumped into his wife, Darlene, a few times when she would show up to get money from him. I began to feel myself getting upset over having to work with someone I didn't know. It being the boss's daughter added to the pressure I found myself feeling in calling out of my Saturday shift as well. All sorts of thoughts flew around my head from the obvious of whether she was cute, ugly, overweight like her dad, or just annoying. Would she pull the whole "well my daddy's the boss" card? Could she even lift?

I spent Friday freaking myself out with more of these thoughts before spending the evening drinking a 12 pack with Alex. Hearing the story and the extravagant possibilities I had conjured up, he simply laughed at me telling me to stop being an idiot. Walking in at nine the next morning, I was relieved to find only my boss in the store. Thinking to myself that Peter's oldest was suddenly unavailable, I felt my shoulders relaxed and my stomach return to its normal position.

"Hey buddy. Heather will be here in a few. She's still on college time!" My cartoon character looking boss said with a chuckle as he smiled and walked past me to his office in the back.

Moments later, a small blue Geo Metro pulled in the front parking lot with a young, athletic brunette emerging from within. Standing by the side of the car taking an elastic off her wrist, she pulls her shoulder length brown hair into a tight ponytail, before turning towards the store.

Peter returning from the back, confirming this to in fact be Heather, left my jaw on the floor. Smiling as he walked behind the front counter, I followed the long strides his oldest daughter made as she closed in on the glass door. I was captivated by her beauty, firm athletic build and confident smile upon a head held high as she reached for the handle. Feeling my mouth open, I retracted my jaw and took a swallow of the saliva that was building up behind my teeth, as she walked right up with an outstretched hand.

"You must be Keith! I'm Heather." She said grabbing my hand with an unexpected grip.

Damn it.

She even smelled good.

CHAPTER 5
AIN'T NO SUNSHINE

hate soccer about as much as tennis and watching golf or stock car races. The only sport I ever truly enjoyed watching in any capacity was baseball, followed a distant second with the occasional football game. But for some reason sitting in the cab of the Mattress Cloud delivery truck, listening to this beautiful young brunette go on and on about the game centered upon kicking a ball back and forth, I listened intently.

Heather had been filling me on the details of her collegiate career since we left the store over 45 minutes ago heading for Manchester. Her voice was soft, but confident and she spoke with such elegance and intriguing information that I couldn't help but want to hear more. I was driving, which was the normal routine with the other kid as he was either drunk, drinking, or hungover. Heather didn't want to drive but had offered if I didn't feel like doing so, which I found to be a nice gesture.

Almost to the other store, she began to ask what I did, outside of work and what I was going to school for. Upon hearing about the fire department, she became ecstatic, turning in her seat to look at me with a giant smile and impressed face.

"Wow! That's awesome! So, you actually run into burning

buildings?" She said as she was trying her hardest to contain her excitement which was obvious with her wide eyes and ear to ear grin.

It was refreshing to have someone genuinely interested in what I did, especially with the fire department. Short of Alex, no one ever really engaged in a meaningful conversation with me regarding anything about myself, my likes, or hobbies. To have a woman do it without poking fun, was a monumental moment. I couldn't stop staring at Heather for some reason. Up to that day I wouldn't make eye contact with any female I spoke to, even the ones I had tried being intimate with. I just wasn't able to do it, but with her it seemed to come naturally.

There was no churning stomach, narrowing vision, sweating, racing heart, or losing chunks of time. I felt an almost warm sensation all over my body. There was something that felt safe about Heather, and I was ok with not knowing exactly what it was. Throughout the day we talked about each other's life any chance we had. We laughed, we ate lunch together and she was stronger and more ambitious than the kid I normally worked with!

As the day was coming to an end, we left the Manchester area and started making our way back to Massachusetts. I was chopping at the bit to ask Heather out on a date. Even if it was just to the Burger King back at the plaza her father's store was in for a quick bite. I was trying to wrap my head around all the feelings I was experiencing with her, when I was asked something I was not expecting.

"So, I was going to come back up to Manchester tonight to watch an adult league soccer game. You want to come with me?" As she finished, she turned revealing an alluring look across her face.

Looking back at her from the driver's seat, my smile must have given her the answer she was looking for. A small giggle was followed by her plan to pick me up in Townsend on her way through, around 530. Getting back to the store and finishing what we had to, I gave her my address and phone number, and raced out the door to get home so I could get ready. Walking into the normal Saturday afternoon scene in my parent's living room of them on the couch watching tv, my mother asked what was going on. Her reaction very unbecoming of her. She seemed happy to hear that I was going out with the boss's daughter. I was on high alert because of this and gave her as little information as possible only to tell her that Heather would be at the house in 20 minutes, so I had to hurry.

Before leaving the store I had told Heather I would drive from Townsend to Manchester as I wasn't going to fit in the go cart she pulled up in earlier that morning. She assured me she would have a different vehicle, and when she arrived at my house not only was she in a four-door sedan, but she had another guy in the front seat. This ended up being a family friend, Dan, and as I walked up and Heather gave me a hug, he got into the back of the car.

The night went well. The soccer game wasn't any more enjoyable than I thought it would be, and Dan ended up sitting a few rows behind Heather and me so we could talk. After dropping me off, I was convinced I would never see her again. I walked back into my house, went to my room, and put my headphones on.

Shortly after this, the kid I worked with, not surprisingly, got himself fired. It was mid-May and when I asked Peter what he was going to do about someone for me to work with, I was shocked to hear that Heather would be filling in until he filled the position. That day, she strolled in much the same as the first time I ever put eyes on her beauty, and I think my jaw hit the floor just as hard. Walking in with the same smile, she came right up and hugged me saying how happy she was to see me again.

The day went even better than our first and as we were getting ready to head back to the store, I asked Heather if she wanted to go to the movies. I think she said yes before I even finished asking the question. Picking her up at her parent's house that was literally a mile from her dad's store, we opted to go to the theater right in Leominster. When I told her we were going to see Phantom Menace, which had just been released, she shook her head in amusement and smiled at me.

"Are you a Star Wars geek Keith?" Was said in a half serious manner, to which I told her "Kind of."

Holding hands throughout the two-hour film, we didn't even bother to eat popcorn. Walking out, still hand in hand, she asked if I wanted to hang out longer and maybe go park somewhere. Knowing what she was getting at, I agreed, and we found a secluded spot behind an abandoned gas station nearby. With a great view of the summer sky, we sat with the seats reclined in my Explorer and windows open to enjoy the warm breeze that occasionally blew through the cab. We talked about just about everything. At one point, she pulled back and leaned against the passenger door, sort of looking perplexed. When I asked if she was ok, she told me that technically she had a boyfriend.

The news hit me right in the gut. Of course, she had a boyfriend. Explaining that he had cheated on her, and they were in the process of breaking up, I still wasn't sure how to proceed. Turning to look her in the face, my initial thought was to tell her I was going to bring her home. But as our eyes met, it was as if a magnet was pulling us closer to each other. Time seemed to stand still and finally our lips came together while our eyes closed. Placing my hands on either side of her head, we sat making out in the darkness of that parking lot. It was 1 in the morning by the time I dropped her off, where we kissed another ten minutes before I backed out and drove home.

Heather and I worked together every day for a few weeks. Make out sessions happening in the back of the store and truck made for some of the most enjoyable times I've had at a job. Eventually Peter hired a new guy, Tim, who happened to graduate high school with Heather.

Summer was in full swing and the tv's were covered in stories about Y2K. Everyone was convinced that the world was going to come to a screeching halt because the computers were supposedly not going to function once the new millennium started. Heather and I were hanging out every chance we had, not caring about any of this, as she prepared to spend the next 6 weeks down on cape cod as an intern at a veterinary clinic. She was going to school to be a veterinarian and this opportunity was one she couldn't pass up. Our relationship had escalated quickly, in a physical way, with me finally getting all the way around the bases. Again, no churning stomach, no loss of time. Nothing. I always felt completely safe with Heather, and once we had become sexually active, we didn't stop.

Any chance we had, we made love. Some days, multiple times.

One day on the phone while she was on The Cape, she told me she had never felt the way she did for me before with anyone. I wasn't sure what I was feeling beyond it being the best thing I felt in my life. I had no idea what love was in a romantic sense, and even love on a family level was confusing to me. Up to Heather, any chance I had to be physically close to a woman ended in disaster and at times embarrassment. For a while I didn't want to be close for fear of what it could bring. Everything with her just felt right all the time, and I was beginning to think I was falling in love.

Mind you, I refused to say it and I was definitely not going to say it first.

One Saturday night she drove all the way up to Townsend, having said on the phone earlier that she just needed to be with me. After getting to my house, I took her up to the empty fire station to show her around. As I opened the officer's door on Engine 2 for her to check out the inside, she hopped up and motioned for me to join her. Climbing on top of her, we quickly find ourselves undressed, grinding against each other, eventually having sex inside the same fire engine I had gone on so many heart wrenching calls prior. As we stood in the bay, getting our clothes on, she pushed me up against the wall and began kissing me. Pulling back with the biggest smile I've ever seen on someone's face; she told me something I had never heard from a woman in my life.

"I love you so much Keith!" she began crying the happiest of tears, pressing her face against my chest and wrapping her arms around me.

Eventually I said it back, and the two of us were convinced we would never leave each other's side. Early August put that to the test.

After a bare foot run around her neighborhood, Heather got an infection in her foot that went systemic. She ended up critically ill and in a coma at UMASS hospital in Worcester. The infection turned out to be of the flesh-eating type, and she underwent dozens of surgeries in an attempt to stop the spread and save her life. During this same time, the fire department was holding its annual outing up at one of the small local ponds down the road from where the fatal fire of March 1997 was. A three-day festivity that ran from Friday to Sunday, members and their families camped out in tents and RV's drinking, eating, swimming, and sharing stories old and new. I had hoped to show off my first real girlfriend while spending the weekend in a tent with her. Now that it wasn't going to happen, I walked around with my head hung low, convinced Heather was going to die.

It would also be the first time my uncle Jack and I would get into a fist fight.

At one point he said something to me, I took it the wrong way and next thing we knew, punches were being thrown. We had to be pulled off one another, and once things cooled off, he came over and I told him why I was so heated with everything going on with Heather.

Weeks went on and I would visit my girlfriend bedside while she slept, not aware of my presence. Sitting there staring at Heather lying in bed with tubes and wires going everywhere in and on her body, she looked lifeless. I would beg God to put me in her place, convinced that I deserved it, and she did not. I went as often as I could, sometimes three times a week just to walk in, hold her hand, and be told by family or a doctor that I had to leave. When I did, I felt like I was leaving a part of me there. There was just something eerie about the whole situation every time I walked out of the ICU down in Worcester. Up to that time, I had never actually seen someone unconscious in a hospital bed like that.

Time went on, Heather finally recovered from her coma and

was eventually released. Her time home was hard for her, and still, I tried almost daily to be in her life just to see her face and try to make her smile. For a while she stayed with her mother's parents down the street from her own house, as they had a single-story home making it easier for her to get around. Once she made it back to her house, it became clear I was no longer welcome. Phone calls went unanswered. When I'd stop by, I was told she didn't want to see me. A few times, I drove by, seeing her "ex" boyfriend's car parked in the driveway.

So, heartbroken I stopped trying.

I felt used, loveless, and unlovable. The whole thing reinforced what my family had been hard at work doing for two decades. My mother took full advantage of the situation making sure I know how awful of a person Heather was, and that she never cared for her. Later that fall, I quit working at the store, taking a overnight job at the local Pepsi plant working in the quality control lab. I was drinking throughout the week and had begun using pills that a coworker at my new job was supplying me with, to numb any feelings that came into my body.

I was still running fires and emergencies and even had a few close close calls that barely phased me. I simply didn't care. Somehow I came down with Mononucleosis, mono for short, and got pretty sick. Even that didn't stop me from my escapades with alcohol. Eventually I got hopeless, not quite suicidal, and wished for something to take me out, or maybe not wake up one day. After being told I was loved by someone for the first time, and having them do an about face, I just didn't care anymore.

December 3rd brought our fire department Christmas party, two days after my 21st birthday. A few hours into an otherwise joyous evening of awards, acknowledgments and gratuitous drinking, tragedy struck central Massachusetts. Six city firefighters were killed in the line of duty at the Worcester Cold Storage Fire in what would become the largest loss of firefighters since the Vendome fire in Boston decades prior. After we were notified of that, a solemn and melancholy mood fell over all in attendance. Worcester was a large city of about 200,000, 40 minutes to the south of Townsend.

In the days that followed, numerous departments from across the state would send apparatus down to Worcester to provide relief and coverage while their members searched for their missing firefighters remains in the rubble of the giant warehouse. Townsend was part of this effort. A week or so later a large ceremony was held in remembrance of what became dubbed "The Worcester Six" at the Centrum downtown. I was among the over ten thousand firefighters from around the country, Canada, and parts of the world that marched through the city to pay our respects.

Christmas had an odd feeling a few weeks later, and with everything I had going on in my head after breaking up with Heather, I barely took part. The day after I joined Eddie, Jack, Grant, and a few others on a northern Vermont snowmobiling trip. My uncles and Grant had just purchased a cabin by a lake about four miles south of the Canadian border in Averill Vermont. It was a great time of hanging out, drinking, telling stories, eating homecooked food and snowmobiling. There was no electricity or running water by the normal standards and the heat was all woodstove or from the gas baseboards. We ran a generator when we needed minimal electricity and took sponge baths in the sink to clean up. For the first time in months, I was able to joke about the whole Heather situation and eventually it stopped occupying my brain 24/7.

Returning home two days into the new year after the world didn't end, I went back to work at my job in the QC lab at Pepsi. At the end of my work week, now off for three days, I sat on the couch in my parent's living room doing some homework. Deep into my studies shortly after lunchtime, I heard a car pull into the driveway, and then a knock on the front door. Not giving it much thought I walked over and turned the knob, opening the door to reveal Heather standing on the other side. Her face as beautiful as the first time I set eyes on her, smile as radiant as ever, she stood there looking back at me.

Heather sat on one end of the couch as I tried to sit as far away from her on the other. I stared forward, not looking her way as she asked the usual questions, trying to engage me in conversation. I felt the betrayal of the past months creeping back up inside me, as she spoke. I stood up, fists clenched, about to tell her to leave the house, when she did the same and looked me right in the eyes.

"Keith, I tried to get ahold of you so many times. I was wrong by pushing you away. I love you so much!" Tears rolling from her eyes over her rosy cheeks, she leaned forward putting her head into my chest.

Putting my arms around Heather, she began to tell me about the phone calls I was never home for or aware of. She told me about how after the Worcester Six fire, she had stopped by the house a few times, to be told to leave by my mother or Don. None of this, neither of my parents ever relayed to me, often my mother telling me I was better off without Heather in my life.

My betrayal shifted focus, and I looked down at Heather to be met with her hazel eyes staring right back at me. Before either of us knew it, we were in a full embrace, locking lips in a fury of passion. Ripping each other's clothes off, we made love right there on the living room floor. In the beautiful aftermath, holding her in my arms, she looked at me and said she would never leave my side again for the rest of her life.

After that day we were inseparable. I began working at the Massachusetts Fire Academy, along with a few side jobs swinging hammers, doing demolition, while attending college and still working for the fire department. In between all that, Heather and I spent as much time together as possible. We went to new places, tried new things, and even when we didn't have the money to stay in a hotel, we would drive somewhere and sleep in my truck. I felt a release in what was building anger and the warm sensation I had flowing through my body the year before, had returned. We were madly in love.

Much to my mother's displeasure.

Come early April I decided to propose to Heather while down

on Cape Cod taking a weekend getaway. When I pulled out the ring belonging to her grandmother and asked her to marry me, she jumped on top of me, knocking me off the side of the bed. Saying yes, we went out that night for dinner to celebrate. Before we had time to tell everyone in our families our marriage plans, we found out she was pregnant. This did not go over well on either side. Especially hers having Irish Catholic routes.

The weeks that followed were stressful with me and Heather's mother being the cause of most of it. We were living together at my parents in my small bedroom, with both of us working to save money for own place to come after our wedding that was now planned for September. Heather and I fought a lot due to this stress. One fight in particular fell on the night before I was slated to go work the fire academy. As I was walking out the door to make the 40-minute drive that morning, Heather stopped me and gave me a kiss.

"I love you, always. Please be careful today." She said as she ran her hand along my jawline.

It was business as usual down at the fire academy that day. I was working with another "support" member lighting fires in the training building for the fire recruits. My job those days was to ignite varying fires in different rooms, on different floors for the fire academy recruits to practice extinguishing. The guy I was working with, Fitzy, was an old school firefighter from one of the area towns, and a bit of a drunk. That day in particular was what they called Phase Four fire day, meaning we lit fires in almost every room on every floor, simultaneously. These require a choreography between my partner and I through visual signals and radio traffic.

My duty was the first floor and top floor with Fitzy having the basement and second floors. Once we start, you had to move quick to get all the fires lit, then make a hasty exit before the recruits came in with hose lines and tried putting them all out. My plan was, once I got to the top floor, I would bale out a side window, onto the balcony roof next to it.

Over the radio, I heard Fitzy's raspy voice give me the go ahead to start lighting my rooms. As I rounded the hall, making my way to the last room, I saw him run past me up the stairs to start on the second floor. When I was done, I made my way up the same stairs to then have to walk past the fires Fitzy was lighting to get to a separate set to head to the top floor. As I walked past the second-floor rooms, they were ablaze, and the heat was building quickly. Even through the turnout gear I knew it was getting warm. I hadn't yet put my facepiece on for the SCBA, as the air was relatively smoke free. I started to climb the second set of stairs, the heat got intense, and I took a knee to put on my air mask.

Getting upstairs, the area was already filling with smoke, and I could feel the heat banking down across the giant open room. A few steps in, the heat got so bad I had to crawl over to the pile of straw and pallets I was charged with lighting. Pitchfork in one hand as I fumbled with a lighter in the other, the huge pile of fuel ignited in front of me from the buildup of heat. I stumbled backwards onto my ass in surprise.

"Hurry up Hanks! Light that fire and get the fuck out of the building! It's going fast!" Fitzy's raspy voice bellowed up the stairs below me.

I watched in amazement as the fire took off and grew in size with every second. I could hear the crews below me making entry into the lower floors doing their best to put out the other fires. I knew I had to get over to the far wall, to the window I needed to get out was located. Suddenly the whole room went black, and I was in a world of hurt. Crawling around on my hands and knees I raced to find a wall to try to orient myself. I heard the footsteps of the recruits followed by the voices of their instructors yelling my name. Finally finding the wall, I threw myself as flat as I could against the floor next to it and was convinced this was it. It was hot as hell, my ears burned, even the air in my tank was getting hard to breathe.

I was going to die. I knew it and the only image in my head was Heathers face.

As I was about to start reciting my prayers, a hose line began hitting the big fire behind me. Immediately it started to cool off, and I felt a sense of relief. I made my way along the wall finding a window and opening the metal shutters within it. Sticking my pitchfork out into the fresh spring air, I felt for the balcony floor before hurling myself through. I fell into a heap onto the cement roof, steam and smoke rising off my tan gear. Looking down, the radio antenna in the coat pocket had melted in a candy cane shape and the visor on my helmet was completely warped.

Getting down the escape ladder and walking up to the other instructors, their faces told me shit had gotten real. Apparently wind had come through the drill yard in an unusual fashion causing the fires on the lower floors to take off quicker than normal. By the time I had gotten to the third floor, flames were pushing out of almost every window in the building. They were all calling me on the radio, but it had melted. For a few tense minutes, they too thought I was dead. For a while after that day, I was sent to the gas yard for a safer task of filling extinguishers. This felt like more of a punishment than the safeguarding it may have been intended for. It did cause me to realize that I was less concerned about dying than I was of leaving my pregnant fiancé alone.

Taking the sign, I poured myself into supporting Heather and letting the stress of our families roll off. Her mother was never my biggest fan, as she felt what I was going into for a career as a firefighter was a joke and had little respect for it. With both our mother's causing almost daily stress, we vowed to stick by each other's side, ending every day with a passionate kiss and "I love you."

Because of her being pregnant, Heather's family pushed us to hold our wedding before the birth of the baby. September 2nd, 2000, we got married with our friends and family present in a ceremony that ended up being held entirely at the Elks Club. Originally planned for the common in downtown Townsend, with fire trucks and the whole sha-bang, a rainstorm caused a last-minute change in plans. Alex as my best man, Heathers sisters as bridesmaids with Dave and Grant as some of the groomsmen, the day went great all things considered. Our honeymoon was in Disneyworld and was not only my first time going on a trip further than NYC, but also flying. We spent 10 days running around like kids, laughing, and going on rides. Heather being pregnant, couldn't enjoy any alcohol, but it didn't even matter. The time spent together brought us even closer than we already were.

Getting back, we moved out of my parents place and into our first apartment right next door to the West Townsend fire station. I had also taken a full-time position at the same manufacturing plant as Don a few towns away. I was working a 4-day overnight shift from Sunday to Wednesday while finishing my degree in college and beginning my EMT class at the hospital. I was busy between all of that and a very pregnant wife who was due with our son the middle of January. I was burning the candle on both ends, but overall, we were doing really well.

I had set up a sleeping routine whenever I was in bed next to Heather as I had been having difficulty falling asleep since we became a full-time couple. I'd lay next to her and act like I was asleep until I knew she was, then I would turn and stare at the ceiling till I eventually passed out from exhaustion. When I did sleep, my bad dreams were back in full swing which Heather was aware of, but we never discussed it. Then there were the times the fire department would shorten my stay in bed.

Beginning of November, I was taking a nap on a Thursday mid-day with Heather at her father's store now working as the vice president. The sun was shining in the windows of our second floor two-bedroom apartment, and my eyes were just starting to open when the fire department pager started chanting its tune from across the room. Another house fire with people possibly trapped rang through the airwaves as I jumped into my bunker pants out in the hallway. Getting next door at the same time as Eddie and the rest of the would be crew that day, we raced off to the known address just down the street and across the river. Dicky Amadon was our Lieutenant that day.

Dicky and three of his sons were staples in the fire department, with the father having almost 45 years on the job himself alone. Donnie, his eldest son, and I had gotten close in recent years. He got on the fire department with Eddie back in 1978 after graduating high school with him. Dicky and Donnie were common figures around the first apartment my mother and I lived in as the Amadon's owned a bunch of buildings around town. They also ran one of the school bus companies. Beyond that, all three of my uncles had worked up at the Amadon family farm back in their teenage years. The relationship Donnie and I forged was one of mutual respect and brotherly love. He always loved hearing stories of how I was testing for other fire departments and my journey through college.

Pulling up front of the dilapidated home, all of us were relieved to see two occupants laying on the grass. Smoke and steam rising from both their bodies, having narrowly escaped death minutes before. Taking my orders from Dicky, I ran a hose line up to the front door as I pushed the heavy orange flames back. The house was a total loss, and we eventually learned that the third resident, who was missing initially, wasn't home at the time of the fire.

Around this time, my Uncle Jack had been diagnosed with testicular cancer. He was immediately put on a treatment regimen that including several weekly visits to the chemotherapy unit at UMASS. At the time, Heather was going down once a week or so, for minor surgeries on her leg. These procedures were to repair some of the leftover work from her stay in the summer of '99. Jack and Heather would often make their appointments on the same day so they could ride together. Something that I think helped keep each of their spirits lifted. When she couldn't go, I would. When I couldn't, someone from the fire department would. Support came in many forms for my youngest uncle as he fought and eventually beat this round of cancer.

Christmas time came and Heather insisted on a real tree that I reluctantly cut down then dragged up the two flights of stairs to our small living room. She also tried making popcorn garland which led to the bleeding of my fingertips, and more shattered popcorn than a decorative piece on the tree. We received a camcorder for a gift from her parents with the hopes of taking videos of their soon to be grandson.

A few days before Christmas, a Manchester New Hampshire firefighter would die in the line of duty trying to save a child. His funeral was the day after the holiday, so Eddie and I went up for the services. It was a bitterly cold day around 12 degrees, and I remember my face was numb as we got back to his truck. Returning around lunchtime, I walked into the apartment with a very pregnant Heather greeting me in our kitchen. Stepping forward, she gave me a hug and I just wrapped my arms around her.

"Please don't ever leave me like that." She said as tears rolled down her face.

I took my class A uniform off and laid down on our bed, with Heather next to me my hand going over the circumference of her tummy. A few jokes about the size of her round stomach led to the all-familiar love-making that our relationship had grown accustomed too. While the two of us slept in full embrace, the fire department tones, and screeching voice of the dispatcher came over the radio. This time it was for a fire in the east end of town with neighbors reporting heavy fire showing.

Eddie driving, Donnie in the back and myself planted in the officer's seat, we sped off for the 5-mile ride across town. Getting our orders as we turned into the neighborhood, black smoke could be seen rising above the tree line a 1/8 of a mile away. Pulling up to the house and stepping out of the truck, I looked to see the crew from Engine 1 getting pushed back out the front door by thick orange rolls of flames. Walking up, stretching out the hose line as I went, the fire chief motioned for me to come to the same door the previous crew lost a valiant fight at. Flames were coming out of the door over our heads and the windows to our right, with thick, acrid brown smoke from just about everywhere else. I made my way into the front left of the house and doused the fire then turned to make it to the rear kitchen. My back up on the hose line then tapped my shoulder, bringing my attention to the room I just extinguished, that had reignited in ferocious flames.

Back and forth we would go as we made our way around the inside of the home. Melted family pictures, tv's, the skeleton of a Christmas tree with traces of what were once gifts scattered around the house made for a sad scene. In the heat of battle, the guy behind me left, leaving me alone in the building. As I struggled to move the nozzle and hose line from one side to the other, the fire creeping closer and closer in on me, I began to feel impending doom. Finally, as I became pinned at the end of a hallway, behind the front room with the fire rolling up on my heels, another firefighter came up and we moved to extinguish what had become an almost 20-minute fight. With where my headspace had returned to, part of me was almost upset that I hadn't bought the farm. The flashbacks were becoming an almost daily occurrence, and my sleep was questionable at best with even worse nightmares starting up again. I found myself wishing for a hero's death more and more and when I survived a near miss, I was let down at the outcome.

Black bunting. A folded American flag. None would have been the wiser, but my pain would be over.

Back out at the truck as I had my air bottle changed out, I looked at what was left of the house. The residents, not home at the time, were standing in the front yard crying at what would be a total loss of everything they owned. Three air bottles and five hours later, I walked back into my apartment. Heather smiling, sitting on the couch, held the camcorder in her hand.

"That was a bad one, but I got some really good footage!!" She said in such a proud tone. As exhausted as I was, I tossed her an ear-to-ear grin, with an accompanying impressed laugh.

January 2001 brought the arrival of my first child, Tyler, and the stress of figuring out how to be a young father. I had the honor of welcoming him into the world, alongside the doctor, in a relatively uneventful delivery. I immediately found myself growing attached to this adorable little version of me. He even had my oversized ears! I loved him from the second I laid eyes on him and heard his first screams. Back home I was bouncing between overnights at work, the fire station, EMT class, college, along with being a husband and new father. With no high-quality role models, short of Don in later years, I felt pressure to not let this little guy down and give him everything I never had. Donnie Amadon even stopped by the apartment to see Tyler. While holding him he shot me one of his famous proud looks.

"I love ya brother. You're gunna make a great dad!" He said with one arm over my shoulder, the other holding my son.

After another close call with the fire department in early spring where I nearly fell off an icy roof, Heather and I made the decision to invest in life insurance. Something neither of us had ever given a second thought to, but now married with a kid, and the near misses I seemed to keep having, I bought each of us a policy knowing we wouldn't need it till well into old age. I was still on the fence on whether I was better off dead or not, but I knew I definitely didn't want to leave Heather with a heavy financial burden if something did happen. With Tyler waking up nightly, sometimes several times, I used it as the perfect excuse not to sleep or get up with him every chance I was home. One morning over coffee, Heather asked me how I was sleeping. Something no one had ever asked me in a genuine way. So, I told her the truth, that I really wasn't. I withheld the part about the nightmares and the daytime flashbacks, but she now knew I was faking falling asleep whenever we were in bed together.

Her ability to give me the female stink eye was at times an uncanny skill.

Early May brought an event no one on the Townsend Fire Department was prepared for. In the early morning hours one weekday morning after beginning his daily farm chores, Dicky Amadon had a massive heart attack. Dying at the hospital after being transported by half a dozen responders that had worked alongside him for decades. Having just gone on a fire call the day prior made this situation even harder to come to terms with. We gave Dicky full department honors at his funeral, complete with bagpipers. Donnie approached me and asked if I would give his father's eulogy at the church services. I did my best trying to pay the highest respect to a man that had taught not only me, but my family, and hundreds of others from the town so much about being a good man. I had been to a dozen firefighter funerals up to that point, and after that day I was all set with going to anymore.

Summer pressed on and having passed my EMT class, I only had a handful of classes left to complete for my degree once college started again in the fall. September came and Heather was asked to be in one of her friends weddings later that fall. I had applied to one of the local private ambulance companies and was slated to start mid-month. We woke up and began our normal weekday morning routine with the exception that I had to leave earlier to head north to Concord New Hampshire for the statewide firefighter exam. It was a beautiful, unusually sunny day for that time of year I remember thinking. Dave showed up to the apartment to ride with me, as I finished my coffee. Leaning over to kiss Heather and Tyler as she looked over a bridal magazine, we exchanged "I love you's" and Dave and I walked out the door at 730am.

It was Tuesday September 11th.

Despite all the death, carnage, and unknown of what would happen next that most around the country and world felt that day, some of us in the first responder world saw a different perspective. That day we spent hours searching for a Vietnam veteran that went AWOL in the woods shortly after the first tower fell. During breaks we had regular townspeople coming up to thank us for all we do, asking what they could do for the distraught person and his family. In the weeks that followed we saw churches filled with more parishioners than in recent years. People started holding doors for others and exchanging smiles at their stores and coffee shops. Kids would stop by the fire stations just to tell us how they wanted to do our job when they got older. American pride was at an all-time high. Families grew closer and spent more time together. Even mine. In the shadows and literal dust of that day people found hope on the heels of one of the worst terrorist events in history.

I myself began to feel things may not be as bad as they had felt for so long.

Around Thanksgiving, Heather's parents offered to have us to take over their Leominster house as they had built a larger one a few towns to the west. A two-story cape style with attached two car garage on a postage stamp property, the house itself needed some interior TLC. Immediately I enlisted the help of Alex and a few others to make this house a home. Heather and I had just found out she was pregnant again and we were going to eventually outgrow our small two-bedroom apartment in Townsend. I had started at the ambulance service in Leominster back in September, so the whole situation seemed like it was meant to be.

Even working 50 plus hours a week on the ambulance, maintaining my time with the fire department and finishing up college, me and Alex went through every room on both floors replacing floors, walls, cabinets, paint, and carpets. We probably drank way more beer than we really needed to but had more laughs than expected. Often one or two ambulances would be found parked out on the street, while our co-workers stopped in to see our progress.

With all that I was doing, I would often sleep at the house in Leominster not seeing my pregnant wife or Tyler for a few days at a time. After a month or so of doing this, it began to wear on me and Heather's relationship. We fought more than usual. I drank more than usual. I would reach a ten quicker than before. I seemed more on edge and even more anxious than I ever had as an adult.

Granted I was responding to emergencies I had never gone to before and seeing parts of society I hadn't been exposed to yet. Becoming a father to another child was definitely weighing heavy on my mind. Overall, I was doing right by Tyler, but he wasn't even a year old yet. I began having thoughts of what was going to happen as he and his soon-to-be sibling grew older. I was already walking the line between doing what I thought was right as a dad and winging it altogether. My biggest fear was dropping the ball like all the other would-be fathers in my family.

Come end of May 2002, the house was finished enough to move in, and not a minute sooner. Saturday June 1st, as I was getting ready to head in for an overnight shift, Heather felt contractions and ended up being brought to the hospital by my mother. I met the two of them there with my partner and the ambulance and right around 1130, I helped deliver my daughter Elizabeth. I ended up working a "reverse" 24-hour shift scheduled to end Sunday night. I went back up to the maternity ward the next morning with my new partner, Ben, to spend some time with Heather and Elizabeth. Ben brought his drug box to do his morning checks and even got to hold my new daughter while displaying one of the biggest smiles I've ever seen the man bear. As we walked out, he looked at me saying how great it was to be able to visit someone in the hospital under the circumstances that they were.

A few weeks later I was fired from my position under suspicion of doing something I hadn't actually done. A situation laden in others not believing me, that would further fuel the perception that I needed to keep my past hidden.

By July I had gotten hired by a different service, this time working up in Lawrence. Heather was working ten-hour days at the store, now running the books and day-to-day operations with the occasional need to be a sales rep. She had also become a little too close for my comfort with one of the salesmen, Eli. With me now working further from home on 12, 16 and occasional 24-hour shifts, this often-left long periods of time where I wouldn't hear from Heather. She assured me nothing was going on, but with our relationship somewhat strained, I often found myself drifting into paranoia that she and Eli were engaging in extra-marital activities.

As fall of 2002 settled into early winter, I was working two 16 hour shifts along with an 8 on Friday that ran 5pm to 1am. I was responding to, at times, a call an hour and some of them were pretty bad. Lawrence a very large city, population-wise, but only about 8 square miles in size. The Merrimack River separated the north and south parts of the city. The southwestern side being the nicest. Our ambulance station was located in South Lawrence, behind Saint Patrick's church, and around the corner from one of the city's several fire stations. A mixed demographic of poor to lower middle class with dozens of cultures all intertwined within its tiny borders. Various Hispanic gangs littered its streets and added to the higher-than-normal violent crime and murder rate Lawrence had become known for.

Right before Thanksgiving I responded to one of the many three-story apartment buildings, known in New England as a "three-decker", for an infant not breathing. When we arrived, my partner was handed a blue 18-month-old, as the parents stood oddly calm staring at the two of us. As the police were walking up the stairs, the mother disappeared to the back bedroom only to return with another child around the same age. Forced screams and tears filled the air as I was handed this tiny, lifeless little boy. Looking across the room and making eye contact with my partner, I felt the same anguish in his heart that was racing through mine. Both children had been suffocated by the parents in what had been initially deemed an accident. As I sat in the EMS room at the emergency room, the image of my two children ran through my head. I called Heather and told her what happened.

After almost a minute of silence on her end of the phone, she could only muster up "Oh my God." As I ran through describing what it felt like to hold a lifeless child in my arms, I realized it was too much for Heather. Her sobbing became apparent as she begged me to leave work and come home to be with her and the kids. I refused and ultimately finished my shift, pushing the new traumatic images into the already overstuffed file drawers of my brain.

We had already made plans for a early December trip to Aruba that had been acquired through Heathers position at her father's store. For five days we sat in the sun, waded in the warm Caribbean waters as our friends and family received six inches of snow back home. We had an absolute blast, and it was the first vacation the two of us had been on since the beginning of 2000, where Heather wasn't pregnant. So, we drank. A lot! The two of us even talked about making Aruba a yearly getaway for us. After months of questionable loyalty in our marriage, that trip, sitting staring at my beautiful young wife by the ocean every day, I felt a new formation of hope in my soul.

After a rough touchdown back home when the planes landing gear almost didn't come down, we settled back into our lifestyle, promising to take no moment for granted. Christmas was amazing with Tyler almost two and Elizabeth just over six months, gifts were spread over two different rooms in our house. Smiles upon every ones face and laughter filled every moment.

Once the new year hit and 2003 was in full swing, so were most of my previous dormant symptoms. Most of my coworkers on the ambulance had met Heather and the kids, with a few becoming closer friends. Alex was finally seeing a Colombian girl he had met while moonlighting as security at a local hotel. Heather had gotten a substantial pay raise at her job, along with more responsibilities. I was balancing 60 hours on the ambulance with time at the fire station in order to stay a member now that we lived out of town. The bad calls stacked up and I was doing more than my share of child abuse and rape situations that often left me wanting to curl into a ball and cry. I held on, bottling it all up not showing one inkling that the shitstorm of awfulness was affecting me.

Come early March it was obvious things were at their boiling point. Heather, concerned at my recent uptick in angry outbursts, got me to an emergency mental health clinic at Emerson Hospital in Concord. Convinced I had bipolar disorder with massive depression I was put on a medicine called Wellbutrin. Within a week I came unhinged, and at times inconsolable. One day at the end of the month, Heather came home from work right after I had, and we clashed in our kitchen. My grandmother, holding my almost 10-month-old daughter, with my son hiding behind her legs watched in horror as Heather and I screamed at each other. At one point she shoved me in the chest.

Everything seemed really tall, bigger than me. The green walls turned brown, like wood, and a darkness surrounded me making it hard to see the faces nearby. The voices raised and got deeper, pushing me down to the floor. One started laughing and I felt cornered. I panicked and did what I had to, to escape. Arms stretched out I grabbed the source of the laughter in front of me, throwing it as far as I could away from me. Suddenly there were screams, cries and a loud thud. I felt a rush of temporary relief as the green walls began to return.

Looking down, I saw Heather laying in a pile outside the kitchen in the mudroom, motionless. Panic set in, as I could hear my grandmother trying to calm my children in the other room. She returned as I made my way over to my wife's now stirring body.

"That's it. We're done. You're going to jail!" She said with tears rolling down her cherry red cheeks as she picked up the phone and called 911.

I walked into the living room and picked each of my kids up. I kissed Elizabeth, and hugged Tyler telling him I loved him and that I was sorry. I then sat at the kitchen table and waited for the inevitable arrival of the police department. My arms outstretched in front of me, sitting bolt upright with my eyes closed, I knew what was coming in the next three to five minutes.

Their entrance did not disappoint.

CHAPTER 6
QUIET NOW

Dave's face was long, sad, and a strong sense of disappointment was felt even from my side of the iron bars. Sitting in the Leominster police station holding cell, I stared at my feet asking my friend what I had done. Dave was working as a police dispatcher for the city and had just come in for his shift when he saw my name on the arrest log in the office.

"I don't know buddy, but it will be alright. I called your parents." He said not making eye contact with the monster that just threw a woman through a kitchen door a mile down the road.

Don showed up an hour later and I was bailed out. We returned to my house, where family from both sides were now present. No one approached me, or looked my direction as I quickly gathered some clothes and a few items for my next shift at work. Heather came out the door as I was getting into my giant red pickup. Trying to apologize for what happened, I dismissed all of it knowing this was all on me. I felt lower than low. A monster that should be put down, never to cause harm again.

"I love you Keith. I always will!" She said as heavy beads of tears rolled down her beautiful face, smashing on the ground around her. As I got in my truck and shut the door, Heather fell to the ground crying more intensely.

The next few weeks were filled with uncertainty as I stayed in my parents back bedroom. They had recently moved to Lunenburg, in a house within a lake community. The back room had become more of a storage unit than a bedroom, until I needed a place to sleep. Not that I did, but from time to time in between shifts, I would lay on the futon, staring at the ceiling. I would imagine how long I would be sentenced to prison, and what it would be like. I figured it couldn't be worse than my childhood, even with all the rape that inevitable happened to the "fresh meat" that ended up calling prison home. I came to terms with the fact that I would be sent away to some degree when the court date happened in May.

I was seeing Tyler and Elizabeth under supervised visits either at the house in Leominster or when they would get dropped off at my parents. When I saw Heather she never seemed upset to see me, almost as if the whole terrible event a few weeks prior had never taken place. She would try and give me a hug to which each time I would pull away while staring at my feet. I had also become convinced she was now sleeping around on me for sure. The thought occupied every second of my time when I wasn't running and gunning calls on the ambulance or fire engine.

That was until Friday April 11th.

I had adjusted my normal work schedule to two 24-hour shifts to make every effort to spend as much time with the kids as I could. Sitting in my parents back bedroom around 5pm, Heather pulled up their driveway, and got out of the car without Tyler or Elizabeth. I was halfway through the kitchen when she walked in the porch door that served as the main entrance. She was wearing my favorite pair of her jeans, that hugged her backside just right, accentuating her female curves. A light pullover blouse with flowery designs around the neck that came to rest just above her waist showing the perfect amount of her fair Irish stomach. To top it all off, she was wearing makeup, which in of itself was a once-a-year occurrence for her. She looked the most beautiful I had ever seen her in our almost 4 years together. Giant smile and bright hazel eyes to boot, she leaned forward and grabbed a hug from me knowing I was caught in her tractor beam.

Damn it.

She even smelled good.

"Can we go out back and talk?" She said as she took my hand, leading me from the door and into the kitchen. My parents saying hello to her, but not moving off the couch as if they were part of some plan.

Sitting on the futon my hand in hers, she spoke about everything. She told me she knew about my nightmares, the flashbacks, the bad calls, the sadness, the fear, and the loss. She even took a guess at some of my childhood stuff and wasn't far off target. Gripping my hand as hard as she could, my eyes turned up from my feet and met hers. Giant smile, beautifully outlined in soft pink lipstick, she leaned forward as I did the same, our lips meeting. We held this position for what seemed like forever. My heart filling again with the warmth she had been originally responsible for years prior. Pulling back, she didn't even break that smile.

"I love you more than anything. This is dumb. We love each other. We're going to get you help!" Drifted from her lips convincing me of something I had been denied my whole life.

That was all it took for us to fall against each other in full embrace. Her on top of me at first, until I sat forward, her arms going over my shoulders, her legs around my waist. Standing up, I reached over and shut the bedroom door and turned all in one motion, setting her down on her back on the futon with me now on top. Before either of us knew it, we were taking our clothes off and made love in the back bedroom of my parents, like we used to in our dating days.

When we were finished, she lay smiling at me from on top of my folded arm. She told me Dave and Kristina were going to meet us at the house in Leominster and the four of us were going out to dinner. She told me she was going to spend the rest of her life loving me more than she ever had and would be by my side till the end of days. Looking her back in her eyes, I knew she meant it, and I felt more in love with Heather than I had ever been.

Our friends met us as planned at our house around 7pm. We decided on a Chinese restaurant down in Worcester that we all liked. It was about a 20-minute trip down route 2 to interstate 190 to get to the city. My red Ford F-250 being a double cab with a full backseat, we climbed inside, with Dave and I up front. Our wives sat together in the back. Heather on the passenger's side and Kristina behind me. We normally sat couples with couples, but without hesitation, this time we didn't. Smiles and laughter filled the cab as we drove the one mile to the route 2 on ramp. Being almost 730 at night in April, it was dark. It had also started raining lightly just enough to run the wipers on intermittent. The rain didn't even seem to matter to us.

Talking with Dave about guy stuff, I would occasional catch Heathers face smiling at me from the back seat. Everything felt peaceful and right, as if the events of the past years were beginning to pan out the way they should. Hope filled my heart and my mind as I drove us onto the interstate to head south to Worcester. The interstate being two lanes in either direction, I drove in the right until I began to catch up to some vehicles, moving to the left in an effort to pass. One of the vehicles also moved to the left, however, didn't pick up any more speed. With vehicles coming up behind us in the right lane, I was trapped behind the slower car for a few miles. As we approached an exit, I did what I never do and moved to the right lane to pass the slower vehicle. Now on the overpass, the other vehicle suddenly moved in front of us and hit their brakes hard, causing me to react by turning the wheel.

An ominous red glare filled everything I saw in front of me. The laughter turned to screams. My world began spinning around me as I tried to muscle the steering wheel. Side to side the truck violently shifted across the pavement, eventually beginning to turn in circles. Suddenly we were moving backwards. I continued to struggle with the wheel, Heather's scream the only one I now heard. A jolted stop brought blackness to everything around me. Strange unfamiliar voices and a bright light filled my world as I turned to see Dave trying to get to Heather, her eyes looking straight ahead. No life behind them. A sudden return of darkness and sharp pain in my arms. Then cold over my entire body.

Dave G: I knew it was terrible when I watched Heather's eyes dilate.

Kristina G: I watched as my husband didn't skip a beat, freeing himself from the front seat and trying to help Heather. Catching each other's eyes, I knew it was bad.

The world around me came into focus with a frightening brightness. I was cold, my arms outstretched to my sides with the hands of a stranger on my left. As I concentrated to bring reality back, I saw the man holding my left arm drive the IV in, releasing the tourniquet around my bicep. It was a face I knew but couldn't place the name. My surroundings were that of the back of an ambulance. The white, cold, and sterile environment only disrupted by the movement of the large vehicle as the driver negotiated the black highway in front of it. As I widened my eyes to hone in on the man to my left, I felt the presence of another behind me, their hands on my shoulders.

"It's ok sir. You're in back of the Sterling ambulance heading to UMASS. Do you remember what happened?" The soothing male voice asked as his finger massaged the base of my neck trying to reassure my safety.

As I tried to remember who and where I was, the screams of others began rifling through my head, with a certain females in the forefront silenced by a sudden jolt. A flood of memories came rushing back over me as I remembered Heather being my wife, who I was and driving in my truck. Sitting bolt upright, I strained against the seatbelts across my chest and waist.

"Where's my wife!? Where is Heather!?" I screamed dropping my left leg to the floor of the ambulance.

With that, both men in the back with me, flung themselves towards my body trying their hardest to restrain me to the stretcher I was lying in. The outside world began to spin again, darkness blurring its way in around me. Time seemed to stand still as I tried to figure out where Heather was and why she wasn't sitting behind me anymore.

My reality refocused as I was wheeled into a familiar setting. The trauma "bay" at UMASS hospital in Worcester. A place I had brought a few rather beaten-up souls over the years looked different from my perspective of now lying flat on my back. A sensation of stiff foam and plastic around my neck told me a cervical collar was in place. I struggled to put the night together, clouded images flying around in the upstairs of my head. A dozen new faces, maybe more, now surrounded me as I was shifted from the stretcher to the hospital bed. I just kept yelling at them demanding to know where Heather was. The responses varied as a hundred hands explored the different parts of my now naked body. This time, blackness didn't surround me, and I was super focused on what the faces were saying back to me.

"We don't know."

"You were in a car accident Mr. Hanks."

"Do you remember what happened?"

"Sharp poke."

"This is going to be uncomfortable!"

"They're bringing her in now!"

With the last I broke free of my captors sitting upright in time to see Heather getting wheeled in on another ambulance stretcher surrounded by four personnel. Three of which I recognized, one of which was the medic Ben I had worked with almost a year prior, the day of Elizabeth's birth. We caught eyes, I felt his soul sink to the floor, and I lost all ability to contain myself.

With dozens of hands trying to hold me down, telling me to remain calm and that it would be alright, I went full Hulk. My right arm, feeling some freedom, lifted the smaller person trying to hold it down as I tossed them across my body to the left. My arm now free I struggled to gain leverage, to get off the bed. Screaming ensued. More bodies plunged onto mine, as a sharp pain shot through my left shoulder. My breathing slowed, vision narrowed, as darkness wrapped in around me from the sides. I soon felt my back hit the softness of the hospital pad beneath me. Then nothingness.

The ceiling tiles above me had a rather uniform series of indentations in them. As my eyes began to adjust, I found myself counting these manufactured imperfections until I heard the familiar voice of my best friend.

"Hey buddy. Can you hear me?" Alex's voice was the softest, and calmest I had ever heard in our over ten years of friendship.

He asked a bunch of mundane questions, followed by telling me what he had been told about Heather. It wasn't good, and I felt the first of the flood of tears roll down my cheek, hitting the sheet beneath me with the echo of a bass drum. Moments later my parents and a doctor came bedside. My mother and Don were covered in a shadow of sorrow, their eyes bloodshot as they looked down past me at the floor. The doctor, with his impeccably clean long white coat, stethoscope around his neck, looked more bothered by the whole situation than empathetic.

"Do you think you can behave now Mr. Hanks??" His tone was condescending and insulting, and at the same time, I knew what he was referencing.

The collar around my neck was removed as the doctor reluctantly went over the details surrounding Heather's condition. Her brain stem had been "snapped" from the impact of a tree coming through the bed of the truck, the rear of the cab, and then her skull. She was being kept alive by a bunch of machines in one of the upstairs ICUs, where they were preparing to move me for the night. I had apparently received a serious concussion and was continuing to lose consciousness from time to time, which fragmented my memory of the events even further.

Eventually I was brought to an ICU bed, reassessed by another doctor and team of nurses, then deemed stable to go see my wife.

An IV hanging from each arm, the world spinning in every direction, I was wheeled down the cold, dark hall a little before midnight. A blur of a dozen sad faces followed my entourage as we rounded the corner of Heather's room. The sound of electronic beeps and bleeps in the air, the mother of my children lay motionless, facing the ceiling with her eyes open. Her parents sitting in chairs against the windows that overlooked Lake Quinsigamond below. Machines all around her, with a breathing tube in her mouth, her skin was olive, with an almost tight, shiny appearance.

She was completely lifeless.

The only movement was the artificial rising of her chest by the ventilator behind her head. Wheeled up to her bedside, I took her cold hand in mine. Rings, jewelry, and clothes all removed, she was in a green hospital gown, with white sheets and blankets covering her to chest level. I leaned in to kiss her face, holding out hope that it would cause that beautiful, contagious smile of hers to reappear. It did not. Everything felt like a nightmare as I stared into Heather's dilated hazel eyes, feeling no soul, no warmth, and no one anymore. With that, I fell from the wheelchair. My kneels drilling into the tile floor, I sobbed uncontrollably leaning against the hospital bed, my fists clenched. I begged God to end this all now! I started telling Him to take me and put my body in place of hers. The only answer I received was a dozen hands lifting me back to the wheelchair, with arms draping over my shoulders.

I took Heather's hand again. Kissed it and told her I would always love her and that I was sorry it was her and not me. Wheeled back to my own room down the hall a half hour later, I was helped to bed, given some meds to help me "sleep," and lay staring at the ceiling again. My mother in a recliner next to me, I slowly drifted off, even as I fought to not let it happen for fear of the inevitable.

I awoke to the morning sunlight gleaming in my window, as my mother stood, stretching at the foot of my bed. Her silhouette all I could see against the bright orange glare. Turning towards me, she offered a small smile as she touched the tips of my feet in the best version of reassurance that she was able to offer. As I began to realign with reality, I realized something.

I didn't have one bad dream or nightmare. In fact, I don't remember dreaming at all. Good thing too, cause within 15 minutes I was reminded of the nightmare I now lived in, when the medical team came in. They told me that I had to go over end-of-life decisions for Heather in the next few hours with her parents. My IVs now removed, with another assessment to clear me to leave the bed unmonitored, I was wheeled to a meeting room of sorts. For the next two grueling hours, Heather's parents and I made all the arrangements and decisions for terminating the only things keeping her in this world. I stared at the neutral paint and pictures depicting happy moments on the walls as I shook my head with each question. I left the final decision on exactly when, with her mother, as Heather's youngest sister, Celine, was on her way home from England.

Around noon, I was discharged, after yet another assessment and evaluation. Still, I was wheeled down six floors to the hospital lobby. Don had pulled my mother's Ford Taurus station wagon out front in anticipation of my departure. Hopping in, the nurse did her best to convey genuine sorrow and hope that I was able to grieve. Tears building in the corners of her eyes, her voice shaky.

I never even acknowledged her.

The 45-minute ride back north to my grandmother's was a silent one. I stared at the passing trees and cars as we made our way back up the same highway that had just changed the course of history, not even 24 hours earlier. I barely recognized where I was, not even knowing when we passed by the previous night's scene. I said nothing. I heard nothing. I felt even less.

Pulling into Nana's dirt driveway, three extra vehicles signaled family and friends were in attendance. Walking in the door, I was greeted by a room full of sadness and tears. Nana, all three uncles, and Grant stood in place as I was helped through the doorway by

Don. Everything remained silent for a few moments, until I heard what I was almost dreading.

"Dada dada!!" Tyler screamed as he ran over to me from behind my grandmother's leg.

Elizabeth was handed to me from an uncle, Tyler clung to my leg as if he was going to get swept away by some invisible wave, I motioned to the back of the house. For some reason, I felt drawn to the cold, dark, wood paneled back bedroom, that my Uncle Eddie still slept in. Years of pain, torture, and the origins of my nightmares had nothing on me in that moment. I sat on the foot of Eddie's bed, Elizabeth on my right leg, Tyler standing in front me, I felt everyone's souls drop. The sorrow had to be overbearing as I looked at each of my kids in the eyes, preparing to tell them the one line no father should ever have to.

I didn't get a chance.

"Where's mama!?" Tyler asked with an innocent tone. Words that had been asked of me hundreds of times before, shot through me like a hollow point. Blowing my heart through my back, exploding on the wall behind me.

The house erupted into sobbing adults, some of which had to sit or take a knee. Eddie standing in front of me did his best for three seconds before his own head was in his hands. Then both the kids started bawling. Everyone in that house was crying their hardest.

Everyone, except me.

I didn't shed a tear. Didn't say a word. Didn't feel a thing. As I pressed both my children against my chest, I told myself in that instant, that I was never going to feel emotions or love again. No one, and nothing was ever going to make me feel pain again.

My soul was gone.

CHAPTER 7
THE GAUNTLET

The funeral and the weeks that followed were a blur. Some members of the fire department and a few of Heather's relatives were pall bearers. People came and went from the house, dropping off food, trying to hold conversation, and offering to watch the kids so I could sleep. As much as it was appreciated, from the Thursday night following Heather's funeral for two weeks straight, I never voluntarily fell asleep. The only times my eyes closed they were assisted by alcohol, or it was from pure exhaustion. Every time I tried to sleep be it at night or even just a quick nap, I had nightmares. Nightmares that rivaled the ones rooted in what happened to me as a child.

The nightmare: Walking through the living room in our house, I would hear Heather's laughter in the distance. Joyful, sweet, and lighthearted. A smile comes over my face and I feel at peace. As I make my way to the French doors leading to the front hallway to find her, the rooms start to get cloudy, almost smoky and the harder I try to get to the doors the further they seem to get. I panic and start to yell but make no sound. I feel hot, and now it's dark outside and Heather's voice is no longer joyful and sweet. It's scared in tone and she's saying my name almost questioning the situation.

As I finally make my way through the French doors, I fall onto my knees and land on something cold and wet. Getting to my feet I realize I'm standing on the highway. It's raining but I'm not getting wet, only the road. Heather starts screaming. First softly, then louder and louder until suddenly it's too much to bear and I cover my ears. I run towards her screams and the scene starts to spin uncontrollably over and over. The only thing I can see is the pavement. I hear Dave Gambino's voice yelling "Come on! Hurry up!'. Heather is still screaming along with another whooshing sound. As I seem to be getting close to Heather, her screams stop, I get pulled back while trying to grab for anything around me. I start screaming "No!" over and over again until suddenly I'm jolted to a stop and can't move. The last image I see is Heather's lifeless, sad stare. Then I wake up in a cold, saturated sweat, terrified.

I convinced myself I didn't need to sleep. I told myself that maybe if I was sleep deprived enough, it would kill me. I didn't deserve to live with my wife, and mother of my children, in the ground, and I was completely ok with answering Death's knock on my door. Being in the house that Heather, the kids, and I made a home, often felt empty and cold even when others were in it. Like me, it seemed to lack a soul now that she was gone and often, I could be found just staring blankly at a wall or my personal favorite, the family picture above the fireplace in the living room. This picture, taken on a day that captured one of our last moments of happiness as a family that seemed to have it all, became an eerie reminder of how short life is. It also served as a form of punishment to me, where while staring at it, usually with a drink in my hand, I would find myself on my knees on the floor in front of it, begging for Heather to come back.

The bed Heather and I slept in, laughed in, and made love in, remained untouched for those two weeks. I never even pulled the covers down. I would walk upstairs, check on Tyler and Elizabeth when they were home, walk into my bedroom and in a matter of seconds my stomach would turn upside down and I'd have to run to the bathroom to puke. I had no one to confide in, as I knew nobody who lost their wife tragically at a young age. Sure, there were a few folks who had their spouse die from cancer, but these were people in their 60's. Or older. Death is so much more terrible when the person is young. Add to the mix VERY young children now without a mother, and me with all my issues and the job I did, and it felt unbearable almost all the time.

Elizabeth was only ten months old when the accident happened, she couldn't even speak. She never got to engrain into the fibers of her brain any real memories of her mother, but I think she knew. There was always a sense that something was missing that could be picked up from her. I tried my hardest with her, even more than with Tyler, to show her the love or some semblance of, that she deserved and that I knew Heather would provide if she was still alive. There were times given Elizabeth's age, that she would just scream uncontrollably in my face, till she was literally purple and every time it happened, I wanted to die. What was left of my heart broke for that poor kid every single time.

Tyler, being just over two, would ask almost every single day "Where is mommy?" or "When is mommy coming home?" A series of words that would shoot through my chest like fiery arrows intent on setting ablaze what remained of me. It got to the point where I would snap at him, he would cry, then I would cry, then his sister would cry. Next thing you know I'm holding both my little kids rocking them in my arms, shaking, praying to God that Heather would just walk into the house, and everything would be ok again. It never happened and eventually I got so sick of getting upset, feeling nothing but anger, that because the booze wasn't doing a good enough job of numbing me, I turned elsewhere.

Heather had surgery a few months before the accident, so she had also been prescribed a whole bunch of different pain meds to help with her discomfort. She wasn't one for taking narcotics, but filled the prescriptions anyway, just in case. Percocet, oxycontin, and Vicodin sat in bottles in the drawers of her nightstand, just waiting for the right reason to be taken. At first, I just took a few here and there with a glass of booze. Once I figured out, they were doing exactly what I needed them to, numb the anger, it became a daily habit in order for me to get through. When I ran out, I would go and fill the open script and say I was picking them up for Heather. Being 2003, there was no way for them to know Heather was dead, so it was never refuted. Also, being before the opioid crisis, when her scripts ran out for refills, I found other ways of getting my hands on them.

The walls and cold feeling of the house eventually became a prison, and I finally went back to my two jobs after over 6 weeks of living like a recluse. That, and Freedom ambulance service was growing tired of holding my position and gave me an ultimatum of returning to work or resigning my position to apply later when I felt fit to work. I had been contemplating never returning to either job, firehouse, or ambulance, for the last few weeks leading up to going back. I felt burned out, scorned, and even as if the job was fruitless considering how Heather died. The fact that I was working on an ambulance in a city infested with shitbags, that somehow kept surviving the situations they put themselves in and my innocent wife was dead, weighed heavy on me daily. There were numerous times I had the phone in my hand and dialed all but the last number to either the fire chief or my operations manager on the ambulance, ready to leave it all behind.

I didn't do it and for the longest time I regretted putting my uniforms back on.

Leaving my children with family, I reluctantly returned for my first shift on the ambulance in Lawrence. The operations manager, Paul Thompson, and I figured the best option for me to return to working again would be to start with a few 12-hour day shifts. Days were still busy; however, they fell short with the number of bad calls that evenings and overnights carried with them. I ended up returning to a shift working with Marissa who had been working a separate ambulance on one of the same days I had previously been working a 24-hour shift on.

Marissa and I were pretty good friends, and she was great at talking about everything going on. I remember it being a laid-back shift, not that busy. I was on a 9a to 9p shift that day and it was a Monday. Eventually Marissa mustered up enough courage to ask about the accident and what happened that night. I remember her crying uncontrollably, and a lot of "oh my gods!" being dropped. But she let me continue as she genuinely wanted to know the whole story. We sat there in the Blanchard Street parking lot crying together.

When I came back to work in Lawrence, most of the folks hadn't seen me since the funeral back in April. Most of them were good at not treating me like cracked glass, but obviously there are always a few select people who have no clue how to talk to someone who has been through what I just had. For the most part everyone gave me the benefit of a doubt and treated me like I guess they would have wanted to be in the same situation. That made an uneasy time a bit more tolerable for me. At the same time, every shift I was going in for felt like acid in my mouth. I had really lost my desire and satisfaction with responding to and helping the public. On more than one occasion before going in for a shift in Lawrence or at the firehouse, I would sit contemplating whether any of this was worth it.

For a few months following the accident, Dave and Kristina moved into the house with me and the kids. They were trying to save money to buy a house, and everyone but me felt I needed to have extra company. After a while, it was in fact nice to have them both there even if it were for the occasional mundane conversation. Short of a small discrepancy over some laundry, the arrangement went very well. Dave and Kristina even conceived their first child in my house. A joke that stands strong till this day.

Back on the ambulance, the shifts pressed on, and even while working 48 hours a week, I was barely sleeping. I would spend my time at night on the computer, playing online games, talking with strangers in the chat box, doing what I could till the sun rose the next morning. Eventually I started talking to a woman from North

Carolina. We hit it off rather well and talked about everything from hobbies to movies to relationships. After exchanging numbers, we began having conversations over the phone. She was recently single and had no children. Both being lonely, she suggested we meet up and hang out just as friends. It was decided for her to fly up to Boston so we could spend a few days trying to get me out of the house where I could just be a "normal" adult. We went everywhere from the beach to Vermont, to seeing a few movies. We ended up sleeping together a few times before she headed back down south.

We literally never spoke again.

This scenario weighed heavily on me. I felt dirty. I felt as if I had betrayed not only Heather but myself. After a few weeks I gave up trying to speak to this person and began to look at it as just part of the messed-up grieving process. In the back of my mind there was a part of me that had enjoyed what had just taken place also

July 4th came, and I ended up working a 24-hour shift in Lawrence. The day was fairly routine and relatively slow during the day. Come dinner time, all of that changed. The trucks on duty all began running back-to-back calls. Most of these were for fights, falls, car accidents and drunks passed out somewhere inconvenient. Throughout the shift, the other crews had been taking any car accidents that my truck had been assigned. Around 10pm I was dispatched to Merrimack Street for, what the dispatcher called, a really bad accident. As I was putting the phone down Marissa and her partner told me they would respond to the call. I wasn't sure how I felt about this behavior continuing. If I was going to be able to do this job, I had to do ALL of it.

Knowing perfectly well that at some point me and my partners were going to end up at this accident anyway, we walked out to our truck and waited. The police and fire radios were overrun with excitement and stress filled transmissions. This was a bad one. Within 30 seconds, Marissa's light, almost sensual voice came over our radio, asking the dispatcher for two more ambulances and to start the MedFlight helicopter. One of the other crews was just clearing Lawrence General across the river about a minute away, signing en route. The dispatcher hailed my trucks designation, telling us to also respond. Sitting in the driver's seat, I flicked the lights to life, picked up the radio mic, and signed us en route to the chaotic accident scene.

As we pulled up, it looked more like a Christmas scene than fourth of July. Red, white, and blue lights bounced off every structure in the immediate area including the 6-story brick mill building that lined Merrimack Street for over a quarter mile. It was almost hypnotizing. Our orders were to drive just past the accident to attend to the individual that apparently caused the crash.

Standing by three police officers, half leaning against one of their cruisers, our man was obviously drunk. As I got out, and walked over, the smell of stale alcohol was in the air, mixed with the metallic tang of blood. Red ooze was running from the bridge of his nose, as the guy carried an almost smile trying to talk to the cops like they were his bar buddies. My partner opened the side door to our truck to grab the first aid bag, as I walked straight up to this asshole. My own blood beginning to boil.

"Gee. I do hope they're ok." The little prick said with such a tone of sarcasm I lost all self-control.

Lunging at him, the cops stepped in keeping me from my mission of tearing him limb from limb. Another two pulled me back, my partner coming into view, calmly putting his hand on my chest. Assuring me it was ok, and all we had to do was bring this creep up to the hospital and drop him off, I panted, as I forced the adrenaline coursing through my veins to subside. Fists clenched I pulled away and got back into the driver's seat.

Sitting in the EMS room up at Lawrence General, my hand on the bridge of my nose, I listened to the radio traffic and conversations of the ER staff. The victims were a husband and wife. The husband was dead on scene. The wife was going to need to be flown to Boston. I began thinking of all the poor wife was going to have to go through regarding services for her deceased husband. Suddenly I started thinking of the life insurance policy Heather had made me get a few years prior. How useless I felt they were. How I never thought I'd need them before retirement age. And now, another couple was going to need to plan another funeral based on tragic circumstances.

The night ended with me first yelling at, then apologizing to Marissa and her partner. She gave me one of her famous hugs, which helped calm me down the rest of the way. I left work the next morning, traffic lighter than normal as most people were sleeping off the previous evening's festivities. As I passed exit after exit, making my way home, I found myself staring at some of the larger roadside trees. Images from last night mixed with ones from my own accident raced through my head. Panic, fear, and frustration grabbed hold as my vision narrowed. I was going to do it. After almost three months of pure hell, I was going to take the Jetta wagon I was now stuck driving and plow it into one of these massive tree along the highway. I picked up speed.

70. 80. 90 miles per hour.

As I began to feel my intestinal fortitude build to allow me to pull hard right into the next thick trunk I could see, the radio seemed to get louder. It had been on the whole time, but now it was unmistakable what I was hearing. Pink Floyd's *Wish You Were Here* trumpeted across the cab of the small, gray, grocery getter. I started to slow down.

85. 75. 65 miles per hour.

Floyd was one of Heather's favorite bands. Hours were spent listening to the various tunes the group pumped out. Reality set back in, and I spent the remainder of the ride crying. Sitting in my kitchen in bewilderment, I put myself back together, changed my clothes and headed off to my parents to see Tyler and Elizabeth. I never mentioned what happened at work the night before, but everyone knew something was up.

Summer in full swing, I began to realize I needed more than the occasional handful of pills or bottle of booze to fill the void in my life. Trying to enjoy the hot weather and all it can offer became a daily chore. Even when it involved time with just the kids.

Cookouts, small parties, and other celebrations left me feeling colder than the New England winters. Co-workers, friends, and family alike all tried to drum up genuine conversations with me, all to fall on deaf ears.

The only time I seemed to care about what the other person was saying, was when it was a female and there was a chance for intimacy. Being 24 years old, tall, wearing a uniform, and now tragically single, brought with it endless callers. I found myself having ladies visit my house late at night for one reason. Well, only one reason on my end. What began with the formalities of conversation and flirting, always ended with a pile of mixed clothes and heated, at times even angry sex with multiple different women. It seemed to dull the pain of existence enough to get me further through each day. Mix in some alcohol and a few Vicodin, and I was flying high for a few days.

I felt nothing, even though I wanted to.

As fall settled into winter, Heather's youngest sister, Celine, was back home from school. She had called earlier in the week asking me to go out to dinner with her that Friday. I was off, not going back into work until Saturday. So, I agreed. A colder night, she showed up dressed in a longer black coat, scarf, and one of Heather's old white winter hats on. She was wearing a pair of jeans that hugged her backside just enough, with a light blouse that hung close to her smaller frame. Bright, endearing eyes, and a warm ear-to-ear smile, she immediately leaned in to hug me. Giving me a kiss on the cheek.

Damn it.

She even smelled good.

Our meal at one of the local Italian restaurants in Leominster, was filled with much needed conversation and laughter. I had recently traded in the Jetta wagon, getting myself another pickup. As I helped Celine up into the cab, I was reminded of the last time I did so for her oldest sister. Driving us back to my house, she kept the conversation light, asking about work, and what I was doing to occupy my downtime. Walking back into the kitchen, I tossed my jacket on one of the chairs, as she did the same, then sat down to take off her almost knee-high boots. I needed another drink, as I could feel desire and lust beginning to overtake my self-discipline. As I turned to ask her what she would like, I was met with her small frame standing right in front of me. Her blonde hair, carelessly flaked onto her shoulders.

I wasn't sure what was happening, but I felt nothing bad within me at that moment. For the first time in months, I wasn't cold inside. Celine looking up at me from the middle of my chest, I set the bottle of rum down on the counter, as I bent down closer.

My eyes closed as our lips met, and my hands touched either side of her hips. Pulling away almost as quickly, I half expected her to be upset, half hoped she initiated more. I began to drift away, my vison becoming blurry and my perspective fading to a younger time. She pressed herself against me, forcing my back to the counter. Tilting her head, standing on her toes, she reached in for another kiss as I felt myself gravitate closer to her. Before I knew it, our tongues engaged in a full wrestling match, and my hands slid up under her ass. Pulling her up around my waist, her arms around my shoulders, I walked us out of the kitchen.

Turning to walk up the carpeted stairs, my eyes still closed, I moved my hands up under her blouse. Getting to the top, her legs still around me, I turned right, into the bedroom. As I laid her down on the comforter, she unwrapped her legs reaching for the button of my pants, as I worked on freeing her of her own. Shirts came flying off, as I brought my body on top of hers. In full embrace, I could feel her body heat radiating through me, her smell invigorating and driving the sexual desire to a new height. Leaning in towards her ear, the moment became too much for me to bear any longer.

"I love you baby." I whispered into Heather's ear, as I felt my hand slide under the thin material of her panties.

Sobbing brought my attention back to her face where I was met with a situation I was not prepared for. Celine, not Heather, brought her hands up to her face, covering her semi-open mouth. I sat back, pulling myself away from her as she sat up, knees bent, still crying. I lost myself. I saw, smelled, felt, and heard Heather and now reality was setting back in.

Heather is dead.

"I'm so sorry Keith." Celine's unneeded apology rang from her mouth as she put a hand up to my chest just over my heart. The other was wiping tears from her now red cheeks.

I fell to the bed, curling into the fetal position, Celine running her hand over my bare back in an attempt to sooth me. Muttering the same words, she just said, I felt a shame I had never experienced rain over my body, causing sharp pains within my gut. I began to sweat, clenching my fists, asking myself what the hell I just did to my sister-in-law. Assuring me she wasn't mad at me, Celine made haste out the door after gathering her clothes from the floor. I walked down the stairs in time to watch her back out the driveway, and leave. I sat down on the second to last step, head in my hands. Guilt, desperation and zero self-control.

After that, the holidays came and went without much flare. I found myself now drinking less often, however when I did it was still a larger amount. Come early spring, the guilt and loneliness got to be too much. I decided to end it all with a handful of Percocet's and Vicodin's, washed down with half a bottle of whiskey. A failed attempt that only resulted in me being woken from a drunk and stoned slumber, by my mother the next morning. Her inability to show empathy or caring in the situation was in contrast laden with threats of removing my children from my life if I didn't get my shit together. She seemed insulted that I even tried to end my life.

Or. Maybe she was upset it hadn't worked.

I couldn't tell.

On the one year of the accident, I held a get together at the bar Alex and I had frequented for years. Dozens of friends, family, and coworkers came to celebrate Heather's legacy, her love, and the friendship that knew no bounds. We laughed. We cried. We raised a few glasses to the best friend I ever had up to that point.

It was a great night of remembering her, and that life was too short.

The next night I defiled our bed with yet another woman. Barely 24 hours after spending an evening remembering my dead wife, I was bumping uglies with someone who was more than willing to oblige. And it didn't stop there. This behavior became a new habit, not only giving me a literal physical release, but a mental break from the constant torture of what my life had come to be. I didn't care who it was. If I'd ever see them again. If they were in a relationship with someone else. More importantly, I didn't keep it a secret, often bragging about the revolving door on my bedroom.

Work had panned out by the arrival of Elizabeth's 2nd birthday that June of 2004. I was working two 24-hour shifts in Lawrence, with at least one 24-hour overtime shift. I was maintaining my time with the FD along with pulling a day shift once a week or so. I was sober more often than I had been in the last 14 months. I was eating better, and spending as much time as possible with both kids. I wasn't using pills anymore to hide my emotions. This was mainly due to my new-found ability to completely ignore most of them 24/7.

Around the kids and family, I was neutral as I could be, throwing the occasional smile out in order to avoid any annoying interrogation. At work, I had a blank effect. Nothing seemed to bother me or rattle my cage. Short of a partner being in danger, I just simply did not react. And if I did it was almost always unjustified anger. Around friends, I was unimpressive. I put almost zero effort into anything outside of the kids.

Over the summer I began seeing a woman that worked for the same ambulance service up in Lawrence. Alice was a couple years younger than me. She was also about five foot three inches tall making the sight of the two of us together rather humorous I would imagine. What started as middle of the night "bootie" calls, turned into dinner and a movie, and then hanging out late at night at my place, on the couch, when the kids weren't home. For the first time since Heather, I was seeing someone for more than just sex. As much as a large part of me didn't want to commit to anyone for the overwhelming fear of loss and pain, there was a smaller part that was curious what could happen. This smaller part was also a bit stronger with its opinion.

Our relationship accelerated quickly, and I eventually introduced Alice to Tyler and Elizabeth. Their mother being gone now nearly 18 months, they both grew attached to my new girlfriend. All four of us got along great, and to be honest, it was heartwarming to look across the dinner table and see a female face interacting with the kids, who wasn't one of their grandmothers.

At the same time, I was trying to maintain a relationship with Heathers side of the family. Even if it were just for the sake of the kids, I would often accept an invitation to their house in Hubbardston and include them in all the festivities down at my place in Leominster. Alice's arrival into our lives brought with it initial uncertainty on how they, in particular my mother and father-in-law, would take me being in a serious relationship with a woman. Surprisingly they took a quick liking to her, even including Alice in family get togethers.

After a while, I began to accept my new life having a full-time woman in it, Alice now living with me and the kids. I still never spoke a word about my childhood, the nightmares, flashbacks, and occasional dark thoughts that popped into my head to her. Later in the fall of 2005 I would propose to Alice, with her saying yes.

And that's when things got rough.

Almost immediately I began to see a side of her that had remained hidden during our entire relationship. She had a mean streak that wasn't reserved for just me. I started to hear stories of her punishing Tyler and Elizabeth in ways that were completely unacceptable given how I raise and discipline my children. Alice would purposefully pick fights, often pitting me against my mother. On several occasions she told me that my mother was crazy and was eventually going to fuck my life up. She began to drink more often than she ever had, which given my own history wasn't an issue at first. That was until it included violent outbursts.

One night she went out with her sister and some friends, returning home with what I felt was evidence of cheating on her clothes. The kids were at one of the grandparents that night, which ended up being a saving grace, because things got ugly quick. After she had gone upstairs, returning in a "naughty nighty", I confronted Alice about what appeared to be semen on her pants. She hit me. Soon after she began throwing punches and objects at me from across the room. As I made my way upstairs, she gave chase. Our bedroom became a battle zone. Everything she could get her hands on was used as weapons including the tv, a bunch of Heathers pictures and glass items. Picking up the phone I called the cops as I couldn't control her temper by this point. While on the phone with the dispatcher, Alice threw a full-size mirror, which shattered against my body.

At least the person on the other end of the phone finally believed me.

Pushing Alice to the floor, in an effort to escape, I ran downstairs and out the front door as the cops showed up. My shirt torn to shreds, blood running down each arm and panting, I turned to tell the two officers what had happened at the same time an apple went flying by the three of us. More followed as Alice appeared out the side door by the garage, hurling an armful of Cortland's. She was eventually arrested, spending a few hours in the same jail I had over two years prior.

Alice's sister called me later that night. Insults ran from her mouth, as I sat in shame for calling the police on my fiancé. Even before her sister called, I felt like less of a man. At six and a half feet tall, nearly 250lbs, what do I have to be scared of, with a woman? Something beyond the literal situation of what Alice had done that night was eating away at me. I did my best to keep the exact reasons to myself when we inevitably broke up in the weeks that followed. After a short-lived conversation with a coworker regarding the event, and his response, I was convinced I was the one at fault.

I was a man. I can't be abused.

Moving on from Alice and her drunken tirades, I immediately caught the attention of another woman. This one, a receptionist at the ER in Lawrence, had children of her own and lived in the city I worked in. She was also Hispanic which was a big "no no" in my family when it came to dating. We simply didn't date anyone who was not white. Again, this relationship escalated quickly, with me falling in love with her in a few weeks' time. She didn't reciprocate the feelings and within a few months, we separated. Not before I had introduced her to my kids, and vice versa. This of course became an issue for the two grandmothers. I was told I needed to stop dating "numerous" women and that all I was doing was confusing Tyler and Elizabeth. They became overcritical of how I was living my life, and more specifically my abilities as a single father. By the beginning of 2006 I was receiving criticism, more than praise regarding my raising of the children. Suggestions were being made by both my mother and Heather's, that I buy one big house for me, the kids, and my parent's to live in. That way I would have "help" with Tyler and his sister and the pressure to meet another motherly role model wouldn't be as heavy.

My relationship and already lower amount of respect for my Uncle Eddie was tested one Sunday morning. At the tail end of a very long 24-hour shift in Lawrence, around 530am, I was sent to an infant not breathing call. Arriving on scene and running to the front door of the house, I was handed a blue 18-month-old boy. The mother yelled hysterically for me to save her baby. I immediately began mouth to mouth, pressing lightly on the small frame hanging lifelessly in my arms. The fire department pulled up at the same time, the lieutenant exchanging looks knowing the situation was dire. With a firefighter driving our ambulance and no paramedics available, we flew to the hospital. All our attempts were in vain. I sat for almost an hour just staring at the walls of the EMS room, trying to remove my children's faces from that of the dead child I just walked away from.

Another dead baby was weighing heavy on my soul. There was something deep inside me that got keyed up whenever I dealt with a sick, injured, or dead child. A younger voice that brought with it a sense of helplessness. It was as if I was feeling the fear that child was. It was something that felt like a memory from my past. As I dwelled on this for a while, I became overwhelmed and quickly pushed everything aside and left work at shift change.

After a brief stop by my parent's to wrap my arms around Tyler and Elizabeth, I went to the fire station looking for some sense of normalcy and distraction. While talking to Jack, Eddie, and Grant about mundane shit, my eldest uncle piped in randomly with his view on my lack of parental skills. Shortly thereafter, while discussing the mornings events, Eddie decided to provide me with an insult that set the bar high even for him.

"You're just an ambulance driver! The paramedics do all the work." He snapped at me walking around the backside of the fire engine.

The darkness filled my field of vision, and I was no longer standing in the fire station. I saw the dim light of a rising sun peaking over the roofs of frost covered homes. The shriek of a panicked woman echoed in my ear drums, as my arms became weighed down with the flesh of another. Small lips touched mine, as my heart raced, and I felt sweat running down the middle of my back. Suddenly I was being pulled through tunnel with the faces of Tyler and Elizabeth flashing by at lightning speed. My shoulder sensed a large hand of comfort as the darkness begins to brighten.

Looking to my right, Jack had put his hand on my shoulder, asking if I was ok. I told him I wasn't, told Eddie to go fuck himself, and left the fire station, still trying to shake the images in my head.

A month or so after this, the added pressure of needing to live with my parent's, and all the criticism of my fatherly duties caused a great deal of stress that I began to take out at work. I became even shorter tempered with coworkers, supervisors, and patients indiscriminately. After a rather large blow out with a dispatcher regarding how long a patient waited for an ambulance at a dialysis center, I was fired from my job in Lawrence.

The annual Heather "remembrance" get together that year,

ended up being a who can sleep with Keith fest. I had picked up right where I left off before getting into a relationship with Alice. I was sleeping with whomever accepted the invitation or asked. Sometimes two or three at a time, women frequented my life in such magnitude that I often got names mixed up with different phone numbers. In the heat of the moment, it all felt like what I needed to do to get through the pain of feeling like a failure yet again. Typically, even as the woman, or women were leaving my bedroom, I was already beginning to feel like a scumbag. I literally had no idea what side was up.

Chloe had worked in registration at the ER while I was still up in Lawrence and knew the other woman I had been dating. When she found out I was single, she searched me out, calling me one night as I sat alone in the now cold, darkness of my living room.

We hit it off immediately, mainly because we had sex on the first date, and she definitely came across as a "good time girl" having quite the life story. Recently clean from a run with heroin, she was open minded, willing to do anything, including going face to face with me, often telling me to knock my shit off. A thicker, curvy woman, with long, brown hair and tan skin, Chloe stood around five foot seven and had a presence I had never felt in another female before. She wore a smile that lit up any room she walked into. Eyes that seemed to look straight through you, and somehow she knew when I was lying about how I was feeling.

By this time, I had gone back to working at the manufacturing plant where Don was now working in the shipping department. My uncle Jack had also began working here a few years back. It was great pay and benefits that had a union backing to boot. I went to a 3-day rotating schedule of overnights with a fourth half shift. Every week I had three and a half days off and plenty of time for the kids and Chloe, who had begun sleeping over the house more often. Tyler and Elizabeth loved her, and she would at times spend more time playing with them than hanging out with me.

I had also started working a regular 24-hour shift in Townsend for the fire department once a week. I was making good money, had a good woman in my life and the kids seemed happy. My family was also content, as I was back to working full-time with Don and Jack, and more of a regular with the fire department. I on the other hand was waiting for the other shoe to drop.

Chloe was living with a friend in an apartment in Medford, outside of Boston, near Tufts University when we started dating. Her spending more and more time over my place finally put her in a position to decide on where she resided. At the same time, come the beginning of 2007, me and my parents had started the process of looking for a house all of us could live in. Finding out that Chloe was going to possibly be living with me full-time, did not sit well with my mother or Don. Because of her past, they felt she would be a burden to the household if she moved in with us. This caused a serious conflict inside of me.

Chloe and I had begun talking about getting me to start seeing a therapist again, after years of avoiding them. She was witnessing my nightmares and restless nights and had picked up on the presence of the flashbacks I was having. I wasn't able to fool her, like I was others. She somehow knew and was completely supportive of trying to help me find the right path I needed to be on. This outspoken mentality on her disposition from both my parents, brought with it a fear of attempting to seek help for my own problems.

So, I didn't.

"There's something just not right with your mom Keith." Chloe said to me on several occasions after finding out I wasn't going to see a therapist because of her.

As the summer of 2007 took hold, we had found a house that was going to work for all of us. Reluctantly, my parents agreed to ALLOW Chloe to move in with all of us. The kids were beyond excited to have her joining us, I was on edge because I could tell my mother had an ulterior motive behind the whole thing. I just couldn't place it.

The house was still being built in a new development in a wooden area of Townsend. It was off the center of town, on the road that ran behind the police station with schools, the library and elderly housing all within a quarter mile. It promised a relatively quiet neighborhood, added to the fact that the house itself was on a cul-de-sac with a dozen other homes. At the time, the house was nearly half a million dollars to purchase, and was the biggest, most expensive house anyone on that side of my family had bought. The life insurance payout from Heather's passing allowed me to put a large amount down in order to be able to buy the small mansion. It had three bedrooms with a larger master bedroom, that had its own bathroom and sitting room. My parents decided the latter would be theirs, as the third floor of the house was big enough to be made into an area for me and Chloe.

Everyone but my parents and grandmother seemed to really love Chloe. I even took her along to the Aerosmith concert with me, Eddie and Jack that fall at the outdoor venue once called Great Woods. She and Alex had grown to like each other over the year or so that we had been together come the fall of 2007. When he got married to Emily, the woman he had been dating for a few years, Chloe was invited to the wedding and got along with everyone in attendance. Being his best man, Tyler the ring bearer, and Elizabeth one of the flower girls, Alex and Emily actually invited most of my family to their big day. It turned out to be a great weekend, and for a while there after, things felt like they were going smoothly.

My Uncle Chucky had been diagnosed with a rare respiratory condition years prior, and in recent times his health was making a steady decline. He had married the woman he was living with, Nancy, not long before and was now a permanent fixture in his recliner in their home a few towns to the west of us. He spent most of his days continuing to smoke cigarettes, while 30-foot oxygen tubing ended in double prongs resting in his nose. He would get winded just trying to hold down a conversation. He was drinking more than any of us knew he ever had and seemed to not be taking care of his health. When he began to lose weight, me and the family started paying him more frequent visits. Chloe often joined me on these trips. Her and Chucky could be heard laughing it up, as I tried to dig information on his health from his less than concerned wife.

The holidays were rough, and I ended up spending New Years on a locked psychiatric unit at Burbank Hospital following another suicide attempt. No overdose this time, as I chose to try and freeze myself to death in the middle of a single digit December night. After hours of sitting in the dugout of the baseball field at the high school, the only thing I accomplished was to fall asleep, waking up with my pants and t-shirt frozen to me. Apparently in my half-frozen slumber, I had pissed myself.

I had never gone inpatient for my mental health. Chloe visited me every day when she wasn't working and called when she couldn't be there physically. I saw my parents once. The phone call to my fire chief, telling him I was in the nuthouse and couldn't work my shifts, was one of the most excruciating conversations I ever had. Crying into the receiver of a payphone, while I stared at the tan walls of the unit, I was met with a complete lack of caring or empathy. I was simply told to get my shit together and get back to work before I sullied the family name.

So, I did.

In the beginning of 2008, I made the decision to return to full-time work on the ambulance. This time in a different city, Lowell. Along with this I made a permanent switch to a Wednesday 24-hour shift at the firehouse, picking up an extra shift or two a week. I was again, fully emersed in the 911 life. By this time, I had been working quite often with a medic in Townsend for almost two years. Jeff was from central Massachusetts and had a little bit more time on the job than me. He was a few years older, about five foot eleven or so, wore glasses and smoked butts which gave him a familiar air I was used to and came with an awkward comfort.

Things at home had gotten rough between me, Chloe, and my parents. One argument in particular left my head spinning so much that I fell down a downward spiral. One I hadn't in years. I felt no purpose or reason to continue on. It was like I was on an island and those in my life simply floating by on boats refusing to dock. One day I bought an airline ticket to Tampa and just left the house for three days. Returning home, not feeling any better, Chloe expressed her concerned. We were at odds, with the conversation of separation occurring more often than love making. Still, her empathy towards me and the love she felt were made obvious by her constant inquiries.

I lied to her every single time.

My mother took full advantage of where Chloe and I were. She started filling my head with the thought that my girlfriend didn't actually care about me. That she was "using" again and that she wanted to destroy the family dynamic. This was supported by how distant Chloe, and I had become often not sleeping in the same bed for days. Finally, I had enough. I had enough of everyone, but I knew I couldn't remove my family. That wasn't an option. So, I told Chloe she had to move out. I was hopeful that we would stay seeing each other, but my request was the final straw for her.

"I have done nothing but love you Keith. I'm not the problem here." Adamantly ran from her mouth as she tried to remain as stoic as she could with streams of tears falling off her tan cheeks.

She moved out the beginning of March on a warm weekend. Some of her friends showed up with a small U-Haul to grab her belongings. No one was rude or disrespectful, despite the fact that my mother had made me have a cop present for "fear" of Chloe likely trying to do something. As I walked over to put one last, heavy box in the rear of the truck, her two friends walked to the cab. Now standing, looking at my feet, Chloe took my hand trying to get my attention. The police officer coming to attention with this move. A gesture of my other hand set him at ease, as I raised my face to look at Chloe's. Her long, brown hair blew gently in the warm early spring air. She had on a perfume I had bought her that Christmas. It was some sort of lavender, jasmine mixture that saturated the insides of my nostrils and left me longing to grab hold of her and never let go.

I didn't. I just stared as she opened her mouth.

"This shouldn't be happening. I love you. Good luck Keith." She said as she kissed my cheek, turned, and got in her car.

I walked into the garage, shut the two overhead doors, and opened the door into the house. As I turned back around from shutting it, I saw my mother sitting on the couch in the family room at the other end of the house.

She was smiling.

CHAPTER 8
WOODBURY'S BEST BIDETS

Twisting the throttle, I hugged the curve as it rolled in between several hillsides. An unusually warm late March Saturday enticed me, Don, and a few of his buddies to hop on our motorcycles for a scoot across southwestern New Hampshire.

I had bought my '99 Victory back in the fall and spent as much time as possible honing the skills necessary to join my stepfather on many a ride. A hobby that was also shared by my father Calvin. The therapy provided by riding knees in the wind was unlike anything I had experienced up to that point. I felt free. Just me, the rumble of the v-twin motor, and the fresh air against my face. It gave me a connection to Don, but also in a way, one with my biological dad.

I had also recently started on a concoction of different psychiatric medicines to aid in my seemingly never ending up and down mood swings, depression, and nightmares. The therapist I had recently started seeing was an older woman who suggested I talk to the med doctor in her practice about finding some stability with pharmaceuticals. With the recent loss of my relationship to Chloe, I was struggling to say the least, so I reluctantly gave in.

Now taking 6 different medicines daily, I was often left with zero personality, no emotions, and the inability to care about anything that resembled conflict.

My shifts in Lowell and Haverhill on the ambulance started to go by a bit smoother, with less negative interactions, and happier supervisors regarding my overall attitude. My firehouse 24's with Jeff were my escape from all the hurt and bullshit in my personal life. Over the last two years of working together, he and I had gotten close as friends, and were at times inseparable, refusing to work with others even on extra shifts. With the weather holding that Wednesday, I decided to ride the bike to the firehouse, parking it in the bay with our Paramedic intercept SUV. The Ford Expedition was outfitted with all the basic EMS equipment, along with the Advanced Life Support (ALS) supplies needed to provide a higher level of care to the patients in our service area. We responded to all the calls in Townsend and were the ALS for four other surrounding towns and back up for a few over the border in New Hampshire.

Our shifts were busy with as many as seven or eight calls in a 24-hour period. Others, we would turn the wheels one time, then spend the rest of our shift doing chores, truck checks, and playing videos games.

As I parked the bike and made my way up the stairs to the crew room, I could hear the usual morning laughter that often took place at shift change. Sitting at the kitchen table, Jeff and I were joined by the fire chief, the shift captain, two firefighters, and the overnight crew from the "medic truck". As coffee was sipped from a variety of mugs, Natalie, one of the medics I had also worked with in Lawrence, glanced my way. Her face indicating that she wanted to talk to me off to the side about something of importance.

Around 5 years older than me, Natalie was about five foot three, had short brown hair, and a pleasant, warm, welcoming effect. She had three kids, and her husband was a firefighter a few towns away.

"So, rumor has it you're single again? I have this friend..." She trailed off as I felt my eyes wanting to roll in their sockets. Not the conversation I was looking to have at 745 in the morning.

As I continued to drink my coffee, doing my best not to give Natalie the impression that I could care less about her "friend", Jeff must have overheard the conversation. His childlike smile, aimed at me from across the room, inferred that he was amused with our coworkers attempts at setting me up with this friend.

A week or so later, Natalie and her friend, Danielle, stopped by the station in the middle of my shift. I was enjoying the typical Wednesday break from the bedlam of home that my regular 24's with Jeff provided. I also happened to be in charge of lunch that day. The smell of spaghetti sauce emanating from the crock pot on the counter gave Danielle, who was Italian, all she needed to break the ice.

"An Irish guy making spaghetti sauce huh?" Was cast my way with the most delicate, and sarcastic tone combination possible.

Danielle stared at me from the other side of the table. Her emerald, green eyes, looking upward to meet my face from her small five-foot, petite frame. Her long brown hair, pulled back to a half ponytail, half bun, showed off the soft skin of her long, thin neck. She smiled, tilting her head off to one side, as I outstretched my right arm in an attempt to show that I appreciated her comment.

"I'm Keith. You'll fit in just fine around here!" I said with a flirtatious smile and matching sarcastic tone.

After exchanging numbers, we started seeing each other once a week for dinner and a few drinks. Danielle had been through a really rough, and abusive relationship of almost 10 years with her now ex who also happened to work as a paramedic in the private EMS world. She had two kids. Her daughter, Kassandra, was around 15 and her brother, Nick, was 12. Initially, Danielle was living in Natalie's finished basement with Nick. Shortly after we started seeing each other she moved into a friends unused apartment in a complex right off the center of town. Kassandra lived with her father out in the Lawrence area.

This was also the first time I had dated someone five years older than me. We hit it off great, talking on the phone almost daily with most conversations leading to teenage laughter. It would also be the first time since Heather that we took a few weeks, and several dates before engaging in sex. With where I had been in the last five years with women, this was a definite positive step.

Telling Danielle about Heather and the accident, I received a reception I never had from anyone before. Maybe it was because she was a parent herself, but she focused her end of the conversation on how awful the situation must have been for me. Asking me questions about how I dealt with the grief, loss, and being a single father at a young age. I was quickly gaining respect for this woman, and decided it was appropriate to invite her to the small five-year remembrance dinner I had planned that April. She attended as a friend and kept a very low profile, but she still came and supported me, the kids, and the family.

Danielle was amazed with my work as a firefighter and EMT and she often became an ear after a difficult shift. She was even more receptive to the problems within my family, namely my mother. When my uncle Chucky took a turn for the worse with his health and ended up staying at the house with me and my parents, Danielle offered help right away. She had worked in healthcare for the last 15 years, so her skillset was put to use upon occasion for my now dying eldest uncle. Eventually his care got to be too much for the family, and we reluctantly moved him to a nursing home in Fitchburg. My mother didn't listen to me when it came to the place she chose, as they didn't have the best reputation with the care of their patients. It was as if she just wanted to dump him on someone else.

While all this was going on, we were able to connect with Chucky's two children who were now living out in Minnesota. They made the trip to New England to reestablish their relationship with their estranged father. Peace was found between the three of them, and when it happened I found myself being jealous. It was all I wanted with Calvin. Peace. Not even a relationship. I literally wanted what my two new to me cousins were getting with the man who was, for the part of my life he was in, my most favorite uncle.

Come September, Danielle and I had become almost inseparable, with our collection of kids getting along as good as could be expected given the age differences. My mother was showing a mild appreciation to my new girlfriends presence, and especially her ability to cook, which Danielle was doing almost weekly for me and the household. Nick on the other hand was not my mother's favorite person. She always had something negative to say about his awkward behavior and mannerisms. Overall, the atmosphere in the family was moderately good given Chucky's health.

Going in for my normal Wednesday shift, I was more relieved than normal, when the day turned out to be a busy one. Over the last weeks I had found myself drifting in and out of my past, especially the dark images from my childhood. The prospect of losing an uncle who had recently made right his past with his own children wasn't sitting well. Being occupied by calls, chores and other daytime tasks was giving me a much-needed reprieve. Jeff and I normally went to the house for dinner while on shift, but that night my family took an opportunity to go visit Chucky in the nursing home. It worked out for the best as we remained busy through dinnertime, not returning to the station till almost 9pm.

Danielle stopped by the fire station on her way home from working as an aid in the ER shortly before 10. With my partner resting in his bunkroom, preparing for a busy night, the two of us took the opportunity to enjoy the quiet. The rest of the overnight was fairly steady with our last call putting us back at the station just after 430am. I decided to test fate, laying down in my bunk trying to grab a few winks before shift change at 8am.

It was Thursday September 4th.

Just after seven, I was awakened by the sweet, light voice of my girlfriend sitting on the bed next to me. Opening my eyes, I saw tears running from hers.

"Chucky died this morning Keith. Your mother called me to

come and tell you. I'm so sorry." Her thin long fingers now caressing my shoulder and back.

Sitting back in the house on Peter J Drive after my shift with Jack, Eddie, Nana, and my parents, we devised a plan to go over to the nursing home to claim Chucky's body and start the funeral process. Walking into Chucky's private room, with him lying lifeless still covered in his sheet and blankets up to his chest, was an overwhelming moment for the other members of my family. His arms were by his side, his skin drained of all color. Eyes wide open and his mouth in a resting peaceful smile, it almost looked like he was smiling at the ceiling. Everyone got emotional, especially Nana who had to sit down at the sight of her oldest son, dead in the bed in front of her. I walked up to my uncle, putting my hand on his and then closed his eyes telling myself he was finally at peace. I put my fingers on the bridge of my nose trying to rub away the stress that was flying around inside me. As Jack walked over to me to put his arms around me in show of support, I turned and walked out of the room leaving my family behind. I walked out into the hall, leaned against the wall trying to shake the image of my dead uncle from my head. As I tried to empty my eyes of what I just saw, thousands of past thoughts raced into my head. I slid down the wall into a kneeling position and found myself crying.

I wiped the tears from my face, stood up and walked out of the nursing home. I was already bitter with God, given my own personal and professional interactions with his "plans", never mind all the loss, pain, and darkness of humanity, I had witnessed over the years. I stood outside staring at the white clouds that periodically dotted the deep blue sky, fists clenched. I spoke to God in the one way I had gotten used to over the years.

Angrily.

My mother had been the executer of Chucky's "estate" so when the life insurance policy was processed, she received it. A few months before his death, the family had obtained a lawyer to make Chucky's marriage to Nancy obsolete, as evidence had surfaced that she may have been trying to kill him. This was done in an impossible way to prove, by pushing cigarettes and alcohol into his already weakened system. With the funeral and other expenses paid for, my mother thought it be a good idea for all of us to take a much-needed vacation to Disney World. She even asked if I wanted to invite Danielle and Nick, offering to pay for them to go.

The day after Thanksgiving, we arrived in Florida. The seven of us stayed in an extremely nice two-bedroom suite that had a full kitchen, living room, laundry and two baths. More than enough room for all of us. This trip ended up being rather eye-opening for Danielle as my mother spent most of the trip cursing me and Nick's name saying that the two of us were ruining the event. One of the days I didn't even join the rest of the family in the park. I just jumped from bar to bar across Epcot, trying not to feel the rage that was building up inside me.

December brought the "Ice Storm of 2008" to New England and other parts of the northeast. Millions were without power, food and water. Some for weeks. I ended up on duty with the fire department for almost a week straight. Due to the initial loss of power, my mother and Danielle would often bring all the kids to my grandmothers as they had wood stoves for heat. In between cutting trees, dodging melting ice, and responding on calls 24/7, I would get frequent messages from my mother on how awful Nick was being. How much of a burden it was to have him and Danielle over Nana's. This was always countered by conversations with Danielle regarding how my mother was acting.

By this time, I was already enrolled in a paramedic program in Manchester New Hampshire. It was eating up a lot of the little spare time I had. I was trying my hardest to make everything operate like a well-oiled machine. Work, school, family, and my relationship with Danielle. In May of 2009, Danielle and Nick moved in with us on Peter J. I had to beg my parents to allow my girlfriend and her child to live with us. They were about to lose the ability to live where they were and had no other options. I was in love with Danielle and had developed a fatherly relationship with Nick. I felt like their protector and given how much Danielle had supported my family over the last year, it was also the right thing to do.

The problems began almost immediately.

If I wasn't being dragged into a fight over the phone while at work or school, I was coming home to one. Danielle was not only cooking, cleaning, and taking care of three kids, at times four, but was being crucified for doing so by my mother. My parenting of Tyler and Elizabeth was being undermined almost daily. Danielle and I were beginning to fight, which we had never done. I was always getting to the point of yelling at my mother, and sometimes the kids. Nick included. I tried to appreciate my parents' view of not wanting their son's girlfriend living with them, but at the same time they wanted me to buy a house with them.

One day, everything hit me way too hard and deep. I began to feel controlled in every aspect of my life. I had no say. I was always wrong or somehow hurting someone around me. The guilt and shame of always yelling at everybody in my life was punching holes in my confidence and self-esteem. Feeling as though I had to be the reason for everyone's apparent misery, I decided the best solution was my not being around anymore.

One Saturday afternoon I took half the bottle of my Klonopin, knowing perfectly well I would eventually fall asleep and never wake up. The one thing I forgot to consider was my size. My six foot five, 250-pound frame, delayed the long-term effects of the meds, causing me to spend the next few hours stoned out of my mind. At one point Danielle, me and the kids went to the store, where I passed out in the toy aisle. Making it back home, Danielle decided to bring me to the ER. The next thing I remember was waking up after having my stomach pumped of all its contents. I am told my breathing came to an almost stand still.

The next week I spent in-patient, again, with daily visits from Danielle, and a few "family meetings. During these, my mother made her point clear on my girlfriend and her son, and I made mine clear that they were not moving out. Finally, we both agreed to be more patient with each other, and vowed to make things at home, work.

This was the case for less than a week.

I dropped out of medic school. Began missing shifts on both the ambulance and at the fire station. I spent most nights at home, after the kids went to bed, just staring at the walls wishing something would happen to take me out of the picture. A bad fire. A car accident at work. Even an alien abduction would be acceptable given how miserable I was daily. Danielle and I tried to hold each other up, spending as much time as possible convincing one another that things would work out.

My grandmother had stopped talking to me because of the whole situation. Following an argument where she blamed Danielle for everything and I kicked her off the property, our once amazing relationship was non-existent. I felt hollow not having Nana in my life. I became colder and unaffected by situations at work more than I ever had.

Leading up to Thanksgiving 2009, I would have two weeks where I saw more death than any other time in my career. Shift after shift was filled with DOA's (dead on arrival), fatal overdoses, bad wrecks and other sudden and tragic ways of life ending. The main issue was almost none of these involved elderly or terminally ill patients. The first of these took place while working my normal 24 with Jeff at the fire station. A woman around 30 had a fatal asthma attack and by the time we arrived on scene, she was dead. Confirming this through our cardiac monitor, pulse, and lung checks, along with a few other medically required evaluations, I began to pick up our equipment. The boyfriend was standing in disbelief, crying his head in his hands. I was more bothered by him being in my way as I just wanted to leave the small apartment that stank of body odor and every meal they ever cooked in it.

My next shift in Haverhill involved a driver that plowed in the guardrail. The heavy, steel beam planting itself in the chest of the former businessman. My partner throwing up on the side of the road, I sat in the truck not feeling a thing besides the desire to get a new partner.

I was growing colder and colder when it came to my compassion. I just couldn't muster it up. People's misfortunes didn't matter to me. Even my close friends began to feel as though I didn't give a shit at times. The job didn't really affect me, and I was beginning to hate it. At the same time, it was an escape from all the other pain in my life.

For almost a year I had been a field training officer (FTO) on the ambulance. The last six months, I had spent trying to update the training program for new employees with other FTO's. One of those, Mike, worked a 24-hour shift on Tuesday and Thursday in Lowell. His partner had recently taken medical leave for hand surgery, and for almost a month I had been filling in on Tuesdays. The week of Thanksgiving I started working both days with Mike, dropping my Haverhill shift.

We got along great, and more often than not spent most of our down time in between calls, making fun of everyone we came across during the course of the day. Mike was as confident and fluent with his skills as an EMT as I was and on most calls we didn't even have to speak. We just knew what the other needed or was thinking. For the most part, I loved work when Mike was my partner. Even surrounded by the magnitude of death I was.

My 31st birthday that year tested that mindset.

For the last week, Mike and I had a third rider, John, who was a new EMT that had been working strictly non-emergent transfers in Haverhill. Several partners had told the training supervisor that he needed some remediation of his skills, so they sent him over to me and Mike. He was a big guy, close to my height only about 375 pounds. He had an awkward stance, and emotionless eyes, that often gave people the impression he was a bit of a simpleton. To me, he was just a different, quiet guy. John also turned out to be a black cloud like me. Our busy shifts became busier. The bad calls somehow got worse. Tuesday, December 1st, was the pinnacle of this week-long situation.

Pulling the ambulance out of the ER bay at Saint's hospital, Mikes habit of smoking drifted across the cab into my face. It was a smell that brought an almost uneasy comfort with it. We had been running all day so far, with John getting his fair share of serious calls, and Mike had taken 5 minutes to enjoy the toxic benefits of a much-deserved lung dart. He now reeked of Marlboro cigarettes. John was his normal quiet self in the back. I continued to stare aimlessly out the passenger side window, as the radio crackled to life, dispatching us to route 3 for a "serious" car accident.

Route 3 is a three-lane highway which runs north to south along parts of Chelmsford and Lowell. It connects Nashua New Hampshire with metro Boston. Speeds averaging 70 miles per hour, short of rush hour, it was a very dangerous road. We were being sent for reports of a car that struck several construction workers just north of one of the Chelmsford exits. The ambulance company I worked for had the 911 contract for both the city of Lowell and town of Chelmsford. Immediately three ambulances were dispatched along with the fire and police departments.

Lights flashing, our siren blasting the song of our people, we weaved in and out of traffic. Working our way up the on-ramp, cars were already backed up, barely moving. Pulling onto the highway we could begin to make out the scene. As we came to a stop near one of the fire trucks, the highway looked like a bomb went off. Car parts, metal, and fluids littered the concrete across all three lanes. A dark SUV with heavy damage was off to the left. As I hopped out of the truck, I looked down to the right and saw a coworker carrying a man's leg towards an ambulance. His face void of all expression. Just shock. Another man was being tended to closer to a roll-off dumpster truck in the break down lane. A mangled body lay just behind it, almost unrecognizable as a human being. Immediately after that I was told to watch where I was walking.

Looking down, body parts, including ones that belonged inside a person, were strewn across the road in front of me. Screaming could be heard from the victim by the truck, along with the woman who was apparently trapped in the dark SUV. Shouting from the various emergency workers filled the rest of the air. There were no horns. No rush of air from the cars in the southbound lane. No calm voices. Just utter chaos. And dozens of people standing from their cars, looking at it all in awe.

It looked like a warzone.

Mike was already getting our orders, which were to help the woman in the SUV. When I turned to tell John to grab our equipment, he was frozen. Deer in the headlights, only that deer was dead. I had to slap him to break his gaze. We worked to free the woman from her metal cocoon with the fire department and transported her south to a hospital outside of Boston. She survived. One road worker died. Another lost a leg. Now sitting in the ambulance parking outside of this ER, the three of us didn't speak. Mike smoked. John was still staring off into space, his face red but not showing anything but what I imagined was disbelief. I walked over to Mike, deciding I needed a cigarette. As he handed one over, staring beyond me at our now completely incapacitated third rider, he tried his best at the dark humor that had made us friends.

"How was that for a birthday party?" A slightly unsure smirk came over his face as he coughed, taking a drag.

The following Wednesday on my 24 at the fire station was a day spent sitting on the couch, watching the clock tick by. Nothing had been done for my birthday the week before. I barely got any well wishes from family. Tyler and Elizabeth had both made me cards, with the usual "I love you daddy" written all over them. In the week that had passed since that shift on my birthday, I had barely spoken to anyone. Jeff picked up on this and tried his best to cheer me up. After telling him about the accident, we went down to the grocery store, and he bought me a small cake. He also got a number "3" and "1" and fastened them into a "13" feeling it was appropriate given the last few weeks.

Dark humor.

In the middle of the night, we were sent with the fire department up to one of the state parks for a body that was found. The midnight sky was crying those cold, early New England winter tears that seemed to penetrate straight to your bones. I stood cold and irritated by the side of the river. Several firefighters were trying to fish this young women's nearly naked body from the part of the Squannicook that ran through Willard Brook State Forest. It was obvious, given the time and location, that this was someone who was raped, murdered then dumped in an attempt to cover up the crime.

After ten minutes of watching my coworkers fumble with this poor soul, in the flowing water, against rocks and uneven terrain, I lost my temper. Yelling at them to just pick her up so we could be done with it and get out of this intolerable rain. I hadn't spoken to Danielle most of the day, not really paying it much attention until I got a closer look at the woman's cold, wet, and pale body. She was about five feet tall, with long brown hair and a petite frame. As the pit formed in my stomach, I leaned in to inspect the face.

"Jesus Christ. Thank God!" Forcing as much blasphemy from my mouth as possible to ensure if He was watching, He heard me, I took a knee and dropped my head for a moment.

"Hanks! You good?" I heard over my shoulder as Jeff walked up noticing my disposition.

Getting back to the station a short while later, I remained silent. It was almost 3am and Jeff went back to his bunk, leaving me on the couch in the tv room. I called Danielle and she answered in a panic, given the early hour. After I told her about the girl in the river, I just let loose with all I had been holding in over the last few weeks. I told her how I was done with my entire family fighting. How I just wanted my grandmother back in my life and a period of time where things weren't always on a 10. She assured me things would get better, telling me maybe we needed to think about moving out of the house and away from my parents.

For some reason this didn't feel like a possibility. Not in the way of me not being able to do it. More in the way that I was convinced my mother wouldn't let it happen. Time would prove I wasn't far off.

The holidays were a mix of me and Danielle's kids laughing,

playing, and getting along together with the adults pretending to. I didn't spend any time with Nana, which was a first. Ever. Even when I worked in town on Christmas, I found a way to stop by her house or call when I worked further away. New Years was a joke, and my resolution was that me and the kids were going to move out of the house on Peter J Drive.

Come Tyler's 9th birthday in January 2010, my grandmother finally gave in to being in the same room as me. This was after I begged, pleaded, and even apologized for things that weren't my doing. But she was there and even managed to force a small smile as her only great-grandson laughed and played with his friends. At the end of the party, I walked over to her and threw my giant arms around her. I told her how much I loved her and how she had always been my favorite person. She replied by using my full name in a way no one but her ever could.

"Keith Allen Hanks. You're a giant pain in the ass. But I love you too." She said as she planted one of her famous full lip kisses on my rosy cheeks.

I felt a huge weight lift off my shoulder after that weekend. Mind you, the bad calls at both jobs did not let up and my homelife was still in the shitter. But I had my Nana back and for better or worse she had always been my favorite person.

As spring began to make its appearance, and I prepared to host the annual remembrance for Heather, I felt a glimmer of hope growing inside of me. The kids seemed happy and were getting along better than ever. Danielle and I were back to being madly in love and had started finishing the third floor of the house for our master suite. A brief investigation by the Department of Children and Families (DCF) regarding neglect towards Tyler and Elizabeth on my part, had me confused. The investigator was extremely nice, even saying the whole thing was a formality as the information they received didn't add up. A few weeks later I received notification that there was no neglect found, and the investigation and subsequent case was closed. Hanging the phone up, I looked at my mother as she was at the kitchen table.

She was smiling.

April 6th would send shockwaves through my family and be the catalyst for a massive downward spiral within me.

Back to working a 16-hour shift on Tuesdays in Haverhill, I received a phone call from Eddie in the early afternoon. His voice was strained, he sounded almost mad like he was about to tell me something I did resulted in something else.

"Keith. Nana had a massive stroke. She's in the ER at Leominster Hospital." My now eldest uncle said in an almost see what you did sort of way. There was an air of hatred in his voice.

Right after he said what he did, Don got on the phone and gave me the details. I hung up and felt my knees begin to buckle as I leaned back against the wall, sliding down to the floor. My head in my hands, I sat sobbing for a few minutes before a coworker found me.

I left work and drove straight to my grandmother's bedside, calling Danielle along the way. When I got there she was ashen gray with a breathing tube in place, lying motionless facing the ceiling with her eyes half opened in a glazed-over look. Jack joined me, as the two of us just stared at her. He put his arm on my shoulder, we hugged and walked out of the room together. She passed within two hours.

After the graveside service, we had a gathering at the house. I spent most of the time in the basement, sitting on the spare couch with my headphones on trying to be somewhere else. It was the day before the seventh anniversary of the accident. The remembrance I had planned ended up not happening and instead, I spent the day drinking.

Soon after, the comments suggesting that I was at least partially responsible for my grandmother's death became routine. Whenever the conversation involved Nana, and my mother or Eddie were part of it, guilt was thrown my direction. A few times remarks were made about how my anger may have contributed to the decline in my Uncle Chucky's health. The icing on the cake was how all of a sudden, Heather's death was beginning to be put on my shoulders.

A situation just seven years in the history books, that weighed heavy on me daily, was being spun to inflict minor damage from time to time.

This all got to be too much. I was missing a ton of work and when I was there I was being pulled to the side and asked what my "problem" was. Heather's mother, Darlene, had even gotten involved in throwing punches, and I noticed in recent times, her and my mother had become closer. Something that had definitely not been the case in the past.

Come May, I broke and admitted myself to the psychiatric unit at Emerson hospital in Concord feeling suicidal yet again. Danielle was the only one who came to visit me for the first three days. I didn't see Tyler or Elizabeth. I never heard from my mother or Don. Just Danielle. Around the fifth day of my admission, Danielle left after a longer visit, later in the afternoon. I was allowed to keep my cell phone on me by this time, so I would get occasional texts and calls from her which helped make me feel connected to the outside world. An hour and a half after she left, it rang, and the voice on the other end was shaky and it was obvious she were crying.

"They kicked us out Keith! They've taken custody of Tyler and Elizabeth and put a no trespass order on you and me!!" The words running out of Danielles mouth like a four-year-old that just watched the family dog get run over by a slow-moving Mack truck.

I abruptly hung up with Danielle and called the house phone. My mother answered with an air of arrogance and sarcasm. Her hello sounding more like "Why yes my son, I'm so surprised you're calling!" I slowly began to lose my connection to reality with her tone.

I felt myself shrinking as the clean, white walls of my room began to pull away from me, turning black. Darkness started to wrap in from behind me, as my entire system went on high alert. Muscles tensed. Fists clenched; I began screaming into the phone in my hand. Violent words and threats never spoken before echoed across the empty space in front of me. Suddenly other faces appeared. Laughing began in my ear as a hundred hands grabbed at my body trying to force me to the ground. A sharp pain in my shoulder brought with it a dizzy spin of my field of vision. Then nothingness.

I woke up hours later in my hospital bed. My face lying in a half-dried puddle of drool, my body aching as I began to tremble. Sitting up and regaining my grip on reality, I felt the presence of someone in the room with me. Turning around, a staff member was sitting in a chair, in the doorway. They smiled at me, ensuring me everything was ok, asking how I felt. I was brought up to speed on how they needed to sedate me due to the concern for not only my safety but that of others on the unit. Looking at the far wall, I saw a fist size hole and everything, but the bed had been removed from the room. Danielle then appeared in the doorway and told me what was happening at home.

We were now homeless. Not allowed at the house. And I was not allowed to speak to Tyler and Elizabeth.

My mother and Darlene had taken temporary custody of my kids and obtained a NO TRESPASS order from the police department. They cited my "violent" behavior over the last several months as the reason, along with a recent coincidental DCF investigation. It all made sense now. It had all been a plan going as far back as 2006. All of it.

Danielle was able to convince Natalie to allow me, her, and Nick to move into her house. Once I was discharged from the hospital we returned to the house on Peter J Drive where Don and a police officer escorted me around the house so I could pack what I needed. As I walked around, I noticed most of Heather's nick naks I had out on display were now missing. When I looked at my mother demanding an answer I was given the same arrogant and sarcastic tone I was met with that day in the hospital.

"They weren't yours Keith. They're with Darlene as she had more right to them than you!" Again, a smile came across her face.

I was floored. My head erupted stabbing pains as Heather's face passed across my subconscious and I felt my heart drop. I put what belongings and clothes I could fit in my SUV and left for Natalies.

We spent the next several months living there, as I tried to work as much as possible in order to afford to find me, Danielle, and Nick a place to live. Fourth of July I got readmitted to Emerson for a quick 5 day stay. Late August we finally got an apartment off the center of Townsend. It was a small two bedroom, that had recently been updated. Within a week, while still living out of boxes, my mother and Darlene demanded a meeting.

I was given an ultimatum to sign full custody of Tyler and Elizabeth over to them or risk my two children getting put into the foster care system. I was still shaken by the years events, scared, and hadn't seen my kids but half a dozen times. Out of fear, I reluctantly signed all the papers given parental custody to my mother and former mother-in-law. Now, I didn't even have a legal right to my children.

A bunch of court dates later, I was faced with a new situation. I was ordered to pay weekly child support, to my mother, and have supervised visits with my kids twice a week. Because she now had custody, Heather's social security I was receiving each month now went to my mother for Tyler and Elizabeth. I was in a bad place with absolutely nothing to look forward to during the course of the day. I tried my hardest when I did see my kids, to put on a happy face, but it was hard as no matter what we were doing, I was being watched. I was also being told what I could and couldn't talk to them about.

Danielle kept telling me I needed to get a lawyer as none of what was happening was right. Problem was they took all my money. Come to find out, my mother hadn't paid any of the mortgage on the Peter J Drive house the entire calendar year as she was banking extra money in anticipation for what took place. The house fell into foreclosure, they moved into a rental leaving our half million dollar home unlived in. A lot of my belongings were still being stored in the basement as the small apartment Danielle and I had didn't have the room for it.

Come the beginning of fall, Danielle had started going to the Mormon church with her son. Nick had become friends with a kid whose family went to the Church for Latter Day Saints. After a while, he started going with them. Danielle soon joined them. Still living together, she began practicing abstinence, claiming the Mormon religion forbid unwed couples from engaging in sex. A distance grew between us, and now I didn't even have intimacy to look forward to.

The second week of November, Danielle dropped a bomb on me. After several negative interactions, along with her not being allowed to be present in the apartment when I had Tyler and Elizabeth over, she broke our relationship off.

"I cannot and will not keep competing with your family as they continue to try and destroy you AND me!" She didn't even shed a tear. Anger filled the emotions behind the words she cast at me.

With Danielle now not living with me, and the amount I was paying each week in child support, I was forced to move out of the apartment as well. With nowhere to go, I walked back into the cold, empty belly of Peter J Drive. I called my mother over to have a conversation. I told her Danielle had left me and begged for her to allow me to move back in with her, Don, and the kids. With the usual smirk, and pride in what she had done, I was told that wouldn't be happening.

The week of Thanksgiving came and that Monday I was called to the supervisors office at the ambulance company in Lowell. Even though I had been completely honest with why I was missing so much work, having also applied for FMLA, I was terminated for excessive absenteeism.

Three days before Thanksgiving.

Thursday came and I sat in bed, the cold of the pending winter chilling the inside of the house to a balmy 58 degrees, contemplating killing myself again. None of this was worth it. I now had nothing. My shifts at the fire station weren't going to pay the bills, I was running out of oil to heat the giant house on Peter J and I had zero hope left. As I was about to figure out what way I'd take my life, my phone started ringing. I ignored it three times before answering Alex's relentless attempts to invite me to his Thanksgiving dinner with his family.

I chuckled as I told him I would go. Staying alive another day.

I eventually ran out of heat, but not before Danielle and I had started talking again. She allowed me to stay with her in her new place across town a few days a week. The only catch was I had to start going to church with her and Nick. So, I did. I also began working for a small ambulance service down in Boston which lasted three weeks. I literally couldn't afford to work, as it was costing me more to survive than I could afford to put gas in my truck to drive to Boston four times a week.

I didn't see much of Tyler and Elizabeth over the holidays, short of a quick "family" dinner at Jack and his new wife Melanie's house on Christmas. Melanie was Korean and had a son about Elizabeth's age. For a while her mother was living with them and she was not a fan of my uncle. At one point there was an accusation from Melanie's mom, that Jack was a pedophile and that Eddie had kiddie-porn on his computer. None of this was investigated of course, with her mother eventually moving out but it sent a shock wave of emotions racing through me.

Still working shifts in Townsend at the fire house, I was trying my hardest to stay in touch with Donnie Amadon. I wasn't responding as much on Engine 2, up in his part of town, so we didn't see each other often. His attendance had also dwindled in recent times for some reason. Come the beginning of 2011, I was staying more with Danielle, and we had even given our relationship a try again. Without any intimacy of course. We couldn't even make out according to her newfound group of friends who I honestly found to be more of a cult than anything. But they also took me in, so reluctantly I joined them every Sunday for almost four hours of church service.

Beginning of February, I started at a new ambulance service in Worcester. At the same time, we found out that Donnie had been battling a rare form of cancer and that his current prognosis wasn't good. By the middle of the month, he needed an ambulance in order to get to a surgery in Boston. As a fire department, we applied and got the correct licensure to be able to transport my friend to Mass General Hospital. I drove our ambulance, with Natalie acting as the medic tending to Donnie's needs in the back. Getting him secured in the hospital bed, he called me by his side.

"Thank you brother. I love you man." His voice still strong and convincing as it ever had been. His face and body showing the breakdown from doing battle with his cancer for too long. I told him I loved him, walking out trying not to let on that I was falling apart inside.

I was still maintaining my regular Wednesday 24's while working the new job in Worcester. It was a much younger crowd than I was used to, but overall, there was a good vibe. The service mainly ran non-emergent transports with some backup to the city 911 system which gave me a much-needed break from the chaos of someone else's emergency.

Donnie was released from the hospital towards the end of February and brought back home on a day I was at the firehouse. I helped carry him into his house back on the family farm in West Townsend. More frail looking than how I saw him only a week before, Donnie still smiled at me as I set him in his recliner overlooking the grassy fields. His arms trying to raise to touch my shoulder, I took a knee in front of him.

"Thanks for always being a good friend Keith. I love you brother." His voice faint, there was no confidence and he strained to open his eyes enough to see me. I just stared back at him. My hand on his shoulder, I nodded in agreement. With a hug, I left his house.

Donnie died a few days later on February 21st.

I was asked to be the one who carried his helmet in front of Engine 2 during the processional. His full fire department funeral, held at the same church we honored his dad only ten years earlier, was filled to capacity with the spillover running across Main Street outside. As I marched to the cemetery that cold morning, my face numb from the wind, I couldn't erase the thought of not telling Donnie I loved him that last day I ever saw him. I walked, tears falling from my face, turning to ice before they had a chance to roll off my cheeks. At the cemetery, I handed Ellen, his mother, Donnie's fire helmet and said a few words. When I finished I stepped back. One of the Lieutenants called myself and the contingent of firefighters to attention and I gave her a salute as I fought back my emotions.

A mentor and friend now dead, I struggled to find happiness as I went about my daily routine. Shortly after putting Donnie in the ground, Danielle broke our relationship off for the final time. I felt betrayed, forgotten and completely alone in the universe. Going back to the Peter J house, I found myself constantly thinking of ways to end it all. My commutes to and from Worcester were filled with thoughts of driving into any of the trees dotting the side of the same highway that had taken Heather almost eight years ago. A fitting end for the man, cast out by everyone in his life.

On a Friday night, before needing to be in for a 530am start time to my shift on the ambulance. I made my final decision. I got my hands on a dozen Vicodin's and some Klonopin. Around two in the morning after fighting myself to commit, I swallowed all of the pills. I sat on the bathroom floor, off the master bedroom that had once been my parents, thinking how peaceful everything was beginning to feel. My breathing slowed, my vision narrowed, and the sensation of inevitable sleep loomed over me. Heather's face appeared, and I smiled. She smiled back, motioning me towards her. As I stood to walk, my legs felt like they were rooted in cement and I struggling to get up. As my first wife turned to walk away, a flash of light than darkness overtook me. Then nothingness.

Suddenly I felt a hundred hands all over me. A man shouting followed by a soft female voice saying someone's name. A pain in my bicep, followed by cold on my back. Heather was still standing down the hall as my ability to see her began to blur. My head spun, and I felt nauseous. Then I recognized the man's voice.

Guy Thompson was looking down at me. Sweat and concern covering his face. As reality set back in, I saw another Paramedic from the fire department, Lisa standing off to his left in the doorway of the bathroom. Beyond her, Danielle was standing in the bedroom outside. One of the cops talking to her, writing notes on a pad of paper. Questions rang out from Guy and his partner as I tried to make sense of the situation.

I had overdosed but wasn't given the chance to die. Not showing up for my shift, the dispatcher in Worcester, Carrie, called the cops and Danielle after I wouldn't answer my phone. Danielle showed up with a key, let the police in and found me unconscious, barely breathing on the floor of the bathroom.

Pissed that my attempt at finding peace failed, and now embarrassed, I begged Guy to not say what had happened to anyone at the fire station. He agreed, then tried to break the awkwardness by reminiscing about some of the funny calls he and I had responded to over the years.

I kept that situation and its details from most in my life. Being closer to Carrie, I gave her a slightly different version that she saw straight through. Crying, she gave me a hug telling me I better call her next time I ever thought of hurting myself.

Still working these early Saturday morning shifts, I was routinely late. Often times so much, that Carrie would have to piece together a crew to get the early morning dialysis calls done. One shift I strolled in at my normal almost 6am time and walked into the dispatch room. Sitting with Carrie was this younger female EMT, Adele. I had seen her around the base and when I was out at the hospital on calls over the last month or so. She was cute with long blonde hair, electric blue eyes, and a curvy five-foot seven frame.

"Since you decided to grace us with your presence so late, you'll be working with Adele." Carrie's voice coming across as if the whole situation was planned out long before I was even late.

Adele and I got in the ambulance, with me driving as I made her aware I wasn't getting in the back of the truck until later in the day. We exchanged a few details before getting our first patient and dropping them off at the dialysis center around 630. Pulling back out of the parking lot, Adele asked if I wanted a coffee. I gave her a brief history of my time with the Mormons, and how they didn't allow caffeine in their diet. Laughing, then turning, and realizing I was serious, she repeated her previous question.

I then advised her if she wanted a coffee I would drive to the Dunkins down the street, but I had no money due to how much child support I was paying. I went on to explain how I wasn't really seeing the kids either. Her next comment was her last for about 15 minutes.

"Oh. Baby mama drama huh?" She said looking down at her phone, in an almost matter of fact way.

"No. The kids mother is dead." I returned in the same tone.

Horrified Adele stared straight out the front of the ambulance, her soft cheeks turning redder by the second. I filled in on the story of Heather in an extremely abridged way as we pulled into get coffee. After a bit more conversation, the mood lightened, even to the point of laughter and we had a great rest of our shift.

I would continue to work with Adele on the occasional Saturday thanks largely to her partner who was also known for being late for the shift. After a while she sought me out around the base. Would stop to talk to me here and there when we saw each other out on calls, and even sit with me at the kitchen table during our downtime. One day, Carrie approached me saying how Adele kept talking about me. Apparently she thought I was mildly attractive, for a guy who was 12 years older than her. Adele was 20. Carrie gave me her number and said I should at least give Adele a call sometime.

Sitting in my bunk room, my next shift at the fire station, I held the small piece of paper Carrie had given me the week before. Adele written at the top, with ten numbers below, I pondered my next move. Figuring I had nothing to lose at this point in my life, and at the bare minimum might gain a friend, I dialed the number. After a few rings, Adele's soft invigorating voice answered with a hello.

"Hey it's Keith. What's this I heard you think I'm cute!?"

CHAPTER 9
RELENTLESS

As an adult, I never thought I'd be in a position where I couldn't afford to buy myself a cup of coffee. Never mind a meal while on duty. But come late spring 2011, that's exactly what was happening.

I had no extra money. I was falling behind on almost every bill I had. I was staying within the empty walls of Peter J Drive by myself having barely gotten through the end of the winter with the house averaging 50 degrees. I often coasted into my shift on the ambulance in Worcester on hopes and dreams with my fuel so low I often had to borrow a gas can from the mechanic in order to make it to the gas station to actually put gas in. I was sleeping in the back of my SUV at the ambulance or fire station parking lot, more than my bed. I would pull extra shifts just to be able to "sleep" in an environment with a comfortable temperature. I was beginning to lose weight as I was eating just enough to survive.

After my Wednesday 24 at the fire station, I would drive down to Worcester, and work a 10-hour shift Thursday with this girl Sherry. She spent more time flirting with me than anything, but once she found out some of my financial woes, I never went a shift without eating and always left with 20 dollars in my pocket. Also now seeing Adele in a somewhat dating capacity, I was trying my hardest to see the good in humanity. Trying not to generalize that everything sucked all the time. Trying to see that some people really did want to help.

I was trying to find hope again.

I struggled every day with it. Adele made it easier when we shared company. After our first date that involved her making me a jarred chicken alfredo dish, we began to hang out more and more. For the most part our time together was simply being at one or the others house, talking or rolling around under the sheets. Her smile seemed to always be there. At work. When I showed up at her apartment or she knocked on the front door of my house. She was always smiling. Her bright blue eyes, a lighthouse of love in my seemingly uncaring and cold world. She literally made me want to be a better man.

As we hung around each other more, I realized Adele did not drink alcohol. This worked, as at the time I wasn't either given my recent membership to the Mormon faith. She smoked a few cigarettes here and there, which in some ways provided an odd comfort in the beginning. At times of course, I really wanted to be able to go out and have a few drinks with my girlfriend but given the fact that she wasn't turning 21 until July, it was a moot point. Still. Neither of us was taking in any alcohol and we were both having a blast just being who we were in each other's company. I held great value in that.

June 1st that year brought a crazy weather pattern to New England where most of us felt like we were living in Kansas. A strong series of tornadoes broke out, mainly in western Massachusetts, causing three deaths, hundreds of injuries, and millions of dollars in damage. It being a Wednesday, I was on my normal 24-hour shift in Townsend. Emergency task forces were being activated throughout the region, from my area to where Adele was living just to the west of Worcester.

A task force was a contingent of emergency units, typically involving fire and EMS, that responded as a group from their area to the involved section of the state. Be it a big fire, hazardous material incident, train wreck or other mass casualty, I had been part of a few of these task forces over the years.

Early afternoon, a structural task force was activated, sending our ladder truck out to the Springfield area due to the massive amount of damage. Within the same timeframe, the powers to be in that area, realized they were overtaxed with the number of injuries. So, an EMS task force was activated, calling up ambulances and special paramedic units from all over the state. Given our coverage area in the North Central part of Massachusetts, me and Jeff were spared from having to respond out west. Adele, however, got put on duty for the small on call department she was working as an EMT for.

Calling me in a panic, she explained that her fire chief ordered her to report to the fire station in case they were sent to "tornado alley." She freaked. Apparently she had a giant fear of high winds, and wanted nothing to do with going anywhere near where a tornado may be. As we stayed in touch the rest of the day into the night via texts and phone calls, I found myself being genuinely concerned for her well-being. I wanted to express this to her, but all my past experiences kept my mouth shut. I just told her over and over "You'll be ok." Doing my best to keep my stoic outward appearance.

As summer took hold, my shifts on the ambulance changed and Adele and I ended up working a 24 on the same day, on different trucks. She was on a basic life support ambulance, and I was on an advanced life support unit with my partner Tim. He and I were the same age, with him coming from the cooperate world a few years prior. We would spend 24 hours a day feeding off each other's energy, often the other being only reason we each finished the shift. On the overnight it was just me and Adele's two trucks working out of the main base. Come August, however, the company bought a "satellite" base in the north part of Worcester. When this happened, my truck was sent to it, leaving Adele to operate out of the old one. With us seeing less of each other at work, we did everything we could to hang out together in between shifts.

The tenth anniversary of 9/11 was a somber period of time in the country that year. Leading up to it, Adele and I decided on taking a trip to New York City for a few days. She was amazed by my career in the fire service, and intrigued by the idea of buffing fire calls in the city. Dozens of stories had been shared, of times both in Boston and NYC, of following the firefighters around watching them work at different fires. She was excited to be involved in something I hadn't actually done in close to ten years. At least in New York.

We drove down, taking her car as my SUV was beginning to fall into disrepair. On the 3-hour ride we talked about everything. Where the two of us had been in life. Where we each wanted to be. I filled her in more on the situation with my kids and the family, which by this time at smoothed out enough where I was seeing Tyler and Elizabeth unsupervised. One weekday afternoon, and a Saturday overnight I saw my kids without the always watching eyes of the two grandmothers. A situation, Adele felt, sounded more like a fucked-up divorce than a woman trying to keep her grandkids "safe." For me though, it was the best things had been in years and I didn't want to rock the boat.

Once we got to our hotel room, I laid on the bed, exhausted from an 80-hour work week as Adele explored the different cubies, drawers and finally the bathroom. My eyes closed, I did my best to try and relax after the long ride as my girlfriend made more noise than a herd of elephants running through a nitroglycerin plant. Suddenly I heard giggling, followed by the sound of water hitting a wall with accompanying hysterical laughter. Sitting up on the edge of the bed, Adele emerged from the bathroom with her hoodie up over her head, the front of it wet.

"Turn it off! Turn it off!" She shouted as her young, infectious laugh filled the hotel room.

Frustrated, I got up to peer into the bathroom only to see a bidet attachment in full operation. Water was spraying straight out of the toilet bowl, hitting the adjacent wall. Water now building up on the floor. Irritated more than humored, I walked back to the bed and sat down, telling her to call maintenance to come fix the problem. Eventually after more rest, and some dinner we both laughed uncontrollably about the whole situation. Apparently she had thought the bidet was a cleaning attachment for the toilet. So, she played with it like a child. The more we talked about it, the more we laughed.

It had been years since I found laughter in the mundane with someone I wasn't actively working with. Just simply being in the moment and appreciating what had happened had been a feeling I hadn't experienced in over eight years. It seemed to come natural to Adele, and it was hard to not get caught up in it once she started to laugh or even just smile. Up to this trip I had done an impressive job of keeping the word LOVE out of the vocabulary the two of us shared. I had even stressed that I didn't want to hear her say "I miss you" as inside it held the same power. I didn't want to be loved and honestly didn't think I could be.

Apparently this young beauty I was hanging around with begged to differ.

Upon returning I finally gave in, and Adele and I began exchanging I LOVE YOU's on the regular. Something I was honestly finding hard not to do for longer than I admitted to her at the time. I then met her parents who lived in a small town outside of Worcester. Her father Matt was six foot three and a lawyer, having his own practice in the city. He approached me in the driveway when we first got there to give me his version of an interrogation.

"Do you have a job?" Matt asked.

"Two, actually." I replied.

"You have a license?"

"Drove your daughter here in my truck, right over there." I said pointing to my SUV in his driveway.

"Well, I already know you don't have a criminal record so come on in!" Matt said with that fatherly smirk on his face, as he looked over the top of his round glasses at me.

Adele and her mother, Carolyn, ahead of us, looking back just smiled and shook their heads as they walked in the house. I met Adele's younger sister, Amelia, who was still in high school, and learned they had an older brother, Nathaniel, who was pre-med.

After meeting hers, I hesitantly introduced Adele to my family. Including Tyler and Elizabeth. Shortly thereafter the kids would occasionally hang around with Adele and I on the weekends, typically over dinner. They seemed to like her and Adele being younger, she got along great with them. My parents gave me no clue to their impression other than not really seeming to care that I was seeing someone new.

Even though I was falling madly in love with Adele, I still wasn't being honest with her. Now sleeping together in between our shifts, I found myself back to pretending I was in la-la land until I knew she was, where I then laid on my back, staring at the ceiling every night. At least at work, both jobs, I had my own bunk room so there was no need to pretend to be asleep. Every time I looked into her eyes though, I wanted to pour the truth about all the pain I was keeping inside. I wanted to tell her that even if my eyes weren't closed, what flashed in front of them, were horrible, often terrifying images that I just wanted someone to make go away. But I didn't. I kept the pain to myself. I had her fooled.

Or so I thought.

By this time, I was seeing a new therapist. Dahlia, a woman in her mid-fifties who looked more like someone who attended Woodstock and wore tie dye shirts on the weekend than a therapist. I began to test the waters when it came to mentioning some of my past traumas and even bringing up some of the calls I had experienced. We established our relationship and every once in a while I built up enough courage to engage in a conversation that went beyond how my mood had been.

As winter set in and the new year reared its head I was in hot water. Financially. There was no way I was going to be able to fix what needed to be on my truck, never mind afford to live at Peter J any longer. I was about to run out of heat, which meant I needed to shut the water off to avoid bursting the pipes. I barely had the money to get to work and was only eating real meals when on duty or around Adele. When I saw the kids, we literally just sat around and did nothing with me often asking my parents for money to be able to feed Tyler and Elizabeth. I ended up asking one of the medics on the fire department if I could move in with him and his wife. After much discussion, he agreed.

Now, I was poor and humiliated.

This also put a damper on my ability to see Adele. I wasn't able to drive out to her apartment unless I was already leaving a shift in Worcester and having her come sleep with me at my friend's house was inappropriate. Still, we made the most out of every minute we had together.

The living situation with my friend was less than optimum. Along with his wife, their daughter and her boyfriend were all living in the same house. I was crammed into a room barely big enough for my full-size mattress and a laundry basket with a few days' worth of clothes. The rest of my belongings were all in the cold, unheated walls of the house where the most recent version of my life fell apart.

In desperation, I sat Adele down and we talked about me moving in with her. I even offered to sleep in the second bedroom, not to encroach on all of her privacy. She eventually agreed, and I did. I moved most of the stuff I needed into her apartment with her parents allowing me to store the rest in a spare house on their property. I was now completely out of Peter J Drive. After our shifts in Worcester, Adele and I started meeting for breakfast before heading back to the apartment. It became a weekly event and reprieve from all the stress and at times, never ending bullshit I was feeling. It was one of the few things I looked forward to at the time.

Right after the move, my mother and Darlene invited Adele and I up to the house in Hubbardston for a "meet and greet" brunch of sorts. Tyler and Elizabeth were not going to be there, just my parents and Darlene and Peter. At first everyone was pleasant, with the two grandmothers even seeming to like Adele. Then their motive became more obvious. They began to talk about how men like me, Peter, and Don couldn't live without women like my mother and Darlene. How we wouldn't be able to function without them telling us what to do. Adele simply nodded in a half agreement, half astonishment at what she just heard.

Shortly after this, I told Dahlia I wanted to bring my mother in to one of our sessions to possibly help with perspective. She agreed that this could be beneficial, and the three of us figured out a day that worked. Sitting across from these two females, with my back to the corner next to the only door into Dahlia's office, I immediately begin to feel like this may have been a mistake. My back ached. Palms sweaty. My head started to spin, as Dahlia asked my mother if she would like to talk about some of what she has seen in my behavior over the years. With that, my mother unzipped her purse and pulled out six handwritten pages of "some" of the things I had done wrong in my life. Mostly the last decade or so. Dahlia looked blankly at the woman responsible for my birth, not knowing what to say as she took the stack of wrong doings from her. My mother sat back in the chair, crossing her arms in front of her.

She was smiling straight back at me.

Time pushed on and April arrived. With it a situation I had created back in the end of 2011 caught up with me. The end of December I had missed the day I was supposed to attend for a practical skills session needed to recertify my EMT. Every two years Massachusetts EMT's and Paramedics are required to attend so many hours of continuing education and a practical skills testing day in order to keep up their certification. I had missed my skills day due to a severe stomach bug.

Come a certain date in April my EMT was going to no longer be valid. The major problem with this was that both of my jobs required this certification. As I sat in the office with the operations manager in Worcester, who looked like the cartoon boss from "The Jetsons", I felt that old familiar knot building in my stomach.

"Well, my hands are tied Keith. I can't have you working the truck and we don't have any positions in dispatch currently." Mr. Spacely said in the most uncaring, unsympathetic way he could muster up.

Later the week I had to have a similar conversation with the fire chief. He was a bit more understanding and offered me a few eight hour shifts a week on the fire side, doing mainly clerical and inspection work. However, he warned me that given I was now living an hour away, I had four months to move back in the area. After that, my current situation combined with my out-of-town residency would force his hand to let me go.

Now I had no full-time work. I had even less money. I began to fall behind on my child support obligation. I had no health insurance, so I wasn't able to fill my eight prescriptions a month. I began having withdrawal symptoms, along with constant mood swings, nightmares, daily flashbacks, anxiety, and bouts of depression. I also began having chest pain again.

Going back to when things went south in 2010, I had begun to have chronic chest pain and angina causing me to visit the emergency room on more than a dozen occasions. Even being admitted for further tests a few of those. Now that I no longer had the meds that had been keeping my demons at bay, physiologically my body wasn't very happy. After a few weeks the withdrawal symptoms subsided and I even began to get a bit of a personality, showing emotion from time to time.

Stuck in a position of needing to make money, I applied for and got hired by a life insurance company outside of Boston. I came up with the five hundred dollars to obtain the proper licensure and went through their initial training. While doing this, I was working through the process of getting my EMT certification back into current status. After about a month of sitting and trying to sell people policies I wouldn't buy myself, I quit. I'm not a salesman and that became increasing apparent the first time I was forced to sit with a firefighter and his family. I literally stood up and looked at this guy and his wife and thanked them for helping me realized I wasn't cut out for this line of work.

As I received the letter stating my EMT was valid again, I was called into a meeting with my fire chief. It was late August 2012, and I was hopeful to get my shifts back up and running as I walked into the head of the departments office. As he asked if I found a place to live that was closer to Townsend, I felt that pit in my stomach start to churn again. Sweat ran down my spine, and my vision narrowed.

"Your silence tells me no. I'm sorry Keith. I got to let you go." The chief said, leaning back in his leather chair. His hands making a teepee on his lap as he looked over his glasses at me from across the desk.

I stared at the floor. Fighting back the tears that would eventually come later that night.

I pushed myself through the letdown of being kicked out the fire station door after 16 years and marched back into the ambulance garage in Worcester. Again, greeted by Mr. Spacely, he hired me back and I started within a week. I had lost my seniority and had to work a different set of shifts, but I had a full-time job again.

Not being a firefighter anymore was a tough pill to swallow. It was who I was. It was how I knew my life. It was how I lived my life. It was my identity and now it was gone. In my mind all I was doing on the ambulance was bringing grandma to her doctor's appointments and listening to pity stories form psychiatric patients all while being treating like an inconvenience by every nurse we interacted with.

Early that fall, another meeting was called by the grandparents. This time my mother and Darlene wanted to meet at Tyler's new therapist. They had a habit of changing the poor kids counselor every six months to a year at this point. I agreed only if Adele could come with me. Eventually they agreed to this, and the day came for us to have this meeting. The grandmothers sitting on the couch with Tyler between them, his therapist in a chair against the wall to the right of them, Adele and I sat on a smaller couch across the room. Right away, there was a feeling that this may have been a setup as both my mother and Darlene sat looking at me with their arms crossed. Tyler staring at the floor. After some back and forth which circled around how much of a failure I had been as a father, Darlene spoke up, tossing a verbal grenade into the center of the room.

"Tyler wants to hear you say that it was YOUR road rage that caused the accident and killed Heather." My ex-mother-in-law said in such a calm, matter of fact way. As if she had rehearsed the line for weeks.

Adele's jaw dropped. The therapist turned his head, looking at me to answer. I felt the room pulling away, with **darkness wrapping in from behind me. I began to shrink in size, the walls grown to skyscraper height. My hands felt like over-inflated balloons as if I could grip anything. The faces in the room blurred as the voices got deep and loud. Screams filtered in from behind me. Flashes of red. My arms filled with pain, as my heart increased, my heart beating through my chest. Then suddenly I felt myself being pulled back in. A hand on my right arm.**

Adele had put her hand on me, as she continued to call my name. I began to survey the room as four other faces stared back at me. The therapist in disbelief. Darlene with a look of impatience. Tyler, cheeks red, eyes watery, almost embarrassed. Then my mother.

She was smiling.

"I'm not saying that Tyler, as that's not what happened." I said as I did my hardest to not break my stare with my oldest child who himself was obviously incredibly uncomfortable.

After that I stormed out of the room, leaving everyone behind. Apparently on the way downstairs, Darlene told Adele she was going to do everything in her power to keep Tyler and Elizabeth out of my life. When Adele told me this in the car, I just sat and cried. My head in my hands my fingers trying to pull my hair out. I began to sob uncontrollably for the first time in front of my young girlfriend. Something I told myself I would never do.

I threw myself into my work after that day. I started picking up extra shifts in an attempt to lessen the financial burden I was dealing with. I had started to hide my SUV at my parents' house in Townsend as it was now at risk for repossession due to how far behind I fell on the payments. Seeing the dire situation, Adele pushed me to ask someone to help co-sign a loan so I could buy a different vehicle. In the end I got my old partner Jeff to help me out. I ended up getting a used Cadillac and was relieved of the broken SUV. Things began to look up, at least financially. However, I was purposely working so much that the only visitation I was having with the kids was on Saturday overnights, and they were sparse.

One particular night I received a phone call from Jeff. We had been staying in touch since I left the fire department, so it wasn't unusual for him to call me, especially when I was at work in Worcester. He didn't waste any time getting to the reason he was calling.

"Adele just called me. I guess Tyler was sexually abused by someone." His words hit deep inside me, bringing everything around me to a screeching halt.

In disbelief, I just sat there staring blankly ahead. My partner rushed over seeing something was up. Eventually Adele called and explained the situation. I was told that my mother had called her stating Tyler came out about Danielle's son Nick touching him inappropriately back when we were all living together at Peter J. I immediately just wanted to speak to my son. Tell him everything was going to be ok and that he wasn't alone. That I believed him, and we would get him the help he needed to heal from it.

I was told I wasn't allowed to speak to Tyler, and that a meeting was to take place at the police station in Townsend. Adele was allowed to accompany me, but she wasn't to speak. With this, she reached out to her father, being a lawyer, and asked him if he would come with us. More for support than any legal reason.

Walking into the same meeting room at the police station where my first failed critical incident stress debriefing was held, I immediately felt at a disadvantage. Lit by bright fluorescents in the ceiling, the white walls made the room seem void of any character. Broken up by only a few soundproof, wood panel doors, along with a series of three windows on the outside wall, the room was cold and lacked any sense of life. A long meeting table was perfectly centered in the room with ten chairs positioned around it. When I walked into the room accompanied by Adele and her father, my mother, Darlene, Don, and Peter were sitting all on one side. One of the female Sergeant's followed us in, sitting at one end. An officer I had worked dozens of emergency scenes with over the years, was about to lay out the details of what happened.

As Matt sat down, Darlene demanded that he leave as the situation had nothing to do with him. Stating he was only there to protect Adele as they now involved her in this, he stood up and both of them left the room.

Now, I was alone.

The sergeant stated that my mother and Tyler reported that back around 2010, when we were all living together, Danielle's son Nick inappropriately touched Tyler. There was an investigation into the allegations and Danielle and her son were being questioned. I was then told that as a "non-custodial" parent I was only being told this information, because the grandparents felt I needed to know. With that I began to sob. As the meeting ended, I was then advised that for now, I was not allowed to see or speak to Tyler. I could have visitation with Elizabeth. But it would be a few weeks before I was allowed to see Tyler again.

I was crushed. I wasn't even being allowed to comfort my son.

That Thanksgiving, Alex and Emily invited us up to their house in Westminster for dinner. By this time, they had two small boys and an infant daughter. Both sets of their grandparents were also in attendance that day. I hadn't seen Alex's parent's in over a year and was greeted the same way I always had been. A hug from his mom and a beer from his dad. Right from the beginning there was an uneasiness in the air towards Adele. I couldn't place it, but it was almost as if she wasn't welcomed. Alex had decided to roast, smoke and deep fry three different turkeys. While me and him were enjoying a beer in the cold, late November afternoon sun, I tried to feel out a situation. I began to talk about what I was working on with my therapist and how I wanted to start addressing the problems from my childhood.

"What do you mean your childhood? Like your dad?" He said in an almost dismissive way while not being able to look at me in my face.

When I began to talk about how my uncle Jack's cancer had made a return and then transitioned into his abuse, Alex got very uncomfortable. Changing the subject as quick as it came up, he began talking about something he found humorous from his job at Comcast.

I had my answer. My best friend was not going to be the person I could confide in regarding the horrible details from my childhood. The impression he gave me was that he didn't even want to hear about it. This left me feeling embarrassed and sad that our friendship wasn't what I had thought it was.

I sat with it all for a while and decided to hold off on bringing it up with Dahlia. I tried to enjoy the holidays with Tyler and Elizabeth. They visited a few weekends around Christmas that year and I was able to get them a few gifts with the help of Adele. They were less than impressed with our choice in toys. To add insult to injury, they began to tell me some of what they were being told by their grandmothers. How apparently everyone felt I was just an angry person and not a good father. The word monster was used a few times. Tyler even began to talk to me in ways that felt condescending and had a tone as if he was saying "what are you going to do about it?" I was still forbidden to bring up any of the events regarding Tyler's abuse. The whole topic was off limits.

The beginning of 2013 I started a series of new shifts with a 16-hour one on Wednesdays. With it came a new partner named Joe. An average built guy, a few years younger than me, Joe had a clean cut on his round face. Hailing from a family of first responders and military, we hit it off right away. We spent more time laughing than taking the job seriously, which was exactly the break I needed from the bleakness of other parts of my life.

My love for Adele was deeper than I had ever felt for another human being. Her sympathetic approach to every part of our relationship was getting me to start to look more closely at what I had been through in life. I was beginning to realize that as far back as I could remember, I had always heard voices in my head. Not just me talking to myself. There were other parts of my brain that were, at times, struggling to take control of the vessel that was my body. These voices felt rooted in distinct events that I couldn't yet place. But Adele's unrelenting support was causing a courage to build up inside of me that I had never experienced before. This led to me breaking down one night in bed, telling her about Jacks abuse towards me. She hugged me for hours that night, telling me I should really try and tell my therapist.

Later that spring, Adele and I attended a birthday party at Alex's for one of his boys. Right after he went on radio silence. Not answering text messages or phone calls. At the same time, Adele and I had found a larger, three-bedroom apartment in Lancaster and put us a half hour closer to the kids. We moved in on what became known as the hottest day of 2013. Still, I heard nothing from Alex. Talking to my mother about it one Saturday when I picked up Tyler and Elizabeth, she just looked at me sarcastically citing Adele as the possible reason.

"Maybe they don't like Adele, Keith. I don't know." She said with no effect whatsoever as her eyes seemed to just stare through me.

Right after Elizabeth's birthday in June, I decided to take a leap of faith and start the conversation regarding my childhood abuse. I told Dahlia I wanted to have my mother present, not giving up any details on the horrible things that had been done to me almost three decades prior. Bringing my mother back into that office, I instantly filled with apprehension. Dahlia broke the ice, telling her that I had something regarding my childhood that I needed to tell her. As I sat forward, I began to sob. My mother unmoved by this simply asked what had happened to me when I was a kid. Having never mouthed the words out loud to anyone but Adele, I spoke like a scared seven-year-old, just wanting my mother to make it all better.

"Jack touched me when I was a kid." I was barely able to get the words out before a hot flash raced through my body. Every distal end of my arms and legs tingled, eventually going numb. Sweat poured off my head and down my back.

Blown away by what was just said, apparently not expecting it, Dahlia just stared at me. Eventually she asked my mother what she felt about her younger brother sexually abusing her only child. My mother didn't show much emotion, only standing and giving me a loveless hug out of obvious obligation. After the appointment, I went outside and got into Adele's waiting car. Fear gripped me in ways I hadn't felt in decades. I was certain something bad was going to happen. Adele assured me everything was going to be ok.

I didn't believe her. The secret I just revealed to my mother and Dahlia, was kept locked up for a reason. Given my mother's emotionless reaction, I never told her as a kid for an even better reason. As we drove back to our new apartment I knew, just knew, the contents shared in that meeting were going to come back and bite me in the ass.

On a hot and humid Wednesday shift in late July, Joe and I were getting hammered with call after call. By mid-morning it was already 97 degrees, and I felt like I hadn't showered in days. During a lull in the action, we both took ten minutes to throw our lunch down our throats, knowing we wouldn't get another chance for hours. Taking the last bite of my sandwich, I received a text message. It was from Alex. He wanted to meet that week to discuss why he hadn't been speaking to me.

That Friday, I met my best friend at the restaurant that was the backdrop for so many of our teenage charades over 15 years ago. Getting out of his truck, we gave each other a hug and shared a few laughs before heading in and sitting at a booth in the back of the pub. Alex wasted no time. As soon as a round of drinks were ordered, he told me what had happened a few months back. He claimed right after the birthday party in May, "someone" had called DCF on him and Emily, claiming their house was unsafe for their children. They underwent a brief investigation that yielded no supporting evidence of the charges against them.

That wasn't the issue. It was who they felt called in the erroneous report.

"It was Adele, Keith. We know it was her. It had to be and it's not up for discussion." His voice switched to a deeper, stern tone that he almost never used.

Of course, sticking up for Adele, I told him they were mistaken as she wouldn't do that. He said he didn't care, and that me and him could remain friends but Adele wasn't allowed around his family.

"Well, that's going to be hard as I was just about to tell you I am going to be asking Adele to marry me on her birthday in a few weeks." As the words left my mouth, I knew he didn't give two shits.

Soon after this we exchanged pleasantries, paid the bill, and parted ways. Driving home I was pissed. Pissed at Alex. Pissed at Adele. Pissed at the world. Walking in the apartment, I started screaming at my girlfriend like I never had. Red faced, fists clenched, I demanded to know why she would call DCF on my best friend. She denied knowing anything about it. She begged me to calm down, even pleading with me to allow her to call Alex or Emily to try and make everything right. When I said no, she called her father to try and find a way to clear her name. There was nothing she could do, and at the moment I was inconsolable.

After some time, I did calm down, but I still wasn't 100 percent convinced that Adele wasn't somehow involved. Honestly, Alex and Emily's house WAS a fucking pigsty. They've always been pretty dirty people, and once I began to accept that, I accepted the fact that someone was probably mortified by the way they lived. There were lots of new people in that house the day of the party, and it could have been any one of a dozen.

So, I moved on.

I got the family ring from Adele's Aunt that she had expressed in wanting should I ever decide to propose to her. I approached her mother and father telling them my intentions and received their blessing to ask for Adele's hand in marriage. On her birthday in early August, I took Adele to Boston for dinner and a night away. I had the whole thing planned out, even arranging for flowers to be delivered at a certain part of dinner. Adele had no idea. As the flowers were brought to the table, I stood up and reached into my pocket. Getting down to one knee, with dozens of other patrons staring at us, smiles now on their faces, I revealed the ring to Adele.

"Will you spend the rest of your life putting up with my nonsense!!??" I asked trying my best to add a little humility.

Tears flowed from Adeles face, as she shook her head yes. Applause and cheers broke out from the crowd around us with several people approaching us to say congratulations. After dinner we walked around the North End of Boston, hand in hand, so in love. I had never been so in love in my life. In Just over two years, this woman had showed me a part of the world I had not felt in years. Truthfully, I had never experienced it the way Adele got me to.

That night we made love like neither of us ever had, falling asleep in a naked embrace. Laying against her backside, I promised to stick by her till the end of time and beyond. Turning to face me, she held my head with both her hands. In that moment, I knew I met my soul mate. The one person who knew more about me than anyone had ever tried to find out. Good. Bad. Horrible. None of it scared her. None of it detoured her from convincing me every single day just how much she loved me.

Returning to work I was on cloud nine. I felt like nothing could touch me or send me into another downward spiral. Joe and I had grown into close friends by this time and had begun to be part of each other's lives outside of work. I met his longtime girlfriend, Jenn, and the four of us had dinner, and laughed almost weekly. Everyone got along great.

Come September, Joe had taken a job at the Worcester airport that was a combination of firefighter and police officer. I also started working with a new partner on my 16-hour shift on Fridays. I got along with him, but he was an odd fellow. At the same time a new, younger woman had started working in an administrative position at the ambulance service. She was causing a lot of waves, particularly with me. By the end of the month, I was having almost daily run ins with her. At one point I was told I was being forced off my shifts into a schedule that wasn't going to allow me to see Tyler and Elizabeth on the weekends. I begged. I pleaded to this woman to help me as I was at the whim of my mother and Darlene regarding visitation with the kids.

Around this same time, I had reapproached my mother regarding the news I shared with her surrounding my abuse, months earlier. After a brief conversation of me asking why we haven't tried to talk about it, she replied simply that I had made the entire situation up. She referenced my supposed history of lying and sabotaging the family as her reasons for not believing her sons childhood abuse. Instead of supporting her son, she began telling certain people about the false accusations about her brother, making a mockery of her only child.

This is the situation biting me in the ass.

On a late Friday afternoon, after bringing a patient to the hospital, I received a call from the woman in the office. She told me effective the next week I was going onto this new shift. I had no choice. I screamed at her, feeling my rage reach new levels. Getting nowhere with that, I hung up on her and called my mother. I was hopeful that she would understand the situation and make accommodations so I could see the kids somehow on the weekends. She denied my request, stating I would have to make do with the occasional short visits during the week.

I tweaked. My temper reached a level I never experienced before. All the past years felt like they were right in front of my face, and I had lost all control. I jumped out of the ambulance and began speed boxing the side of it. My new partner, scared shitless, did what he could to calm me down. Eventually, I was able to call Adele who was home as she was going with Elizabeth to Celine's baby shower that night. After a long conversation, I calmed down enough to begin to make sense of reality again.

As we drove back to our base in the north part of Worcester, I began to get dizzy. I started having a pinpoint headache in my right temple that was making me nauseous. I turned pale, and the world around me started to turn on end. Walking into the base, just the two of us, I told my partner I needed to use the bathroom. I walked in and splashed cold water on my face. Looking in the mirror, I couldn't recognize who I saw.

Then. Everything went black.

Hands grabbed me. Sharp pain in the bend of my elbows. Short faint glimpses of the ceiling of an ambulance appeared here and there. Shouting. More grabbing. My name being yelled. Yet the darkness hung strong. Suddenly I felt my eyes start to focus on one face. I didn't know what was going on, but I knew the face. He asked if I knew what happened, then asked me to smile.

"We got left sided weakness back here. He's still out of it." The voice yelled over my head to someone I couldn't see.

With that I felt a stiff collar around my neck. I could tell I was on a backboard, and they had started an iv in at least one arm. I felt the sudden need to puke and tried to tell the person I recognized. As I was tipped onto my side the best they could, I projectile vomited. More dizziness. More in and out. I had no idea what was happening beyond being in the back of an ambulance. After a while we stopped, and the rear doors opened. As I was wheeled out, I saw another face I knew. It was one of the supervisors.

"Keith. Do you know Who I am?"

I nodded.

'Your partner found you unconscious on the bathroom floor. You're at UMASS. We called Adele. She is on her way. Ok?"

Another nod.

Reality came back and I was able to talk and start to give information to the dozens of doctors and nurses that now towered over me. I was moved to a hospital bed with a thousand questions being asked left and right. Exam after exam. Finally, they said I was found unconscious and during the transport it looked like I may have had a stroke. Still having some weakness on one side of my body, I tried to raise my left arm which felt heavy and uncooperative.

"Ok Keith. We're taking you to CT so we can see if there's a bleed. Hang tight!" One of the nurses said.

As I was wheeled out of the room, I heard Adele's voice, and then saw Elizabeth's terrified face to my left. I told them both I was ok, which caused them to begin to cry. After a few more tests, I was able to see my fiancé and daughter. The night was long, and they were able to rule out a stroke. But they still didn't have an answer as to what exactly happened. I ended up admitted, with Adele's dad giving Elizabeth a ride back to my parents.

Because it was an unwitnessed loss of consciousness, the doctors couldn't clear me to drive a car. Which meant I couldn't drive an ambulance. This caused a major issue at my job. They couldn't have me operating any of their vehicles for obvious reasons, however, they also had nowhere else for me to work. So, I was put on an indefinite leave of absence.

Not working again, I found myself with a lot of free time. In an effort to make some money, I began to sell some of the fire collectibles that I had accrued over the years. It helped, but it wasn't going to last forever. I also spent a bit more time than I should have on social media. Doing so, I ended up connecting with Calvin's youngest brother, Phil.

The last time I saw this guy was back at Heather's wake in 2003. Now being almost Halloween, over a decade had passed since either of us had interacted. He sent me a private message on Facebook one night telling me my father was extremely sick and had just had another major heart attack.

I believe my first message back was "Good. Fuck him."

After a bit of back and forth, I agreed to meet Phil for breakfast at one of my favorite diners in Leominster. Before we walked in he tried to give me a hug, which he was met with my outstretched hand. I didn't want to be there, and Phil felt it. About 50, with a shaved head, small thin mustache, and a constant half sarcastic grin on his face, he stood about five foot nine or so. His voice was fitting to his physical appearance, with a light, nasal tone to it.

Sitting down, he went on about Calvin and all his ailments. He told me how my dad always loved me, asking me here and there what memories I had of the man. The answer was not many. When my father fell ill this last time, Phil went to his bedside in the hospital. My father supposedly broke down about how he really wanted to make peace with his only son. Calvin now had lung cancer and was on his third heart attack. He had lost a lot of weight and the medical team involved didn't give him the best life expectancy.

He asked if I would be willing to go see him at his apartment in Plaistow New Hampshire, which was just north of Haverhill. I sat with it for a while. Imaging to myself what this father-son reunion would look like. All my life I had been told nothing but negative about the man. This filled me with anger and a desire, at certain times, to want to murder him. Now that I was being told he was basically on death's doorstep, I decided I had nothing to lose at this point.

So, I agreed to meet him.

The original date we planned in mid-November didn't work out as Calvin ended up in the hospital again. Right after Thanksgiving, Phil and I piled into his car and made the hour trip to where my father was living with his girlfriend Beatrice. Leading up to this meeting, Calvin and I had been emailing back and forth, in an effort to at least be in communication before seeing each other for the first time in nearly 30 years. In one of his emails right before this meeting took place, he asked if it would be ok to have his girlfriend present. In an odd way, I related to this gesture as Adele was my support whenever I needed to confront stressful situations.

Phil and I pulled up to the green, multi-family apartment building around 10am. It was cold and raw with a light rain which

I felt was perfect given the circumstances. As he put the car in park, Phil turned and looked at me.

"No matter what happens after today, remember you faced your old man. Nothing else needs to happen. It's your choice." His hand patting my shoulder as I nodded and opened the passenger door.

Walking up to the main door, which led to a common area that all the tenants used, I was now facing the door to my estranged fathers apartment. A man that held the reputation of uncaring, unloving, and not wanting of his only son. As I reached for the doorknob, I hesitated and could begin to hear my mother's voice, deep in the nooks and grannies of my brain. It was telling me not to do it. Then, in my head, I saw my mother just sitting there.

She was smiling.

So, I reached back for the knob. Just then the door swung open, and I was greeted by a five-foot-tall Italian looking woman with black hair and oval glasses. She introduced herself as Beatrice and welcomed me and Phil into the apartment. As I walked into what was their kitchen, I looked across the room to see a thin, frail looking bald man in his mid-sixties, getting himself out of a rather plush recliner. As he walked, his gait looked familiar. He coughed a few times, clearing his throat and took short, purposeful steps. He had a greying mustache and stood about five foot ten. His frame indicated at one time; this man was a force to be reckoned with as he definitely fit the profile of former biker. I walked a few steps towards him, having to duck as I passed under a ceiling fan in the center of the kitchen. Coming to a stop, obviously taken aback by my size in comparison to the others and himself, my father put his hand out in my direction. His eyes wide behind his round glasses.

"Damn. You're a big son of a bitch!"

CHAPTER 10
CIGARETTES & CHEESECAKE

remember the first time I looked at pictures of my father. I was about six or seven and my mother had dug out the old photo albums. The big red one, with gold letters that read MEMORIES had a collection of images of me when I was first born and a toddler. There were a few of my mother and I but the ones that always grabbed my attention were of Calvin. The balding top of his head with the ring of thick black hair from one ear to the other. Tight olive skin, covering a moderate healthy build with a wide, drooping mustache on his upper lip half covering a lazy grin. In several of these pictures, he was holding me when I was an infant. One of my favorites was of him working on his motorcycle with me standing near him in a red snowsuit. They were all I had to know what my old man looked like.

Sitting on a couch that had its best years when disco was king, I stared across the room at a man that looked nothing like the one I remember from the red photo album. Even though he wore a baseball cap, I could tell no hair remained. His once healthy skin was now pale white, and blotchy looking, with the mustache still there but grey. His arms and legs thin and lacking much muscle.

His narrow chest and small waist, making the clothes he had on look baggy, and unfit. Just resting in the plush computer chair, engaging in conversation, he looked like he had just run a marathon. Often getting winded after just a sentence.

This was a sick man.

My uncle Phil sitting to my right, with my father and his girlfriend Beatrice across from us, I was doing more listening than speaking. I was as curious as I was nervous. As I kept looking over at Calvin, I could sense that he was likely feeling the same. As I was growing comfortable with not really engaging in conversation, Beatrice broke the ice in a rather direct way.

"Keith is there anything in particular you'd like to ask Cal?" She referred to my father by the shortened version of his full name he now went by.

I had been waiting decades to confront my father. To go toe to toe with the man I was always told just walked away one day because he didn't want me. At one point, for years, I was so angry with him all I wanted to do was end his life. Now sitting across from him, I realized he didn't have much life left. My anger subsided and fell away. I grew younger in mind and even felt smaller in stature. When I answered I was no longer in my mid-thirties. I was a child.

"Why did you leave and not come back?" I said not even looking up from the floor in front of me.

Cal's answer not only shocked me but his younger brother, to my side. He explained how he and my mother's marriage was already on the rocks come my delivery. That when I was born, something changed with her. And not in a good way. He said that if he hadn't had left, three lives would have been destroyed. Not just two. He ended by saying that he's always loved me and couldn't have been happier than the day I was born.

I knew what he said was true. I felt it deep in my soul. I accepted it, and the conversation continued into different topics. After about two hours and a few cups of coffee, Phil and I left. My father and I exchanging cell phone numbers agreeing to stay in touch.

The hour or so ride back home was livelier than the one earlier that morning. Phil asked how I felt about all I heard. Told me there was no pressure, however, I did in fact see with me own eyes, a man not long for this world. Getting home and sitting with Adele over dinner, we spoke about the options. All my life I had been given information that led me down an angry path regarding my father. Anger that blinded me from the true loss I was experiencing. The loss of having a dad. Now I was faced with a situation where, if I chose to, I could have a version of that back. Albeit short lived due to his current condition, I had an opportunity.

So, I took it.

It was awkward at first, and we kept to emails for the longer conversations, but eventually we began communicating more regularly. Still not being cleared to work on the ambulance, I was making weekly trips to Plaistow to visit Cal and Beatrice. Right before Christmas, Adele took the hour ride with me to meet my father. This was history in the making as none of the other women in my life had ever met him, and I had never received his opinion on anyone I had dated. At 35, it was an odd experience. One that most go through in their teenage years, I had already been married once with two kids, and now engaged to another. My mother had always had something to say about every woman I brought home that she met. Something less than positive. That day in his apartment, my father lit up like the Christmas tree next to his chair. He was so happy. And so was Adele.

From there out, I had my dad back. We texted more than we talked on the phone, which was held for making the final plans for any visits. The more time I spent with my father, the more what I had been told over the years bothered me.

Adele and I went to the fire department Christmas party in Townsend that year like we had the previous two as a couple. By that time, word had gotten around my family that Cal was back in my life. My uncles exhibited behavior that was in some ways uncharacteristic. Eddie's standoffish attitude was only heightened and there was a bit of avoidance towards Adele and I. Jack on the other hand, seemed nervous. Like a scared puppy, he seemed to follow me all over the function hall. Every time I turned around, there he was. Looking at me like he wanted to ask me something but couldn't gather the words, or the balls to ask.

At my parent's, when I would stop by to grab Tyler and Elizabeth either during the week or on Saturday, no one brought the subject up. At one point during a visit, I had mentioned to Elizabeth that I was seeing my dad again and she had apparently brought that information back to my mother. The next time I stopped by their house, I was scolded for mentioning Cal's existence in the presence of my children.

"He's not a good man Keith. He's done some bad things ya know!" She spoke as if to remind me of every negative word she threw at me about my father since I was old enough to remember.

"I know! The man ran guns for the mob in the sixties. Went to prison for it. Broke out. Went back for another year. Beat some other guys up while out on the road as a trucker. I know Ma!" I said as I waited for the increased blood pressure in mothers face to show.

Thing was. All that stuff was true. He did all of it. I was told about it as a kid in a very hurtful way to inflict some sort of pain on me. But when me and the old man talked about some of the shit he had done, he never shied from the truth. He admitted anything I asked him about.

With the cancer eating away at him, Cal took advantage of every second of our time together. He was honest with me about what he knew regarding his cancer. It had infected his lung and throat, and the doctors were aggressively treating it with a chemo call Decagon. His three treatments a week left him tired, frail, and without an appetite. It was also doing a number on his heart. He had two heart attacks and six stents by the time I came back in his life. Almost weekly angina plagued his existence. This last part he tried to keep from me, even though Beatrice told me all the parts he left out. The other problem with being treated with Decagon was that there was a significate risk for developing Leukemia. All in all, my father faced all of this like a champ. At least in front of me.

Come January 2014, I had gotten on the fire department in Lancaster, as an on-call member. A few weeks after that I reached out to an old friend from my Lawrence days about working for a different ambulance company in Lowell. Now back with a full-time and part-time job, my free time lessened. My ability to drive up to see Dad had fallen back to about once every seven to ten days. However, we spoke three to four times a week and texted daily. When we did hang out in his apartment, he was always smiling, and wanting to hear more about all the things I had done in life. I learned more and more about him too. He was apparently pretty good at pool back in his day. Even making it to the national tournaments out in Vegas a few times. He also hated the cold due to a near death experience in some valley in western Pennsylvania back in his trucker days.

Unless it was for an appointment we almost always hung out in his apartment. Him in his recliner, me on the couch, just shooting the shit. I had told him about my Cadillac and how it had heated seats, saying how someday I would come pick him up in it and take him and Beatrice to our place in Lancaster for a few days. One day I show up late morning for a typical lunch visit. As I walked into his kitchen, ducking once again under the ceiling fan, I was greeted by that same quirky smile of his. Only this time he had on one of his winter Harley Davidson jackets with a pair of gloves and a hat in his hands. A long tan zipped bag on the counter. Beatrice gleaming over to the side with her hands up to her mouth in a way only a short Italian woman could do.

"Wanna learn how to shoot some pool kiddo!?" These words carrying a new life I hadn't heard many times before in my father's voice. An ear-to-ear grin over his face as he stood as proud as the first time we hugged as grown men.

I'm horrible at pool.

The only game I'm worse at is golf.

That day as I showed my father just how awful I was at eight ball; I enjoyed the game not because I was playing it. But because of WHO I was playing with. And it wasn't even that we were playing anything. I was having a moment with my dad that I had never experienced before. A moment most kids have when they're kindergarten age or younger. His smile outlasted his stamina to stand and play a full game. As we sat at one of the tables in this bar and grill, we both ordered boneless chicken wings and shared stories. After only three months or so of being back in each other's lives, it was like we never left. I felt more comfortable asking him hard questions on tough topics. He had begun to share more information with me that in some ways, even though it was the first time hearing it, I already knew. This day also started a new tradition between the two of us. Something that took place at the end of every visit, text, and phone call from there on out.

We said "**I love you**" to each other.

By mid-February, Adele and I were completely immersed in finalizing our wedding details for our August 8th date. Caterers, wedding cake, the DJ, and the venue brought with them a slew of meetings and decisions that were often also accompanied by stress. We had picked out who was going to be in our wedding party and what they would be wearing. My father was equally excited about renting a tux and being there on the big day. I had asked Tyler if he would be the ring bearer, to which he was excited for. Elizabeth was equally as pumped to be the flower girl. My mother was giving me a lot of slack knowing Cal was going to be there. She had already refused to attend our wedding for various reasons, and I was beginning to feel like she had something else up her sleeve.

With all this going on, I began working part-time day shifts at the fire station in Lancaster. I was also growing extremely close to the clique and gaining respect from the membership as a whole. Time and time again I was proving myself capable and confident at my job along with being one of the first to bust balls or tell a joke that got the whole room rolling. My full-time work on the ambulance in Lowell was what it was. They were pretty mundane shifts filled with almost all non-emergent transfers. This I was fine with as by this time I was ok not dealing with everyone else's worse day, every time I went into work.

As spring settled in, I was notified via an email, that Jack wanted to hold a meeting to "set the record straight" regarding some family matters. While sitting in a parking lot out in Lowell, on shift, I pondered what this met. Knowing my mother and what I told her regarding my youngest uncle and my childhood, I assumed the two were related. So, I called him. On the phone Jack was very matter of fact with his tone and information he was willing to convey. Not really unusual for him, but there was an air of fear that carried through the phone. When I asked who would be present for this meeting I was told his wife Melanie, my mother, Don, and myself. He said that Adele could attend if I wanted her there.

Eddie wasn't invited.

This clinched it for me. It had to be something related to my abuse but likely was going to contain facts about his own. With Eddie not being invited, and my own experience with the man, I was beginning to see a common link in the Elliott family abuse cycle. My relief was quickly overrun with a fear of Jack trying to justify, play down, or even deny what he had done to me years prior. Talking to Adele about the situation she told me I had absolutely no obligation to go to this meeting which was set for that Saturday. Going back and forth on it, I finally decided the day of, not to attend. Adele called my mother and told her we wouldn't be coming.

The next month or so, on several of my visitation days, Tyler or Elizabeth conveniently didn't want to come over. Or another family member had made plans with them without asking me first. All of this relayed to me by my mother in a tone that was, short of the words being said, telling me that any time I went against the grain, there would be a consequence.

I was having more and more in-depth conversations with Cal regarding everything from my childhood to the different calls I had been on as a firefighter and EMT. We touched on the rumors I had heard about him possibly having other children. He didn't deny any of it, but also said that he had never been approached to confirm it. I told him how his brother Gene's daughter, had reached out to me stating she had connected with a woman, Cindy, that was convinced she was my father's daughter. He told me that he did in fact have a relationship with a woman from Townsend, before he met my mother, and that her daughter had reached out to him a while back regarding a paternity test. It was never pursued and so he let it fall to the wayside.

But he never denied the possibility of any of it.

For some reason we began talking about how my mother used to tell me that Cal had moved out to California back in the 80's. The genuine look of disgust that came over my father's face was one that couldn't be acted out. He thought for a few seconds as he looked past me in disbelief. His mouth open, brow pushed toward the top of his head making his eyes widen more than usual, he sat flabbergasted.

"Keith. I never lived more than two hours from you and your mother." His eyes looking straight back at mine showing the truth in his words.

I was floored. I sat for a minute, rubbing my head. After a few we carried on with our conversation talking more about the family dynamic. I avoided giving information on Jack and Eddie, just because I did. It wasn't necessarily purposeful, but it happened. The whole time, Cal did not speak ill of my mother even one time. He took the information I gave him and simply responded with his version or perspective. There was no hate, animosity, or infliction of pain. Just information.

About a week after this conversation, I received a rather lengthy email from my father. As I began reading it in my living room, sheer terror reigned over me. He wrote about our discussion regarding the family and in particular my avoidance of my uncles. He told me he couldn't help but fear there was something, or several bad things that took place between them and I.

He knew.

I started sweating, a hot flash ripped through my body, and I felt nauseous. Somehow my father, who had been absent in my life for damn near 30 years picked up on the vibe between Jack, Eddie, and I in one conversation. He never pushed for more information. Never brought the subject up. But from that time forward, there was an even stronger reassuring sensation in each of his stares, smiles, and especially hugs.

I was beginning to see things in a very different light regarding my family. Especially my old man. I had always questioned what I was being told, mainly by my mother, about everything. Not even just things with Dad. Now getting more and more of my father's perspective, I was realizing all the feelings I had repressed for nearly three decades were possibly true.

Occasionally when I showed up to my parents to pick up Tyler and Elizabeth, when they "wanted" to see me, my mother would poke around for information. I wouldn't give her much, but what was spoken definitely let on that my father and I had established our relationship. I could tell this didn't sit well with her.

Come May, Cal wasn't doing well. His angina was occurring every other day. He was taking more and more of his nitroglycerin pills, and not telling me or Beatrice. On a visit with the oncologist, we found out that he had developed leukemia likely due to the chemo treatments. My father took this information without much show of emotion. Beatrice cried. I simply stared back at my dad from across the room. Our eyes met, and I knew what was coming. I had seen the look before. I was unfortunately way too in tune with this shit.

Back at their apartment, the three of us discussed different options that the doctors had given us along with others that I knew of. Beatrice begged my father to look more seriously into some of these, trying to convince him that everything could be fixed. I knew better. I told him the options in a more "if you want to try" sort of way. We may have only been back in each other's life for six or seven months, but I knew there was no getting him to do more treatments. I stared at my father from my place on the disco couch and saw a very tired man that had seen more of the world than most. A man whose body had been through the ringer these last few years and he knew it was only a matter of time. A man, that looked at peace knowing he was staring death directly in the face.

Shortly after this, Adele confronted my mother in our driveway on a Sunday morning. This was sparked due to some back-and-forth texting Tyler was having with my mother regarding him being at me and Adele's apartment. There had been significant manipulation on my mother's end of the texting, and this coupled with a blatant show of disrespect towards me recently by my son, Adele had enough. She ripped my mother apart as she sat in her car, Tyler, and Elizabeth, with me in the living room. I knew it was a bold move, Adele taking things into her own hands, but I also knew there was no stopping her. She was done seeing me torn to pieces by my family. Especially by Tyler.

Things got dicey after this altercation. I had been working on getting Tyler and Elizabeth up to my father's apartment to meet him. A situation that took a certain finesse with my mother and Darlene. Elizabeth was absolutely beyond excited at the prospect of meeting her biological grandfather, while Tyler was indifferent. Within a week of Adele confronting my mother, I was told my father would NEVER meet Tyler and Elizabeth. I decision I wasn't surprised in hearing but hurt just the same.

Adele's bridal party had planned a wedding shower for her that was set for Saturday June 21st and was going to take place in our back yard. I had been working with Beatrice on this, planning out how to get her and Cal the hour or so ride to Lancaster. For the week leading up to the party, it didn't look like Dad was going to be able to make the trip, due to how weak he had gotten. Friday the 20th, I went in for my normal 7a to 7p shift in Lowell. In the afternoon I phoned my father to see how he was doing, and if he felt he could make the trip.

"I wouldn't miss this for the world. I'll be there no matter what!" He said in the most reassuring voice I had ever heard him use.

"You better be, or I'll grab an ambulance and cart your old ass down there!"

After telling me he'd kick my giant ass if I did so, we laughed. I told him I loved him and that I would see him soon.

"Love you too son. Always have. Always will."

Hanging up, I stood there in the ambulance parking of the hospital just looking up, smiling. The sky was a deep blue, with small, fluffy white clouds floating around. There was a peaceful feeling that fell over me, as shoved the phone back in the cargo pocket of my pants. A light breeze blew through the open space on the backside of the emergency room, where I had spent most of my day so far. The smell of recently blooming flowers, and diesel fumes filled my nostrils as I climbed back into my truck. My partner apparently caught off guard by my ear-to-ear grin and light mood that I was now in.

"You good Hanks? he asked, almost offended that I was all of a sudden so cheery.

"Couldn't be better bro."

Adele picked up Elizabeth later that afternoon which was usual practice. With the wedding shower, and Beatrice and my father attending, Tyler did not want to come. Adele ordered her and my daughter some take out and they were enjoying their last bites as I walked into the apartment just before 8pm. I sat and smiled at Adele as Elizabeth jumped on my lap giving me a hug. Around 1030, the three of us headed up to bed. After talking to Elizabeth about how she was going to meet Cal, I tucked her in and walked across the hall to mine and Adele's bedroom. I pulled up our door and sat on the edge of the bed in my boxer shorts, taking in a long-winded breath. It had been a long week for both of us and tomorrow was going to be a great day. We just needed some sleep. As my head hit the pillow, my phone began to ring.

It was Beatrice.

Her voice battered by sobbing and sniffling, I knew what I was about to be told was going to be bad. When I finally got her to calm down, she told me they had decided to go lay down for the night.

When Cal came in the room he apparently collapsed onto the bed next to her. At first she thought he was messing around, then she realized he wasn't breathing, so she called 911. I could hear the noise that accompanies most medical emergencies over the phone. Finally, she couldn't talk anymore and put one of the police officers on the phone. He told me my father wasn't breathing and had no pulse. That the paramedics and fire department were doing CPR and that they were going to bring him to Lawrence General emergency room. I said OK and hung up the phone.

Sitting on the bed, Adele staring at me, she knew what had just happened. Elizabeth hearing the commotion walked in a few seconds after that.

"I think my father just had his last heart attack." I said looking straight ahead as I felt the tears building in the corners of my eyes.

I got up and dressed, kissing Adele and Elizabeth before running out the door to my car. Lawrence was a 45-minute ride up the highway. I made it in 35. Walking into the ER I had brought thousands of patients to over the years, I was met with familiar faces. Nurses, doctors, paramedics and EMT's saw a look on me that each of us had seen on countless others over the years. I was directed to the room my father was in down the hall from the main nurses station. It seemed eerily quiet for a Friday night in Lawrence. It was never that quiet in that ER. Ever. As I approached the room I was told Cal was in, the curtain opened, and Beatrice stepped out. Her face drained of the typical happy, optimistic life it usually contained. She wrapped her arms around my waist, driving her face into my chest. She began sobbing uncontrollably.

Pushing the curtain to the side, I walked to my father's bedside. Technology beeping, a ventilator keeping adequate air in my father's lungs, I sat in the chair on his left side. His eyes closed, his skin an ashen grey, I took his hand in mine and lowered my head. Tears fell off my face, crashing onto the cold, tile floor below. Each with a monstrous splash.

I knew my father was gone.

The doctor came in and began the usual jargon of what was

happening. Speaking to me and Beatrice the way doctors do, trying to give us hope while avoiding telling us the brutal truth. When she was finished filling Beatrice with a false promise that my dad was going to miraculously sit up and walk out of the hospital on his own, I pulled her off to the side. I told her what I did for work and for how long. Told her to not bullshit me and give it straight. And she did. She told em there was nothing more they could do. If he was going to make it, he would need to do it. All the technology in the world wasn't going to save the man at this point. We agreed to move him to the ICU and let happen what would.

I called Adele and updated her. She was going to drop Elizabeth back off at my parents in the morning and have one of her friends drive her up to Lawrence. That way, if needed, she could drive me home.

Once in the ICU, the ventilator was removed, along with most of the other hardware he was hooked up to. All that remained was the heart monitor, a blood pressure cuff, one IV line for the medications to keep him comfortable and a urinary catheter. Beatrice and I took turns sitting bedside with Cal into the early morning hours. I would hold his hand, trying my hardest to force all the recent memories I had made with my father into the forefront of my brain. The laughs. The smiles through months of pain and discomfort. The countless conversations that led to an understanding of each other's perspective on a situation that carried on for far too long. A love that developed out of all of it. I had made peace with my father in only seven months, after 30 long years of not speaking to one another.

Eventually some of Beatrice's family began to show up, followed by Uncle Phil and my father's younger sister Darlene. Again, we took turns sitting with Cal as stories started to be shared and occasional laughter filtered in. As light began to beam in from the summer sun rising outside the hospital windows, Adele arrived and joined in the memories.

A few times it looked like Cal had taken his last breath. Then in a way that was fitting to who he was, he would take another as the rest of us did the same. After four or five times, Adele and Phil encouraged me to go and sit bed side again. I pulled the chair closer, so I could rest my head over his heart. Taken his right hand in mine, I listened to the slow, weak beats as his chest seemed to struggle to rise with the weight of my head. More and more time filled the gaps in between each breath with his heart slowing to a beat every two seconds. Then every three. I felt the inevitable approaching and apparently so did everyone else.

"You can go now Cal. It's ok brother." Phils voice called out. Others joining in with similar chants.

A dozen hands now on my back and my father's chest, I closed my eyes and said what I knew I needed to.

"It's ok Dad. You can go rest now. We'll be ok."

As I said this, a single tear rolled from my eye as a gasp fell over those around me. I felt his chest rise and his heartbeat one last time. Then, there was nothing. Within a few seconds, the heart monitor began screaming its notification of a flatline. My father's body now lay still, all life gone. Sobbing filled the room as I gripped his hand harder feeling myself beginning to accept the reality of the situation. A hundred images flooded my psyche as I sat up, my eyes still closed.

We left the hospital after the proper paperwork was signed and initial plans were made for my father's services. That afternoon we had Adele's wedding shower, which carried a somber mood. I was able to smile a few times, and Joe was even able to get me to laugh. Elizabeth had been picked up again so she could attend. Later that night I drove her back to Townsend to my parents. I dreaded walking into their house, knowing my mother was aware that Cal had just died.

Standing in the kitchen, I told my mother about the plans for the service. I asked if I could borrow the photo albums, especially the big red one with MEMORIES written in gold on it. She told me she would do her best to look for it. I told her I would go with her to the basement to help. With that she assured me she didn't know where they were and that finding them wasn't going to happen. I could have predicted this would be the response. The only pictures that existed of me as a child and my father were in those albums. And I just got told to pound sand by the owner. As I turned to leave, I looked back at my mother.

She was smiling.

CHAPTER 11
ENOUGH IS ENOUGH

Pulling into Ray's driveway, I wasn't sure what to expect. The fire chief in Lancaster had invited Adele and I to his annual Fourth of July cookout and party. My father having just died a few weeks prior, I was still living in a mild state of grief. The small service we had for Cal was attended by mainly Beatrice's friends and family with only a few from the Hanks side making an appearance. Adele, Joe, and Jenn were the only ones from my circle. Dad wanted to be cremated, so we were waiting until a later date in August to spread his ashes on the Kancamagus Highway, in Northern New Hampshire, per his wishes. In the meantime, my mother took it upon herself to flex her legal rights as custodial parent with Tyler and Elizabeth by barring them from being at our wedding. All of this happening, a party was the last place I really wanted to be. Adele convinced me to go be around people.

I had also started having odd dreams that started as an obvious communication beyond "the grave" with my old man. Very quickly though, they escalated into full blown nightmares, that left me wondering what the less than obvious message could be.

The nightmare: Electronic beeps and bleeps fill the air as an almost moonlight darkness surrounds me. My hands searching in front of me, I began to sense a presence high above me but couldn't yet see anything. At first, all I hear is the faint whisperings rooted in a light female tone. Shortly thereafter, a stern, male voice similar to my father's joins in and begins to sound a warning. Like a lighthouse indicating a rocky shore, Dad's voice is telling me to be aware and not come any closer. As I ignore the warnings, the sky above me fills with clouds. Distant lightning and thunder now surround me. As I reach into the darkness in front of me, a bright light explodes above, and I'm struck with a million volts. I awake screaming. Covered in Sweat.

Even with the reoccurrence of these nightmares, drinking was still something I was refraining from at this point, having jumped on the abstinence train the end of 2010. In the beginning it was because I kept hearing from my mother that I was an alcoholic, even though I almost never drank. Then, after not doing so voluntarily for a while, I realized I just didn't ever crave booze. With Adele also not one to drink, it just wasn't something that ever came up as a priority. Ray's party was going to be the first time in almost four years that I attended an event that stereotypically centered around drinking and acting like an idiot.

As the crowd built, and more and more folks did what most do at summertime parties, I looked over and noticed Ray was drinking soda. Come to find out, my fire chief had also taken a departure from alcohol in recent years, and this was publicly known and accepted by his circle. I began to feel the tension drop off my shoulders. I was able to sit back and be who I was. Laughter, jokes, and ball busting filled the entire day as it became evident that I had been completely accepted into this new circle of friends and brother firefighters.

Around 930 that night, Adele looked over my way, past a group of our new friends, and gave me the eyes indicating she was done with this party. Eyes that always spoke more loudly than her lips ever could. She was happy and wanted to go home and be alone with me in the quiet of our bedroom to cap off an amazing day. As we rolled around on top of the bed, covered in sweat, with the summer heat flowing through the third-floor windows, we both fell into a world where we were the only ones in existence. The bullshit of the last few months, especially the planning of our wedding, seemed to melt away. I laid completely spent, in a naked embrace with the one woman who had shown me more in the past three years than anyone had in over three decades.

I prayed, in my own way, that the night wouldn't be accompanied by my new nightmares.

Just before midnight, both of us were jolted from bed with monotone voice of the fire dispatcher. A reported house fire, just one block away from our house, had me making the run down two flights of stairs. Trying not to fall and break my neck as I fumbled getting my clothes back on at the same time, my department radio shrieked with more info.

"Callers are reporting house is fully involved. Unsure if the residents are inside." Still, the dispatcher remained surprisingly calm.

Hopping in my Cadillac, I made the turn onto South Main from our street. As I passed the street where the house fire was on, Kilbourn, I looked down to be greeted by a ball of orange. Like a rising summer sun, the house was indeed fully involved. I was the third person to arrive at the fire station that housed Engine 3 and a spare pumper that was seldom used. Seeing no one else was doing so, I jumped into the driver's seat and pressed the button for the overhead doors. The two others got in the back, as the lieutenant arrived, getting in the front across from me. Flicking the lights on, I hit the accelerator and pulled out onto South Main then quickly turned left down Kilbourn. I was surprised at how many of the residents were out in the street looking at their neighbors' home burn.

As we approached within 100 feet, the lieutenant grabbed the radio to give the first official report, simultaneously motioning for me to drive past the house. As he finished his transmission, the main electrical line broke off the house, falling across the road blocking our path. Still live and potentially deadly, we proceeded no further. The lieutenant jumped out as I shifted the giant red water wagon into gear, then hopped out myself. As the other two firefighters came to my side by the pump panel, our officer had run up to the house that was shooting flames 50 feet in the air from almost every window. Signaling the need for a hose line at his location towards the middle of the house, the two firefighters began to walk one his direction.

As other units arrived, along with the fire chief, it was obvious we were going to need more help. Ray calling over the radio and taking command of the scene, he ordered additional alarms. Right after doing so, the second floor exploded. Fueled by the apparent storage of dozens of home oxygen tanks, the orange and red flames began to mix with licks of blue. It was a long night of chasing a lot of fire. No one was home at the time, short of two dogs that were rescued by the first firefighters on scene. The power company confirmed that the electrical line that had fallen across the road when we arrived, remained live until they shut it down. Adele had walked over, congregating with other spouses as we spent the next 8 hours working to fully extinguish the stubborn fire. Getting home mid-morning after a long clean-up, I was toast. I collapsed in bed until dinner time.

Later that week, during our normal training, we had a debriefing on the fire. I received praise for my quick thinking with the power line, along with my calm operation of Engine 3 for eight hours straight. I gained even more respect, and short of a few small fires, my abilities were truly put to the test that night on Kilbourn. I proved myself even further to this group responders that didn't let just anyone into their inner circle given the sad history of losing a firefighter in the line of duty over ten years prior.

With the loss of my father and now not seeing my children again, this inclusion into a group I didn't know seven months prior, was an uncomfortable feeling. On the surface I gave myself to these people and welcomed them into parts of me and Adele's life. We hung out at each other's homes, the firehouse, texted and phone calls seemingly everything friends do. But below the surface, my past with all its messed-up issues with trust, was keeping all of them at arm's length. Even so, I invited Ray and one of the Captain's, Chris, to our wedding in early August. Beatrice and her daughter were there along with my uncle Phil and one of my cousins. Beatrice stepped in for the mother-son dance typical of most weddings. A collage of pictures of Dad sat on a chair at the entry into the venue for all to see. In spirit I knew he was there. The absence of all other relatives though, weighed heavy and I had a hard time hiding it. There's very few pictures of me openly smiling that day short of when Adele was in my arms.

Our honeymoon was in Vegas, which is ironic given Adele's inability to be in direct sunlight due to a rare allergy and it being a desert. We adjusted our sleep schedule, going out mainly in the later afternoon, staying up closer to the early morning. We spent eight days checking out all the major sights, hitting the buffets, sleeping a lot, and just enjoying our alone time. Once we returned home, we adopted a rescue dog from one of the local shelters. Mack became the fourth member of the Hanks household, next to the cat Adele had since before me and her met. With Mack came a companion I hadn't had since my stepfathers dog Kira. I immediately built a bound with this guy.

I had taken ownership of my father's Harley when he passed and was putting on as many hours as I could in preparation for the ride north to spread his ashes. The '89 Electra Glide was a monster of a motorcycle. Much larger than the Victory I owned years ago. With a full tank of gas, it weighed nearly 750 pounds. It had higher than normal handlebars, referred to as "ape hangers" in the biker world. Dad had put these on and even though the man was over six inches shorter than me, the bars were a perfect fit for my larger stature. I had been racking the miles up on it since the end of June in preparation for the ride up north a few weeks after returning from Vegas.

There was a connection with Cal every time I sat on the 25-year-old motorcycle. Beyond the obvious of it being his old bike, it was a stubborn machine. Just like the previous owner. Sometimes it would start right up. Other times it would laugh at me. Sometimes the radio would shut off on its own for no good reason. Other times it ran without a single issue. Whenever it got temperamental, I just sat there, smiling at the sky. Waiving my fist at an imaginary face of Dad somewhere in the clouds. Being on the bike set me at ease and I rode it like I was part of the machine.

The ride up the Kancamagus was a huge success and a ton of fun. We had about 10 riders and three cars following us up for the almost 2-hour ride into the White Mountains. Beatrice rode on the back with me on the way north. Not even 15 minutes from our kickoff, she tugged on my shoulder, sobbing as we came to a red light.

"You ride this thing just like Cal. The way you lean. The way you accelerate. It's a beautiful thing Keith." Beatrice said as she wiped tears off her face that also had an ear-to-ear heartfelt grin upon it.

Making the hill up into the mountains on the Kancamagus, I found myself talking to my father. I realized how grateful I had been for the short time we had in what ended up being the end of his life. We picked a spot off of a parking area, that held a breathtaking view of the valley to spread Dad's ashes. Hand in hand with Beatrice, we emptied the urn just as a light wind kicked up and carried them across the hillside in front of us. Tears filled every face in attendance. Even some random folks that were just there for the scenery got choked up. After a few words, we made plans to ride back down the other side of the highway into one of the towns for a much-needed meal.

Adele rode with me for the rest of the day. After a quick meal with all those who came, we started our journey back home to Massachusetts. The almost three-hour ride was filled with some of the most peaceful feelings I had ever experienced in my life. I had held onto such a massive grudge with my old man for nearly three long decades. Within weeks of connecting back with him, I had let most if it go. The morning he died, with my head on his chest the rest of it left me. That ride back home that cool summer afternoon, I realized something. After all the bullshit I was told. After all the anger I felt towards the man. After all the anxiety of meeting him again. I realized I didn't have one bad memory of me and my father. Not even the ones I could conjure up from my childhood before he left. All the pictures of me and him when I was little. Every single time I spoke with, texted, emailed, or sat on his disco couch and talked for hours, with the man who helped create me, was filled with great memories.

Short of him not being in the picture for 30 years, every experience I had with my dad was amazing.

As fall started, Adele began her nursing education in one of the local colleges. With her being full-time in college, I stepped up and began working more overtime. It wasn't uncommon for me to work 60-80 hours in Lowell on the ambulance and pull a eight hour day shift at the firehouse per week. It allowed Adele to only work 16 hours so she could concentrate on her schoolwork. As the holidays approached it was evident that my time with the kids was going to be limited. Seeing them for only a few hours the entire time around Christmas sent me back into the deep, dark confines of my brain.

As the year 2015 began, so did all my old symptoms. Nightmares, flashbacks, and anger frequented my daily activities. I tried to brush them off as just occurring due to being off most of the meds I had been for years. I thought maybe I was just getting overworked and needed a few slow weeks. I even started to tell myself I was just a pussy and needed to suck it up like all my old mentors and some relatives used to preach back in the day.

By this time, I had walked away from my therapist, Dahlia. After the way she handled a few things after the appointments with my mother, I was all set dealing with her incompetence and half stoned attitude every time we met. Without a therapist and not on any meds besides a small dose anti-depressant, I was floating on a life preserver that was way too small. All of this was mixing into a sour feeling inside of me that caused me to carry a behavior most of my coworkers were beginning to experience.

On a shift in Lowell in the middle of February, my partner and I were parked out behind the Tsongas Arena by the river. I stared out the windshield, watched the cold-water drift by. Occasionally a chunk of ice would float into my line of vision, and I noticed myself beginning to visualize myself clinging to it. This transitioned to imagining drowning in the frigid waters. I was in a low spot, and here I was thinking life would be better if it all just ended. Thinking of all I read about drowning being euphoric, I drifted into a world of dark thoughts. I felt useless. I felt unloved. I felt as though everyone I loved and cared about either died, walked away, or left me. And those that hadn't would soon enough. I felt like a burden. Not because of my nightmares, flashbacks, bouts of depression or uncontrolled anxiety.

My anger was my burden.

I was yelling at my new, young wife almost daily. My kids were no longer around, and I attributed that to my anger. I was getting told by coworkers at both jobs that I was unapproachable, even scary at times. I was beginning to feel as though everyone else would be better off if I just slipped away under the surface of the cold, icy waters of the Merrimack River. As I sat with this feeling, my phone rang. It was Adele. We had been speaking about me getting some more intensive helps regarding my mental health. I had even Googled my symptoms and post-traumatic stress disorder came up. A diagnosis I knew existed but knew almost nothing about. We had agreed I needed something, but neither was sure what.

"Babe. Did you call Ray about that place in Westminster yet?" Adele's voice being my much needed life line, that again, anchored me to shore.

She was referring to my fire chief and the organization the department used when Marty McNamarra died in the line of duty back in 2003. This organization brought a team out to the fire department to talk to all its members during the incomprehensible times they were faced with after his death. They also ran a facility a few towns away in Westminster just for first responders and Veterans needing mental health help.

I shook off my previous mindset and realized the gravity of the situation. Adele also picked up on something being off, encouraging me to call Ray right then. So, I did. I told my new friend where I was at and that I needed some real help. For the first time ever, I went to someone on the fire department, and told them I was having mental health issues and needed help. I was beyond terrified at what could happen next as I hung up the phone.

Within a few minutes, Ray called back and told me someone from On-Site Academy would be calling me to set up a time for an intake. After a brief conversation with that person, I had an appointment to go see their so-called farm up in the country and have an interview. It was determined the day of the intake that I definitely needed to come up for a three day stay to undergo some of the modalities they offered.

On-Site was a nice place. An old farmhouse, with a barn and a bunch of secluded acres on a dirt road in the back woods. Being there you were removed from the hustle and bustle of any nearby town or city. The house itself was larger in size, at two stories, but had a cabin feel to it. A small three season porch was the main entry which led into the open concept kitchen with attached dining area. A small bathroom created a wall between the kitchen and other side of the house. Another round outcropping that served as an enclosed, heated sunroom had chairs and an area to sleep in off the dining room. A massive living room was on the other side of the house, passed the front door, with the first bedroom behind it with its own bathroom. This was for the female residents to sleep in. Upstairs there was another bathroom and two large bedrooms. One with three beds, the other with four. The whole place was heated by a woodstove and fireplace that the residents were in charge of keeping lit.

It was more of a holistic based residential home then a treatment facility. There were no diagnosis' made there, although they did conduct different types of therapy in the several offices located in the finished basement outside the laundry area. Meditation, yoga, acupuncture, and group therapy were some of the modalities they offered. Residents could also chop wood, go for walks, play games, watch tv, read, write, sleep or nap. If someone was on any medication, they were responsible for its safe keeping. We made our own meals, cleaned the whole house, watched tv and told stories together in between all the scheduled activities throughout the day.

It was operated similar to a firehouse. Or a frat house. Depends on perspective I guess.

At first this seemed to be just what I needed. I finally started talking about some of the bad calls I had been on. I gave a small list of some of the shit I had been through to one of the therapists who determined I would be a candidate for what was called Eye Movement Desensitization and Reprocessing Therapy or EMDR for short. It was also decided on that I would need to come back for another three-day stay. During that stay, we began some of the EMDR sessions.

That spring I was back to working full-time and doing my shifts at the firehouse. I was doing better on the outside but was a different story inside. I hated how I felt. Eventually in May it was decided that I go to On-Site for a full 30-day stay. Before this Ray and I had a conversation about me telling the department about my adventures at On-Site as he felt it would be beneficial to not only the members but me as well. The night before I was to leave for Westminster for a month, I told most of the department and some of the spouses, about how I've been struggling and what I was doing to get better. The reception was amazing, filled with hugs, handshakes, and a sense of admiration for my willingness to be open about my journey. A feeling that carried me through the beginning of an intense 30-day treatment.

Now having the bread winner not working for a month, Adele's hand was forced into working extra shifts to keep a roof over our head. She did this all while finishing up her first year of nursing school, without one complaint. At the end of my stay, I left feeling recharged, refreshed, and willing to face the day to day.

My first scheduled shift back on the ambulance changed all that.

Waking that morning, I was filled with an uneasy feeling. A queasiness that left me throwing up a few times before making the walk to the driveway. Adele saw this, meeting me at my car asking if I was ok. I brushed it all off as just nerves from being away for a month. I kissed my wife, opened the car door, and started the motor.

As I pushed the gas pedal to the floor, darkness came in from behind me. My vision narrowed and all I could see was what was immediately in front of me. My peripherals were completely absent. A thousand images rocketed through my brain, as I felt the pavement beneath me move past. Occasionally I would hear the faint sound of a car horn. My hands jerked unpredictably while white knuckling the steering wheel. Screaming soundly filled my ears, with shear panic raining over me. I felt hot, wet, and completely lost in my environment. After a quick turn to the right, I pulled the car to a stop.

The last ten minutes of my ride had disappeared into the deep chambers of my memory, and I was sitting in some random parking lot a quarter mile from the highway on-ramp. I was covered in sweat, shaking, and terrified. I began to cry. I was scared. I was nauseous. So, I picked up my phone and called Adele doing my best to tell her where I was. Now I was embarrassed. She showed up with Ray in his fire chief's vehicle. Adele needing to go in for her shift, Ray drove me back to the fire station leaving my car by the highway.

He convinced me to call On-Site, which I did, and when they got back to me I agreed to go back up for an indefinite amount of time. I was so let down. I gave so much in the previous month, and now couldn't even get myself to work. So instead, I went back to the farm.

This stay ended up being for the worse. Half-way through I had a verbal altercation with one of the residents. During one of the group therapy sessions in which I was sharing for the first time with others, the facts about the accident in 2003, this resident kept falling asleep. To make matters worse, he started snoring. This resident happened to be a retired firefighter who had 15 years on his department. After my outburst, I was pulled aside by one of the people who ran On-Site and torn apart in front of another of the moderators.

I was berated for being some young, dumb rookie firefighter who had apparently been nothing but a problem since I was there. I was told I had nothing on this other guys 15 years in the fire service and that I was one of the most disrespectful assholes he had ever met.

Most of the rest of what was said is faint, and fragmented as I felt myself slowly becoming unhinged. In all my bad times, I had never wanted to physically hurt someone as badly as I did in that moment. To make matters worse, I was forced to re-tell the story of my accident in 2003 not once, but two more times. A session of unsuccessful EMDR followed. After another brief interaction with the powers to be, I decided to leave. Adele was pissed. I was again let down and lost.

The late spring into summer was extremely dry and led to an increase in brush fires across the region. In Lancaster we were going to at least one a day, with several being fairly large. One weekend in particular, it seemed as soon as we parked the trucks, we were being toned out for another fire in either our town or a neighboring community. Mid-day that Saturday in July, we were sent to the town next to us for a fire along Interstate 190. As the dispatcher read off the location, I swallowed hard. It was the next exit down from where my accident was 13 years earlier.

I made my way to the old army truck, that served as one of our brush units. A tradition in many fire departments is to acquire surplus military equipment in an effort to keep costs down for the town or city. These vehicles in particular, referred to as "Deuce and a half's", were cumbersome and hard to drive with their transmissions not the same as your typical Honda Civic. I was one of the few cleared to operate the beast, so I jumped in the driver's seat and turned it over. Getting in next to me was one of the senior EMT's sons, Rob. A young, skinny kid around Adele's age, Rob came from a long line of responders. He was a quiet, not often making more than an awkward laugh here and there. Average height with a thin build, electric blonde hair, once he was on the department, he just always seemed to be around.

We made our way to the appropriate on-ramp and made the steep climb at about 10 miles an hour. These machines were not known for their speed. They were literally beasts. They could drive throw feet deep mud, over small trees, and boulders, and ask for more without slowing down. That last part became crucial as we approached the fire scene. Now going about 40 in the breakdown lane, I was coming up on backed up traffic, so I began downshifting. The truck vibrated violently and roared as a plume of black diesel issued from the pipe. Two chiefs vehicles, a pumper truck and another brush unit were lining the right breakdown lane ahead of us. Along with about a dozen firefighters. As I applied the brakes it became clear we had none.

Rob also realized this as I began to try my best to downshift even faster. My feet pumping hard on the nonexistent brakes. At the last minute, with us not slowing enough, I pulled the giant truck back into an opening in traffic to the left, than once past the fire vehicles, I turned hard right narrowly missing the small SUV stopped ahead. After about another 200 feet, I was able to get us to a stop. Panting, covered in sweat, I felt a smile come over my face knowing I didn't just steamroll over a dozen innocent people. As I turned to look at Rob, he was paler than normal. Now hunched in the fetal position, he was trying his best to disappear into the far corner of the cab.

"It's ok buddy. We're stopped." My voice trying to convey assurance and not the terror that was coursing through my entire body.

Sitting forward, Rob began to untense. He assured me he was ok but probably shit his pants congratulating me on the most terrifying ride in a fire truck he had ever taken. That day shook me for reasons less than obvious to most. As Adele and others from my circle approached me regarding the location and relationship to Heather dying, most were off the mark with the troubling part. Though I agreed with each of them, the fact that I almost got into another wreck within a mile of the one that took my first wife, wasn't what was bothering me.

When everything happened with Rob in the brush truck, the only thing I was afraid of was him getting hurt or killed. I gave no shits about my own safety. In the initial climax, when I brought the truck to a stop I was actually let down that the worst hadn't happened. To me the poetic justice of getting killed on the same stretch of highway as Heather, was a fitting ending to the fucked-up life I had led to that point. The only reason I was glad things didn't go terrible, was because of Rob sitting in the cab of that truck. But I was let down that somehow, yet again, I was still alive.

Later in August right after our one-year wedding anniversary, with my symptoms not any better, I reached out to McLean's Hospital outside of Boston. They had a first responder focused program for mental health that had just started in the last year. This was in part because of the Boston Marathon bombing two years prior. After a quick intake I was admitted to the inpatient program for two weeks. While at McLean's it was determined through several interviews and tests that I in fact had post-traumatic stress disorder (PTSD). I was officially diagnosed with what is called Complex-PTSD.

During the interviews and endless question and answer sessions, I began to admit to my childhood trauma along with all the shit that I had endured from the job. Added to this was the plethora of personal trauma and other losses I had experienced over the years. The doctors and researchers often left staring at me in bewilderment with stories of death and carnage from the job, topped with a childhood full of abuse and burying a wife at age 24. On a few occasions, all I got for a response after speaking was an apology.

It finally was starting to hit me just how much I had actually been through. I played most of it down my whole life, given my family and those I kept company with. Adele expressed her sense of hope given my new direction and encouraging signs of progress with where I was now receiving help. Upon discharge, I was paired up with a new young doctor who I was going to start meeting weekly for therapy. His name was Matt.

Now going back to work after an inpatient stay, I was told I had to set some boundaries. I had to work less, and advocate for what I was truly comfortable doing. In Lowell, I told my partners the less I had to be in the back with our patients, the better things would be. Most were accommodating. Those that weren't, I just sucked it up and climbed into the six by ten cubicle with a patient, trying to avoid feeling trapped in a wheeled prison I couldn't escape. It worked for a while. Until it didn't.

Working a shift at the firehouse one warm, late September Sunday, we got dispatched for a possible "Sudden death" on the other end of town. The young kid I worked with ran like a gazelle across the prairielands of Africa, as he made hast for the driver's seat of the ambulance. I was less than impressed with working the shift, never mind the fact that we were being sent to confirm that some old asshole was truly dead. Before I even got to the truck, the door was swinging open, and the red lights were flashing. As we hit Main Street and turned left, my hyperactive partner turned the siren on full blast. With that I lost my shit on him. Reaching over and turning the switch back to off, I let him know it wasn't needed.

"They're not getting any deader there junior!!!!" I screamed as the now terrified driver just stared out the windshield.

I ended up being brought in for a formal meeting with the owners and operation manager of the ambulance service in late summer. I opened up about the PTSD diagnosis and was surprised at their response. They wanted to help but needed me to be at work. More importantly, they needed me to be consistent. They offered me two 12 hour and one 24 hour shift a week on a paramedic level ambulance with a partner who didn't like to drive.

It was also someone I knew for about ten years. This was a winning situation and immediately I began working with Gus for two-day shifts during the week and a 24-hour shift on Friday.

The partnership was great. I was starting to relax both at work and home. I no longer feared my shifts, and at times looked forward to them. Me and Gus grew close despite the overzealous political rhetoric that typically ran the entirety of our time on the ambulance.

Adele and I had started a trauma-based couples therapy as she was finishing her final semester of nursing classes. We both learned so much about my PTSD and how much it had affected our relationship. She was able to have a stage to state her perspectives on where she felt I was. I was able to express my needs when it came to what my symptoms often did to me internally. Matt orchestrated these sessions and while he helped to repair my marriage, he and I created a doctor/client bond that made for an amazing relationship I had never had with any other therapist.

A few weeks into December, following my 37th birthday I had another incident on my way in for a shift in Lowell. The ride started as normal as any with me just not wanting to go, then eventually coming to terms with needing to. Somehow I blacked out again and drove 45 minutes past my exit, with reality finally circling back to me as I sat in a parking lot in Hampton Beach. After half a dozen unanswered phone calls from dispatch and my operation manager, Adele called, I picked up, and she knew I was in a bad place. Calling Matt, I ended up going in for an unscheduled appointment the next day after taking a few days off from work.

Again.

I was struggling. I was trying so hard to be the husband Adele deserved. The employee both jobs needed me to be. But I was dropping the ball on just being a man. I felt lower than low. I thought I was doing what I needed to with therapy. Matt and I were working on things I had NEVER talked about with anyone else. Christmas time arrived, and I was beginning to notice that

Adele and I were being left out of the reindeer games with our new friends. What was once dozens and dozens of daily correspondence dwindled to a few times a week. Being invited to every gathering slowly turned into me having to invite myself. I was feeling left out, abandoned and there was an implication that I wasn't healing fast enough.

Adele was seemingly being forgotten by the wives and spouses. During my struggles over the winter when I was seeing Matt twice a week and was at times not there for her, Adele often reached out to the once supportive circle of women to get unanswered calls and text messages. With my kids now not "wanting" to visit anymore, no family in my life and my new circle of friends disappearing, all I had was Adele. The job itself was starting to not fulfill me and thoughts of walking away became more frequent.

Even when I had nothing else to give, I still somehow managed to call upon some reserve source of life from somewhere deep down. I wasn't willing to give in to the thought that I couldn't or shouldn't do this line of work anymore. Why shouldn't I be able to? Was there something wrong with me or had I had the perfect storm of bullshit happen at the right times throughout my life? I didn't really care and being bullheaded, I wasn't about to toss the towel in yet. I went through my days doing what I had to do to get by.

As 2016 started, I threw myself into my therapy, my marriage, and the shifts on the ambulance with Gus, with whom I had developed a friendship with. I was still working a shift a week at the firehouse. These typically fell on the weekends, so I was left to my own devices around the station with the daily chores and no one to bother me.

I would often drift off after doing my station duties and truck checks. Sitting in one of the office chairs, thousands of images from the past would filter through in a fleeting way. Good times. Bad times. Horrific ones too, all came and went as I stared off at the cratered tiles of the office ceiling for hours sometimes.

Why was I still doing this job?

Why did it seem like I was having so many setbacks time and time again?

Why couldn't I just be a normal fucking person like everyone else seemed to be?

I always loved what I did both on the ambulance and the firehouse, but recent times had begun to make me question why I was tolerating the bullshit that came with it all. Come April, and the anniversary of the accident, I was being completely forgotten about by those that once called me their friend. No calls. No texts. No invitations. Adele had been going up to a horse farm in New Hampshire to help take care of the animals and clean stalls in exchange for free ride time. She had always loved horses and used to ride as a kid. At the same time, our landlord, who was also a lawyer, in his infinite wisdom moved a former client into the first-floor apartment where we lived. This new neighbor was horrible. Loud, rude, inconsiderate, and messy I was getting to my wits end. I no longer had a quiet house to come home to in addition to everything else.

We had also just found out Adele was pregnant. This wasn't planned as we had always been told that we wouldn't be able have a baby on account of her lupus. We kept the information to ourselves, not telling even family. It turned out to be for the best. As all this other shit was spinning around me at nauseating speeds, Adele had a spontaneous abortion. Basically, her body rejected the pregnancy early on and the fetus died.

It was the final straw.

The woman who ran the horse farm Adele was working at, happened to have a two-bedroom apartment above a garage on her property. After a brief discussion and a tour of the apartment, we decided to move. There was nothing for us anymore in Lancaster. That had become obvious. The new apartment was the same distance to Townsend as where we were, so if the kids suddenly wanted to come back in my life, we weren't any further away.

Now moving, I had to resign from the fire department. I wrote my letter with Adele's help and called a meeting with Ray telling him I needed to talk about something serious. Before I left the house, now filled with packed carboard boxes, I put all my department gear, radio, and chargers in my car. I sat for ten minutes trying to build up the courage to go do the one thing I always feared doing since getting into the fire service at 18.

I had to walk away from it.

Telling Ray what was going on and that we were moving, his expression didn't change. As I muttered the words "resign from my position" I felt a deep-seated hot flash come over my body. I found myself staring at the ground in shame. I felt like I was letting myself and everyone around me down by simply walking away from the job I had loved doing for two decades. Ray's response told me I was making the right decision.

"Sorry to hear this. Did you bring your gear and equipment?" He said it not even looking at me from across his desk.

I literally felt like I meant nothing these people.

Now living on the farm, things were a bit different. I was further away from work now having to drive almost a full hour. Adele had just gotten hired as a hospice nurse for a place that operated out of area that put her, at times, 90 minutes from her work. However, it was quiet. We were in the country off a main road on a farm that had dozens and dozens of secluded acreage. The horses provided me with a sense of peace. Even just sitting on our porch, as summer was now underway, looking at these amazing animals filled me with tranquility. I was starting to do more self-care while maintaining my appointments with Matt. Again, with his office being just outside Boston, my commute was close to 90 minutes. I took advantage of this time to disconnect from my week and just be in the moment by myself. It also allowed me to work more on what had started as journaling that was slowly becoming short stories about my life.

I was down to just my 48 hours a week on the ambulance as Adele's new job paid her enough to not require me to work any overtime. My shifts had changed to four 12-hour day shifts, running 10am to 10pm. I was sleeping in my own bed every night for the first time in 20 years. At first, this was an obvious gift that Adele and I took full advantage of. After a while, I found myself staying up to the early hours of the morning. Even at times being awake as the sun rose over the eastern horizon at the end of our driveway.

Ever since the beginning of my senior year in high school, I had my sleep interrupted, slept away from home for days, or worked through the night never making it to bed. Now with my 38th birthday a few months away, I was being faced with a situation I thought I wouldn't experience until my mid-60's. Adele worked feverishly with me to implement a healthier sleep pattern given my new work schedule.

With more time on my hands, I found myself needing a hobby or something to occupy the freed-up space in my life. I had begun hanging around with an EMT I knew since my days in Lawrence. Lester was about 8 years older than me and had been working on the ambulance since getting out of the military. Around five foot eight, overweight, balding and glasses, he always reminded me of Elmer Fudd from the old Bugs Bunny cartoons. It worked, cause Lester like guns and hunting!

We would fish. Go to the gun range, Got to Bass Pro. It was Lester who helped me purchase my first handgun. When we did hang out, we almost never spoke about our jobs. It was strictly guy stuff. He was married and had two kids, living off the center of Townsend. Ironically about eight years prior to us hanging out, I responded with the fire department to his house one day. I was on duty, and Lester's oldest began choking. Luckily he was ok by the time we got there, but the event put me and Lester back on each other's radar. A few years after that in 2014 when I went back to working in Lowell, I bumped into him working for the other service in the city. Eventually he jumped ship, coming to work with me and then becoming a supervisor.

With me working with Gus 4 days a week and occasionally grabbing a beer on our off days, then my time with Lester, I had a small circle back. After about 12 months of not talking, Joe and Jenn had also come back into our lives. Adele was happy at her new job as a hospice nurse. Even though it kept her out of the house up to 65 hours a week, we were better off financially than we ever had been. Things were looking pretty optimistic come the end of the year.

Once the new year kicked off, Matt and I decided to up the ante with our therapy sessions. Realizing I was keeping more from him than I was actually speaking about, Matt told me to lay all my cards on the table. Hold nothing back so we could really dive into all the stuff that makes Keith Hanks who he is.

So, I did.

I talked about the hundreds of deaths I was witness too. The dead baby's, the burned up grandmothers, mangled teenagers in twisted metal. I told him about the smells, the sounds, and the sights. More importantly he pressed me about all the personal stuff. Heather dying. The drinking. The drugs. All the women. When we got to my childhood, I hesitated and deflected in a classic manner. Matt being great at what he did, knew this and gave me the space I needed. All of this taking place over the span of several months, with me going in every week, a few times for two-hour long sessions to hash through all the bad shit I was holding inside.

It was during this time, come spring 2017, that I was asked by Matt if I had ever thought of doing something besides emergency work. I wasn't sure how to answer it, because honestly I was in the mind frame that I could not do anything else. Either because I wouldn't know how, wasn't qualified or wouldn't know where to start looking. I started to think about this every day. My behavior at work had actually gotten worse over the last few months, so given our financial position, I dropped my Friday shift. Now only going in three 12 hour shifts a week, I was hoping my attitude and outlook on the job would improve.

It did not.

The summer heat was more relentless than ever that year, I found myself even hotter under the collar than normal. I was popping off at everyone. Gus, Adele, patients, doctors, and nurses.

I was finding it hard to want to go in for my shifts. Often I would spend hours before walking out the door, convincing myself I had to go. The end of September came, and I ended up having a situation occur that I wasn't ready for.

After a verbal altercation with a nurse where a complaint was filed, I voluntarily took my next shift off. I was then not allowed to return to duty until I could furnish a doctor's note stating I was clear to work. According to management, this was due to my "diagnosis of PTSD". After a bunch of back and forth, I was put in a position where I was told I couldn't have it both ways. Unsure of what this meant, I was told because of my diagnosis, I couldn't just take a day off because I felt overwhelmed without it being attributed to my diagnosis.

I was floored, to say the least. Adele and I hashed the situation out of dinner one night. She laid out all the options. One of which, stopping work and going on disability, was my least favorite. Because of my PTSD I was a candidate for full disability. Something Matt, Adele and I had spoken of in recent months. It was something I was adamantly opposed to, until this situation occurred. I was now seriously contemplating it. My biggest concern, which I never voiced, was what would I be if I no longer was working? Afterall, the job, both the ambulance and firehouse, was all I knew. It was all I ever was. It was how I knew me. It was how others knew me. It was how I gained all my skills. How I met all my friends. How I met Adele. It was my passion. It was my education. It was my hobby. It was the tradition in my family. It was literally everything.

It was my purpose and identity.

Regardless, come October 2017, I officially left both fire and EMS life for the last time and applied for disability. I was convinced this would be my death sentence. Not just for my life, but for all the friends I had. I feared no one would want anything to do with some bum that just sat around the house in his pajamas all day while his wife worked. I felt humiliated that at just 39, I was forced out the way I was. Matt and Adele did their best to help me see a different perspective. That being after 39 years of life, 21 of them working an unforgiving career, with a childhood that I had, I had every right to slow done, take a break, and focus on healing myself.

"It's time for you to take care of you Keith!" Matts soft, reassuring voice telling me something I had a hard time buying.

Time went on with me no longer having any full-time work. February came and with the amount of chest pain I was having almost daily, my doctor sent me to a cardiologist where I was then sent for a cardiac catheter. It ended up showing no blockage but was more proof in the pudding that I needed to tone things down further.

Adele and I began the process of looking for a house, as things on the farm had become dicey. The landlord turned out to be a shitbag, and after the apartment started to fall into disrepair, we opted for buying a home instead of renting again.

At the end of April, we found out the young firefighter I had almost died with, in the brush truck a few years back on the highway, had killed himself. Rob Moody, Jr died from a self-inflicted gunshot wound. The family, department, and community devastated, I decided to take a ride to the fire house in Lancaster the day before the calling hours. When I got there I was greeted by the captain Chris. Everyone seemed surprised by Rob's suicide. I kept hearing things like "he seemed happy" and "there were no signs" over and over. Adele and I went to the services, and his father cried in my arms. As I stood there feeling so terrible for this family, I couldn't help but think about what drove Rob to end his life. After the five prior attempts I had made on my own life, I was still here. This kid, almost 13 years younger than me with so much to look forward to in life, was now dead. I just didn't understand God's plan.

That summer, Adele and I purchased our first home together in Jaffrey, the town just north of where the farm was. Now working at the emergency room in Nashua, a larger city about 45 minutes to the east, Adele was home more and had a rotating schedule. The house we bought had three bedrooms and plenty of room. It had a three-car garage with the third bay being segregated from the other two. I set this up as a poor man's workshop, filling it with tools and equipment to run a small woodworking shop. A sort of hobby I had begun tinkering with back on the farm. Mack had a nice open property to run around in. It was off a dead-end road, in a cul-de-sac neighborhood with a bunch of other families.

Family.

Almost immediately, Adele was bitten by the baby bug. With one of the bedrooms set up as our own, another as a den, and the last as a guest room, we began having conversations around the possibility of getting pregnant. After the miscarriage a few years back and Adele's lupus, we went and saw a specialist OBGYN. Back and forth to different appointments and tests, we were finally given the ok to try and have a baby. Reassured by the doctors that with lots of supervision and monitoring, both Adele and the baby would be ok, we started trying to get pregnant.

It was a lot of fun. Obviously.

It also only took about a month to happen. Overjoyed at finding out we were in fact pregnant we made the announcement that December at the surprise 40th birthday party Adele held for me. We were both ecstatic. So was her family and our friends. Eventually we found out we were having a girl. The due date was the weird part as it fell on our five-year wedding anniversary of August 8, 2019. We went into this with open minds, and big hearts. I always loved being a dad, and now I was being given the opportunity to be one again thanks to Adele.

The future looked brighter than ever, and in our minds, nothing could go wrong.

CHAPTER 12
FIRE & RAIN

The nightmare: Flashing lights and a long hallway in front of me. The sounds that convey fear and chaos behind a series of clean walls I can't get around. I'm crawling but feel like I shouldn't be. My partners face isn't visible, but their presence feels familiar. I make it to double doors and push through to be greeted by bright white light. Electronic beeps and bleeps fill the new room. Suddenly I hear the screams of others and a mothers blood curdling pleas. Shear panic pours over me.

I launch myself forward, awaking in my bed. I'm covered in sweat again. Panting, my eyes wide open, I reach for the other side of the bed. It's empty. Adele hasn't returned from her shift yet. Its 230 in the morning on an early June day. The windows breathing in the cool late spring air. I'm soaked. The bed is soaked, and now I'm terrified. I had no idea what the dream I just had was about, but out of reflex, I texted Adele.

Are you ok?

Of course! Getting ready to give report. Are you ok? Why are you awake? Her reply goes unanswered as I just needed to get one from her to reassure myself.

Come the beginning of June, Adele was very pregnant and

working a 3pm to 3am shift in the ER on a three-day rotating schedule. Our appointments at the baby doctors were now on every other week basis with the due date just two months away. We had set up the other bedroom across the hall from ours on the second floor, as the nursery. It was adorned with all the usual stuff a newborn baby girl could need and was painted in pinks and purples against a white backdrop. A small bureau on one wall, the crib against the back, a rocking nursing chair across from that. Long, light blocking curtains covered the sides of the two windows overlooking the garage and driveway. A moon and stars theme could be found in different aesthetic places. A lightly colored oval rug in the center of the room completed the package. It was literally a picture-perfect baby room.

We were both pumped awaiting the arrival of Riley. We had chosen the name after hours of perusing books with all sorts of old and new age suggestions. Our hearts felt complete knowing that when she came, she would receive the love I, and in some regards, Adele were denied as a child. We would sit on the couch together, my hand on her stomach. Riley's little feet trying to kick the flesh between us. I would lay my head against Adele, telling Riley all sorts of random stories. I often imagined what she would look like smiling back at me as I did what dad's did best.

Ramble.

A few weeks later after the baby shower, Adele started to have issues with her blood pressure. Often she would feel dizzy and lightheaded. This prompted the doctors to up the appointments to weekly visits. They gave an air of cautiousness, not necessarily worry, stating that they assumed at some point Adele would likely have some sort of symptoms. These increased quickly over the course of seven days with the doctors now starting to suggest possible bed rest or an early induction of labor. Either way, it was beginning to look like we were not going to make it to our August 8th due date.

On Sunday June 30th, Adele was getting ready for work just after lunchtime. She was already not feeling good, with the dizzy and lightheaded symptoms rearing their head once again. Sitting down at the dining room table, she asked me to check her blood pressure. Being who we were, we always had a blood pressure cuff and stethoscope around the house. When I saw the numbers, my face showed my concern.

"How bad is it?" my young pregnant wife's voice whispered in a letdown tone.

It was high.

Very high as a matter of fact. We discussed her staying home from work. Given the fact that the baby doctors were all affiliated with the hospital she worked at, we decided she could go in and at the very least get checked out. About 20 minutes after she arrived, I received a panicked phone call from Adele. She said that her blood pressure was now over two hundred, and that they were sending her up to labor and delivery. She was starting to cry. I did my best to comfort her, then the doctor came on the phone and told me a little more. I told them I would be leaving the house right away.

I ran out the door, after taking the dog out, who in his own way, knew something was not right. I got in my pickup and began what was normally a 45-to-50-minute ride to Nashua. I called Joe who we had selected as the Godfather, and Adeles friend Bridget who was to be the Godmother. Gave them each an abridged story of what was happening, then pulled into the hospital in less than 40 minutes.

By this point they had moved Adele upstairs to the labor and delivery unit. As I was led to her room, I could hear my wife crying from down the hall. Walking in, the feeling wasn't good. Six nurses and a doctor were working on Adele, as tears ran down her bright red face. She looked panicked, scared, and extremely uncomfortable as I moved close and grabbed her hand. Through our contact, I could sense her pain. I immediately felt my stomach begin to churn. Sweat formed upon my brow, with a bead running down the middle of my back. Deep inside, I could feel my anger growing from the fear I was beginning to face.

"My blood pressure's too high. They're worried about Riley,

Keith!" The love of my life's voice shaking in between her uncontrollable crying.

One of the nurses took me aside in the hall as the others prepared to moved Adele to a room for the night. I listened in horror as I was told if her blood pressure didn't come down they were going to need to induce delivery. If this happened, there was no guarantee the baby would make it, and with Adele's condition, she was also at risk for several complications. As the night grew into earlier morning, Adele began to hemorrhage. She was put on more meds, and we were being told that she would need to be moved to another, more appropriate hospital.

I sat looking out the window in her private room. Downtown Nashua displayed before me in the morning summer sun. We were in the beginning of a heat wave, and it was already in the 80's at barely 9am. Dozens of pedestrians walking up and down the sidewalks in shorts and light shirts. Seemingly carefree, enjoying the warm weather. I was jealous. Angry at them for looking so damn happy. I felt my soul sinking to the floor. I started thinking about Heather. The accident. The funeral and watching her casket getting lowered into the earth. I couldn't help but seeing Adele's face in place of my first wife's. The room was growing darker and darker. Just as reality started to slip away, Adele yelled my name, as her mother walked in the room.

Right behind my mother-in-law was the doctor and a nurse. They told us that Adele needed to be sent to Dartmouth Hitchcock Hospital which was about two and a half hours northwest in Lebanon. She was still losing blood, and labs were way out of range, and they were extremely concerned for Riley's condition. They were considering sending her by helicopter, to which Adele adamantly declined. An ambulance was being called to transport her, while I ran home to grab my wife's "go bag" that we had set up months prior. I then had to take Mack and bring him to my in-laws, who lived 45 minutes away, and then get back to Nashua before they transported Adele.

The heat of the day now reaching nearly 100 degrees, I drove my truck with the windows down. The air conditioning had just broken a week prior in a series of ironic events. Sweat pouring off me, with the dog in full pant, my head filled with a thousand thoughts. Thoughts of arriving back at the hospital to be told my wife was dead and they had lost the baby. I reached for the radio and turned it on high, Mack looking at me as if I was crazy.

Dropping the dog off and alone in the cab of the truck, I raced off for Nashua. As the 90-minute ride dragged on, I found myself talking to God. Something I had stopped doing over 16 year ago. I spoke to him the only way I could. In anger. I begged him to spare my wife and Riley. I told him if someone needed to be punished, let it be me. I had no idea how to truly talk with my higher power. I was never even taught how to pray short of those sporadic Sunday school lessons in my early childhood. I felt like a child, getting upset with a parent that had just laid down an unfair rule.

Pulling into the same spot I was in when I left, I walked out of the parking garage, across the street to the hospital. I never even shut the windows. Getting back up to labor and delivery, I was greeted by the head nurse, telling me the ambulance would be there in 5 minutes. In her room, Adele looked whipped. She was pale, with her head back on a pillow. Numerous IV's in both arms, another nurse was changing some bloody dressings from the lower part of the bed by Adele's legs. As I approached her, she turned her head and I saw that same big smile that caught my eye over eight years before.

Relief rushed over me as I held Adele's hand just as the ambulance crew and doctors arrived. I told her I would meet her up at the other hospital, leaned in and gave her a long kiss.

"It's going to be ok baby. I promise." I said it feeling like I didn't even believe what I was saying myself.

The ride north was a long, lonely one. At first the music helped. Then another ten miles would go by, and I felt myself getting upset again. Eventually I pulled into a rest area. Getting out, I vomited right by the side of my truck. Almost immediately after that, I began sobbing uncontrollably. I didn't want to lose anyone else. No more dying. No more suffering. No more pain. I felt selfish for feeling everything I was. I felt selfish for feeling like I was being punished for something I had no idea what it was. After a few minutes of screaming at the top of my lungs in the empty parking lot, I pushed on and arrived at the hospital.

When I finally got upstairs to the unit Adele had been brought to, dozens of doctors and nurses filled her room. As I stood in the door, out of the way, I could see my wife's face. Panic covered it once again. She was pale, looked weak and scared, as she listened to the voices around her. After a few, I was directed to come in, and went to her bedside. Explaining the situation, the doctors were trying their best to be optimistic, but the news wasn't great.

Adeles's body was in crisis with the baby in grave danger. If delivery didn't occur soon, on its own, they were going to do a c-section. As we sat in the room, we only had the occasional 10 minutes of being alone as the team kept coming in to check on mom and baby. As the night fell upon us, things began to worsen. Adele's blood pressure came down, only because the hemorrhaging had picked up. By early morning they were weighing the blood-soaked pads from under my wife, in an effort to figure out exactly how much she was losing. I was doing all I could to stay positive for Adele, knowing if she saw what was going through my head, she would lose hope.

Just before 8am, the team came back in to tell us they needed to do an emergency c-section in order to delivery Riley. They were unsure if the baby would make it at this point, but they had to save Adele. Looking at my wife, we both knew if she went into surgery, she wasn't coming back out. Lots of information was coming at us at lightning speeds. At one point we were asked if we wanted a priest for last rights. With that, my heart sank. It was happening. I was going to lose my wife, Riley, or possibly both.

As I began to process all this, I squeezed Adele's hand. I felt a tear roll down my cheek, as she looked up at me. Her body weak. Her face drained of all energy; Adele forced that smile again. As I stood trying to soak it all in, she suddenly sat upright.

"I think I need to go to the bathroom. Or push. I'm not sure." She spoke half concerned half relieved as what was about to happen she was unsure of.

Less than ten minutes later, Riley was laying on Adele's chest full of healthy color and letting the world know her lungs were working just fine. She didn't even need blow by oxygen. The neonate intensive care unit team (NICU) standing off to the side of the bed, almost looked let down that their skill set wasn't needed. An air of relief rushed over the room like the incoming tide powered by an offshore storm. Smiles began to come across the faces of the doctors and nurses. Adele cried and laughed all at once. In the moment, I felt myself begin to pull away. My emotions a whirlwind of anger, fear, sadness, hope, and happiness all thrown in a blender on puree. Allowing myself to tap into the happiness, I then felt a small tear run down my cheek.

After 20 minutes of holding Riley, the NICU team took her over to their unit to get our newborn situated which included putting a feeding tube down her nose. The rest of Adele's medical staff started giving her needs attention as my wife's body was beginning to make a rebound to the positive. Seeing an opportunity, I dismissed myself, stating I needed to take a walk. Walking out of the room, I was greeted by different staff members with the usual "congratulations" remarks. I made my way to the main lobby where I was told the hospital chapel was. Walking in, tall stained-glass windows on a high wall faced the door I came through. About eight pews, ten feet in length, lined the room with four rows on either side of a three-foot-wide center aisle. A podium with a large bible stood proud in the front, with a small bookshelf off to the right of it, containing numerous other religions books of prayer.

I took a seat in one of the front pews, now sitting in the dimly light room by myself, that carried with it a feeling of safety and warmth. I looked up at the tall wall with the stained-glass, to see a large gold cross with a figure of Jesus attached to it. With that, I started sobbing uncontrollably. Flashes of 40 years of good times and bad, flew through my head as I begged God to tell me why.

Why everything seemed to be a struggle at every conceivable junction in my life. Why everything had to feel like I was being challenged all the time. I was looking for a sign.

Feeling as though the light coming through the stained glass looked odd, I took out my phone to check the weather. Thinking there was a summer storm moving in, I was shocked. Apparently there was a total solar eclipse that day. Come to find out, the only total solar eclipse that calendar year. Guess I had my sign.

Sure, I was relieved that Adele and my youngest child were both going to be ok, but the damage was done. I felt distant from reality even though I could see what was going on around me clearly. I was there but not in control. It was as if I was on a ride going around the perimeter of the reality I was actually in. As the next few days rolled on with Riley on 24/7 care in the NICU, Adele was given the all clear to be discharged. My hope to return home as a family was crushed as we were told our baby was going to need to stay in the hospital for at least a few more weeks. Devastated at the thought of Riley being two hours away from us, we were able to get them to send her down to the smaller NICU at Adele's hospital in Nashua. Now able to visit Riley whenever we wanted, both of us found more relief.

Even though she was closer to home, and we could see her whenever, and for as long as we wanted, Adele and I were still leaving Riley at the hospital when we left. Something that caused more damage in Adele than me, eventually leading her into a postpartum depression. After two more weeks in Nashua, Riley came home with us. We were a complete family. The ride home was full of smiles, and tears of joy and concern as the two of us knew the next several months were going to be a testament to who we were not only as husband and wife, but as parents and caregivers. It was a moment most would revel in, even without the circumstances we went through. As I drove us home, looking in the rearview at Adele, I would catch that heart-warming smile that had become my source of light and hope over the years. A smile on a face that meant more to me than any one person ever had. A face that I had fallen in love with a lot sooner than I had initially admitted to.

It was also the face of someone I now detested. I just didn't realize it.

Now on maternity leave for almost nine weeks, Adele was home every day. My inner anguish towards her, undisclosed to anyone, and not entirely clear to even me was growing in power. I would often sit in the back room that we had made a den of sorts, staring blankly at the dark tv screen in front of me. Thoughts would enter my mind of how she was to blame for what happened with Riley and the pregnancy. How she was at fault for almost dying and almost taking my third child with her. I was growing more and more angry by the day and didn't even realize it. Hours would turn into days then into weeks of me festering in an undisclosed shitshow of twisted thoughts and emotions that had me beginning to hate not only Adele but even Riley.

I would lie to Matt during our appointments once they resumed. Having just had a child born through a surrogate himself right before Riley, he had been on a maternity leave of sorts himself. I would go to my appointments in the late summer into the early fall, with a smile on my facing saying how obviously happy I was that I now had another child and that her and Adele were safe and healthy. But inside, a different set of feelings were festering in a toxic and vile manner. Riley's insistent, never-ending crying was tearing through me to the point where I would often bash my head against a wall to try and feel something besides anger and frustration. With every cry, I would drift off into a swirling world of pain and inner chaos. Still, I kept all of this to myself, telling myself I wasn't allowed to feel any of it. I shouldn't be feeling any of it.

Right before Thanksgiving, I realized I was in fact feeling and thinking all of this. Immediately I was overtaken by a level of shame and guilt unlike any I had experienced in my life. I had almost no concept of where the last four months had disappeared to, or a clear picture of any events contained within that timeframe.

All my memories seemed blurred, as if I was looking at them through a scratched-up piece of glass from the outside.

Now, I hated myself.

I questioned everything within myself. In the past I had times were I was disgusted with how I viewed who or what I was as a man. But this was based on the actions of others. What I was now feeling was 100% because of my own thought process. Brought on by the past actions and events beyond my own control, maybe. However, I was the one conjuring these thought processes up. Or some part of me at the least. A part I was beginning to understand existed but wasn't sure how or why. A part of me that felt different at different times beyond just simple mood swings. At one moment this was a very dark and overpowering part, sometimes followed by submissive and scared traits. Right now, though, the dark part was in the driver's seat, and we were on a crash course.

During the fall, I ended up reconnecting with Andres through Facebook. We hadn't spoken since graduating high school back in '97, and through social media we were able to have occasional conversations that led to meeting in person. Much like our earlier friendship, we met at a comic book shop then went out for sushi. Haven't not changed much beyond aging as I have, Andres had the same sharp-witted intelligence and almost childish disposition that made our friendship what it was over 25 years earlier. It brought with it a small amount of comfort from a time I had tried to forget about. From that night on, we began talking on the regular.

About a week after my 41st birthday, we had scheduled Riley's christening at one of the Catholic churches in the town just to the north of us, for a Sunday morning. The Friday night before, Adele was scheduled to work in the ER for her 3pm to 3am shift in Nashua. I was openly not in the best of dispositions as she got dressed in her scrubs and put her make-up on. I again sat blankly in our living room, with Riley's playpen set up under the big bay window off to my side. I felt nothing inside. I was cold, hollow, and dead set on what I knew I had to do. My reactions and answers to my wife, as she readied to walk out the door, were calculated and premeditated. With a half-hearted smirk, I kissed Adele goodbye, telling her I loved her, as she walked out.

As the afternoon grew darker in the late afternoon in our living room, so did I. Riley now screaming her loudest, I felt the world swirling around me. A cold, numbing feeling came over my body as I felt as if I was on an iceberg in the middle of the north Atlantic. All by myself. No one could help me now. It was time. Then, I seemed to check out. Looking at the world through that same scratched up piece of glass.

Darkness wrapped in around me from either side. The mid-tone greys of the living room walls faded to black. The afternoon setting sun disappeared into a black hole that seemed to swallow everything around it. The screaming around me drifted to a muffle as I stood up and walked to the basement door. For a moment I hesitated, as if something was trying to get my attention. Then, as quickly as I stopped at the top of the basement stairs, I took my first step down. Rounding the corner and now looking at the five-foot-tall metal cabinet. Keys in my hand, I unlocked the door and peered inside. The silver gun staring back at me with its top locked open. Reaching within, I grabbed the heavy hand-cannon and magazine filled with hollow points. In a movement based on muscle memory, I slammed the magazine into its home in the base of the gun and pulled the top back racking a round. Screaming, I raised it to my temple, closed my eyes, and pulled the trigger. In a fleeting image, Adele and Riley flashed before me.

Click!

Nothingness settled into my body and mind. No pain. No cold. No sounds or smells. Just darkness and freedom from what had been torture. Then a bright light followed by the headrush of reality setting back in around me. The stale smell of our basement made its way into my nostrils as my eyes began to open and I realized that I was still alive. Now shaking, covered in sweat and nauseous, I fell to my knees. Gun still in my right hand, I dropped it to the chair in front of me as I felt the tears falling violently around me. Like a small child that just fell hard off their bicycle for the first time, I sobbed uncontrollably as I whimpered like a beaten dog.

The gun didn't go off. A piece I had taken dozens of times to the range and fired hundreds of rounds through, never went off. Wiping the tears and snot from my face, I dropped the magazine from the grip, and pulled back the slide, locking it into the open position. Doing so caused two bullets to fly out of the chamber. The actual bullet part of one being forced into its cartridge by a few centimeters.

The damn thing did a double feed and jammed.

Now hearing Riley's scream at an all-time high volume, I made my way back upstairs. Picking up my infant daughter, we cried together. After ten minutes she fell asleep against my chest, with me following shortly after. Later that night during a phone call I told Adele what I had done. She couldn't believe what had happened. The christening went off as scheduled that Sunday. Later, back at the house, I took Joe out to my woodshop and told him about what happened Friday night. His jaw hit the floor as he put both arms around me.

"I'm so sorry that happened brother. What now?" Joe's question was answered with a shrug, with me really not knowing what needed to be done.

That week Adele joined me for my therapy with Matt bringing Riley with us. Telling my therapist that I had just tried to end my life, he sat in shock. We discussed why I felt I couldn't approach him with what I was really feeling in the weeks leading to the past Friday night. The three of us spoke about what needed to happen next. The idea of me going inpatient came up to which I immediately turned down, telling Matt and Adele I was no longer suicidal. After over an hour of conversation, it was decided that I would go back to seeing Matt twice a week in an effort to unearth what may be going on inside me.

Christmas arrived, and I wasn't doing much better. I was incredibly depressed and trying my hardest to bury it. I would lash out at Adele in unexpected ways. After an all-out verbal brawl with my wife the day after Christmas, we called Matt, and I agreed to go inpatient. I have no recollection of what transpired between that phone call and arriving at McLean's late that afternoon. As I kissed Adele goodbye, before being brought out to the admissions screening area, I felt like a completely useless bag of shit. I had let down everyone and couldn't even kill myself successfully.

I sat in a room, myself the only patient, while the few staff members talked amongst themselves. As I overheard part of their conversation, I turned to figure out what was going on to see them watching a story on the local news channel. Apparently the day I checked myself in the psych hospital, there was an annular solar eclipse.

I was dumbfounded.

Because Christmas fell on a Wednesday, and I came in the day after, I then spent the next four days not meeting with any doctors until the following Monday. When I did, I completely broke down. I told them I didn't care if I lived or died as nothing mattered anymore. I was a failure. As I held my head in my hands, crying a river of tears, the two doctors and social worker began to suggest different options. Right away it was suggested I stay for at least two weeks, likely longer. A treatment called Electroconvulsive Therapy or ECT, was also suggested as a possible option given its ability to break major depressive disorders.

Now being inpatient at McLean's, Matt came down to the unit I was on that Monday as well. We discussed our plan with meeting and decided to stick with twice a week. I also mentioned what the other doctors had suggested regarding ECT. His response wasn't for or against it, however, he told me he didn't necessarily recommend it given my trauma past. He left the final decision up to me.

I was desperate to be a normal, happy human being. I just wanted to be a good father, husband, and friend. More than anything, I just wanted to stop feeling like a burden to those around me. I was willing to do anything to get there, no matter the risks. There was always risks with any medical procedure, no matter how invasive it was. ECT carried with it the same general ones anything using anesthesia did. Upon this was the possibility of cognitive impairment, brain damage, and because of the use of electricity, a risk to cardiac function. With my history of chest pain and a cardiac catheter, I had to undergo a few extra tests before being cleared for the procedure that, in the end, I decided to go forward with.

The prick of the needle brought a much-needed grounding to reality. The pain of punctured skin was almost soothing given the amount of stress I had been under in recent months. The nurse assuring me the procedure would go great and that I would do fine were as unnecessary as they were redundant. As they rolled me into the procedure room, more staff greeted me with masked smiles. Laying me flat, with just a hospital pillow beneath my head, the doctor came in view above me.

"Ready to go Keith?"

"Yes ma'am."

"Ok. Please state your full name, date of birth, and where you are right now." The rehearsed line coming out with me already firing back the responses before she finished.

Barely getting the word "McLean's" out of my mouth, the rush of cold fluids fills my veins as instantly I go numb. My vision goes dark like an old tv set being turned off, now filled with a million stars. I feel like I'm floating in eternity. No pain. Carefree with no worries. Then after what seems like hours, my eyes open and a new unfamiliar environment is sprawled out in front of me. A nurse is next to me speaking but I can't yet fully hear her. I'm not even sure who I am but I know I'm safe. Within seconds, I'm asked if I know who I am and where I'm at. In a strange series of millisecond clicks, my brain comes up with all the correct information. A few seconds after that, everything starts coming back to me.

Come January 2020, I was getting the ECT treatments three times a week and so far they had done wonders for my depression. A few weeks before, when Adele and Riley came on New Year's Eve, I was barely speaking. Unable to look either of them in the face. Now, I was having conversations again, and even bearing the occasional smile. Adele noticed the difference after the second treatment. Even though the procedures left me exhausted, confused, and sick to my stomach, I could tell they were helping.

There was a drawback.

I was having significant short term memory loss. Beyond those in my life for years, I was forgetting the names of nurses, doctors, and other patients on the unit. I would often completely forget a conversation with Adele. Later I would forget her visits altogether. Come the third week of January I was given the all clear to be discharged after nearly a month in the hospital. The morning of, I had a treatment before Joe showed up to bring me home. Adele had to work and with all the time she had missed or had to rotate her schedule while I was inpatient, she could not change that day.

Walking in my door, our babysitter and her boyfriend met me in the mudroom. Adele had brought Serena on in an almost full-time manner to help with Riley knowing even once I was home, I was going to need time to adjust. I would sit in the den and stare at the tv, maybe play an occasional video game. I would still take care of Riley, but with a teenager in the house to help me out. Even though I knew it was all in an effort to help me, I felt like incapable burden again. I was having lapses in time and memory daily. I was showing no emotion or affect whatsoever.

After an event where I "blacked out" and backed my pickup into the garage door, I ended up getting readmitted to the same unit at McLean's. Now humiliated, I walked back down the hallway to be greeted by a handful of patients I had grown close with in my first stay. Now having another first responder as a roommate I began to develop a slight closeness with another man who had similar experiences in life. Especially the way he ended his career.

Before the first admission, I had started in a men's trauma group in the fall of 2019. A group of regular dudes, none of which were first responders. It was literally just a group for men with childhood trauma. Now on my second admission in as many months, I yet again was being escorted from my locked unit to the main hospital for the weekly meetings. Matt was running the group so now I was seeing him up to three times a week including my two private sessions. Between him, Adele, and myself we decided I needed to stop the ECT treatments immediately as we couldn't get a straight answer on why I was having such bad memory issues.

Come mid to late February after a significant amount of hard conversations, I was discharged home again. This time, I had a more confident feeling inside me. I felt prepared for diving headfirst into the remaining closets of secrets up in my head. With Matt now realizing he had to be more proactive and assertive with me to keep the communication open, our conversations took off in a powerful way.

I finally felt comfortable saying I was happy to be alive. I was starting to see the light at the end of this long, depressing tunnel through Hell that I had been walking most of my life. I was determined to do better, live better and be stronger. I refused to ever attempt to allow myself to get to the point where I was contemplating ending my own life.

During a session in the beginning of March, Matt and I somehow got on the subject of sexuality. As we got further into the conversation, I found myself staring at my feet. My face hot with a growing sensation of embarrassment starting to filter through my entire body. I felt uncomfortable in my skin, my stomach churned, and I wanted to run out of the room. Matt seeing this dug a little deeper, until I began to cry. Letting me have my moment, he finally asked what was bothering me. After a few moments of contemplation, my eyes bloodshot and still shedding the occasional tear, I sat up and looked across the room at my therapist of over 4 years.

"I've been attracted to men my entire life Matt. I even had an experience with another boy when I was a teenager!" The words coming out of my mouth like verbal diarrhea. I said them so fast, I nearly stuttered.

Not even looking remotely surprised, Matt handled the

situation in the most amazingly well, and honestly unexpected manner. We talked more about it, with him telling me how he was also bisexual and living with another man.

"I don't think we have ever discussed the fact that I'm married to another man." Matt's words coming out in a way that made it seem like something that should have been discussed. At least on his part.

"I always knew. From that first appointment back in the late summer of 2015, Matt." As the words left my mouth, a smile and look of almost relief came over Matt's face.

"How did you know?"

"I just told you I'm bisexual. I have a strong Gay-dar! That and you had a man bun and wore tighter pants than my wife." I said as we both chuckled, the air now easing to a level that made me confident what I just shared was the right thing. Later that night I told Adele the truth about my sexuality. In a response that speaks volumes of our relationship, she smiled, hugged me, and then asked if I was going to divorce her to run off with a man.

Now being out of the hospital and feeling stronger and having two positive experiences regarding my secret sexuality, I was quickly gaining my confidence back. My feet back under me, I knew I needed to approach some unfinished business. The first was the broken communication with Lester and Gus. They were both in attendance for Riley's christening then quickly disappeared when I went in the hospital. Neither reaching out to Adele to support her, and when Lester did text me while I was still inpatient, I snapped at him. In all fairness, I wasn't in the best of spots, and the man was trying to make me feel like I let down humanity.

For weeks, I would call and text and get no answer from either Lester or Gus. Finally, one day Gus answered his phone. In a brief conversation he assured me he wanted to meet up to talk about what had happened. That didn't take place. Lester remained on radio silence, and so I began to come to terms with losing two so-called friends because of my mental health.

Around the same time, a woman I had made a connection with

through the New Hampshire Fire Academy, reached out to me. Donna was the director up there and was putting together a mental health symposium in the fall. She wanted to meet and discuss the possibility of me speaking. She had been following my advocacy on social media for a while and felt I'd be a good fit. She especially liked the project I had been part of with McLean's back in 2019 called Deconstructing Stigma. This was a program involving interviews and a photo shoot of several individuals with varying types of mental health illnesses. I was the only firefighter selected to do a piece on trauma and PTSD. Not only did they create a webpage for the project but was planning on unveiling a terminal wide billboard at Logan International Airport in Boston. McLean's had also expressed interest in using me for future endeavors because of my openness on the subject.

Come April, the Covid-19 Pandemic started to grip the country and the world. People were wearing masks, not leaving their houses for fear of contracting the illness, bringing it home to their families and killing everyone. McLean's went to all virtual therapy, including group. They cancelled all "unnecessary projects including the grand unveiling of the billboard for Deconstructing Stigma. Shortly after this they then decided, sighting insurance reasons, that any patient not living in Massachusetts could not receive virtual therapy. Come May 2020, I was told I could no longer attend group and within a few weeks had to end my almost five-year long relationship with Matt. At the same time, Donna called me to say that the symposium had been put on an indefinite hold due to the pandemic.

I was at a loss. Literally. My head was spinning with all these sudden and unanticipated changes in both my mental wellness and personal relationships. As summer began with Adele and Riley's birthday quickly approaching, it was becoming clear that the pandemic wasn't going away anytime soon. I did my best to keep my spirits up with writing, social media postings, time with Riley and Adele, and going for car rides often sitting by the water. I refused to go anywhere in public with gatherings of people as by late August, society was beginning to lose their mind. People acted erratically. Wearing full body coverings, dish gloves, and a respirator, the grocery store often looked more like something out of a horror movie. There was fear all around me, whenever I went out. And not on my part. I could give two shits less about this supposed "super-flu". Working in healthcare as long as I had, that kind of stuff wasn't a massive concern for me and my health.

It was however for my immune compromised wife and our premature daughter who had just turned one. A thought I had never really had up to the fall of 2020, was Adele's safety while at work in the ER. Sure, there were times where she told me patients got a bit feisty with her, even pushing her to the floor a few times. But given what could happen if she caught Covid, or worse yet brought it home to Riley, I started to find myself fearing losing one or both of them all over again.

This time, something was different. I was nervous about the possibility of something happening, but it didn't overtake my entire being. I could talk about my fears with Adele and hers to me, and I didn't spiral down a rabbit hole.

I was still having incredibly powerful bouts of anger though, unrelated to but not helped by the pandemic and by now Adele was convinced something else was going on. She often felt as if I wasn't me and someone else was in my place. She didn't always know who she was going to come home to or wake up to. Something that had been going on since late 2019 even before my last suicide attempt.

During the last few weeks of my inpatient stay at Mclean's, I was interviewed by this doctor. What she specialized in was a part of trauma that was often dismissed by most of the psychiatric community. A diagnosis that had been made fun of more than any other mental health disorder, especially being misrepresented several times in Hollywood. A disorder that I fit the bill for on several levels and it answered a lot of the questions as to why I behaved in certain ways. It answered why I had such big chunks of time missing from my memory even before ECT punched holes in my short term. It answered why I often didn't feel like I was in the driver's seat or in control of my own faculties. It answered why Adele didn't always feel like she was talking to the man she married.

This doctor specialized in dissociative identity disorder (DID). Formerly known as Multiple Personality Disorder.

CHAPTER 13
TRAUMATIC STRENGTH

Everyone has a turning point.

I finally had mine a year after my last suicide attempt. December 2020 and the subsequent holidays that followed were more enjoyable than any other period of time in recent years. After 12 months of rifling through file drawers of memories and pain, I had come to peace with a lot of it. Moreover, I had made peace with the attempt itself. The sixth one in a 28-year period of time and as far as I was concerned, the last one.

Now being in a position of no longer having a therapist thanks to the pandemic that was in full force across the world, I was having to regulate my own self-care. A challenge that in years prior had resulted in seemingly backwards motion in regard to my mental health. I was doing more with advocacy which even back in 2015 had brought me a truer sense of purpose and helped me find out who I really was as a man. I was beginning to get a following on social media with all I was willing and able to put out there and how raw and unapologetic it was always worded.

I still wrestled with this feeling of not always feeling in control of myself. The difference now was that I was sitting with this sensation more deeply. With 2021 kicking off with people still being told to be afraid of each other, not to hold get-togethers, and to always wear a mask over their nose and mouth, I was experiencing a lot of isolation. Adele had started working at a different hospital in the ICU that every week was jam packed with patients dying of covid. My fear for her safety coupled with my own lack of desire to go out in public, was creating a different kind of stress inside me. I knew I couldn't let this bullshit settle in on me, or it would send me into a downward spiral.

The unspoken truth about trauma and especially a life lived with an endless supply of it, is it can re-create who you are. How you think. How you feel. How you process. Even your outlook towards a positive situation is filled with pessimism and questioning of its validity. Nothing is ever just a good thing. After years of dealing with one horrible event after another, your reaction to it becomes your personality. Now at 42 years old, I was beginning to learn and understand why.

Fear was instilled into me at a very young age. Fear of a lot of obvious things, but most importantly, that of loss. Loss of innocence. Loss of pride. Loss of trust. Loss of love. Loss of people and relationships. The one that caused the most amount of future damage was loss of control. Throughout my life I had a constant sense of loss of control. As a child I had zero control over how I was treated and ultimately abused by those that were supposed to care and love for me. With the loss of trust encased within this situation, my outlet to feeling in control was to act out of control. I would break toys. I would yell or react in overly emotional ways. I would get and be angry. All of these behaviors brought with it a known result.

I would get in trouble.

In these situations, I caused it to happen, so in my fucked up, trauma riddled brain, I was in control. It was a welcomed scenario to be punished for something I purposefully did. After my initial sexual abuse, I would also knowingly put myself into positions to be alone with the ones molesting me. As I began to ponder this last one, I would feel myself getting nauseous and a deep churning, like a stump grinder in my stomach, would cause me to let the internal discussion fade off. At the same time, there was a different voice crying out from behind all this pain. A younger voice, that held a deep, stronger tone that often-used simple language in its communication. A voice I didn't recognize but felt at ease with as it left the rest of me feeling safe and protected. I couldn't place it, and when I thought too deeply about it, I started thinking I was going legitimately crazy, but this voice felt strong and confident.

Late January of 2021, I decided it may be helpful to try seeing a therapist that could also prescribe medication. With the leaps and bounds I was making, there were times I felt I needed a little help. As much as I really did not want to start taking meds again, I knew in the past they had taken the edge off. Meeting with a middle-aged woman in one of the offices at the local hospital, we started the interview process. This involved me spelling out a lot of what I had spent five years working on with Matt, along with any past use of pharmaceuticals. The icing on this psychiatric cake was the discussion on my six suicide attempts. As I walked this woman through each one, the mood in the room began to change. She stopped looking at me instead putting her attention into her computer screen. Sensing a change in her disposition, I stopped talking and stared across the desk at her. Turning, what she said next spelt the end of our relationship.

"But were any of the attempts *really* serious?" As she spoke she tilted her head to one side in a show of nonbelief in what I had just shared.

"Have you ever held a loaded pistol against your skull, after chambering a round and pulled the trigger!?? My response as I stood up, received the reaction from her I was looking for. She sat stunned now staring at her feet as I walked out of her office never to meet again.

I felt dismissed. Not believed. It felt like she was saying that all the pain, loneliness, guilt, and shame that led me to each and every one of those suicide attempts was just an excuse for attention. As I sat with these feelings over the next week or so, I realized I was rising above them. They weren't causing me to fall down a spiral or bring up old unhealthy behaviors. No. This incident was causing me to become more fueled to make the changes in society, and apparently even the psychology community, that needed to take place. I was driven with a new motivation to push harder in smashing the stigma on mental health. To use all of what I had been through to pave a road of hope and healing for those hiding behind a mask of trauma.

As New England began to thaw out and the flowers started to bloom in spring of 2021, Donna, the director from the Fire Academy had reached back out to me. She was again planning a mental health symposium that September and wanted to meet to discuss having me speak. This time, I was told there was going to be another firefighter from New Hampshire possibly presenting as well. On an unusually warm late March morning, I drove up to the academy in Concord to speak with Donna and meet this other firefighter. Walking into the lobby I was greeted by a younger guy in his mid-thirties, about five foot nine, with a thin, muscular build. He had a tight, well-maintained haircut, clean shaved, with tattoos lining both arms creating a colorful sleeve effect. Smiling, he extended his hand out to me.

"Hi! I'm Steve Holmes. You must be Keith?" His voice was smooth and genuine and carried with it a confidence I could appreciate.

While shaking hands and introducing myself, Donna walked around the corner and hugged us both. Short of meeting with Donna back in the beginning of 2020 in her office, it had been nearly 23 years since I had walked the halls of the New Hampshire Fire Academy. The last time being only 18 years old, insecure, scared, and unsure of myself and those around me, the memories aren't the fondest. This time, as the three of us walked and talked, we joined in together as we enjoyed the countless group photos along the main hall leading past the large auditorium in the center of the main building. Donna was also now retired from director, holding a separate "part-time" position under a different tier of the Department of Safety. As we made our way down the back stairwell, I felt more relaxed and confident then my last visit.

Walking into one of the smaller classrooms in the basement, we sat and started to get to know each other. Come to find out, Steve was an Exeter firefighter and paramedic, having previously served three tours in the Marines as a Seargent. He had an impressive resume of trauma and as he spoke, laying out part of his story and how he would present, I immediately felt a comfort just being around him. A deep respect that only comes from meeting someone who has been in the "suck" and lived to tell about it. I often took for granted my ability to speak publicly about what I have been through, and that day hearing another grown man do the same, with him even shedding a few tears, I fully realized how powerful stories like ours truly can be.

After sharing her background, Donna gave me the floor. As I spoke, Steve leaned forward in his chair. Eyes as wide as a hawk, jaw by his feet, he sat obviously taken aback by what I had been through. As I finished he stood up and walked over to me. Arms out to his side, we embraced in a hug that anyone walking by not knowing any better, would have thought we had known each other for decades.

For one of the first times in my life I truly felt connected to another man, and it was obvious Steve felt the same. Donna suggested before the September symposium we run a smaller classroom "rehearsal" of sorts, to fine tune our presentations. We both agreed, and Steve and I exchanged phone numbers to help each other prepare.

Right before all of this I had reconnected with another firefighter I had met through one of the group's I was part of when I first got out of Mclean's in early 2016. Brian was also a firefighter and paramedic for a larger town in Southeastern Massachusetts after serving in the military. We had both experienced too many coworkers and friends that had succumbed to their pain and ended their lives. Conversations between the two of us often led us to discussing ways to bring some form of support to the first responder community.

What came to life were virtual, Zoom based peer support meetings for first responders and their families. Eventually we would hold two meetings a week with nurses and doctors joining the attendance. Meetings where people felt safe laying out their problems for the others to offer up support, advice, and even guidance at times. The most important thing that took place was listening, which in of itself was helping people out.

A classroom size presentation was held at the fire academy in mid-July and Donna, Steve, and myself were shocked when over 70 first responders and some family showed up. Brian was one along with a few others from our peer support group. Adele attended along with Steve's wife, mother, and a few members of his department. The symposium in the fall yielded almost 200 attendees. Never in my life had I spoken in front of so many people, even during all my years of being a training officer I never had a class with more than 35 in attendance.

I did some research before both of these, on how to best prepare for such a massive presentation. Most of it went out the window when I walked up in front of the room. As I stared out, I began to imagine what it must be like to be attending a presentation on mental health. To be sitting in a room with someone sharing their life story on how they survived not only PTSD, but numerous suicide attempts. It was with that perspective that I realized that most of them were likely more uncomfortable than me. Taking a deep breath in and holding it, the release brought with it a confident and determined mindset. When I was done speaking, what I felt inside, and what I received from the audience further strengthened my determination to find new ways and opportunities to break down the mental health stigma.

Having to work on my story in order to be able to present it publicly also came with a cathartic effect. After the symposium in the fall, I sat with some of what I had been though. Mainly my childhood. It was in these numerous mindful moments, where I set out to become comfortable with my past, that I began to find true peace. In a half meditative state of mind, the feelings, emotions, and more importantly facts of what I had survived over nearly 43 years, started to fall into their proper places. Hours were spent literally talking to myself, in an effort to hear from the younger versions of me, that had been pushed into the corners of my brain. Pushed there by trauma, pain, denial, lies, fear, and a victim mentality that I had been sitting complacent with for decades.

I was beginning to truly feel my inner potential and desire to constantly do better. Something, *parts of me* often fought me on, causing all of us to falter. These parts, seemingly stuck in an age with a younger mind and at times crippled by the thought of growing beyond their current abilities. Given what I had been told about dissociative identity disorder, and now operating with a more healed trauma brain, I began the painstaking process of hearing out what all the different *parts of me* had experienced with everything we all went through. A process that seems textbook crazy when you start doing so. When you have literally nobody in your life that you can vent to regarding the conversations you are having with the other guys up in your head.

As the leaves stopped falling and the snow started flying, with Christmas only a few weeks away, I turned my attention to a bigger project. Something that could reach a larger crowd. With a bunch of suicides in the last several months, a few of which I knew personally, I was done. I was done hearing how others were still struggling with their demons. Done finding out that some lost the battle with them. Done knowing that PTSD and suicide wasn't getting the attention it needed. I had started doing more podcast interviews and with the public presentations I was gaining a level of confidence speaking in front of others unlike anything I'd felt before.

So, I took a chance.

Back in high school, I had gotten along with one of the football players who was a grade ahead of me, graduating the year before. Scot, ended up coaching college ball himself, finally ending up out in Los Angeles at UCLA. At the same time, he had gotten into Hollywood landing minor parts in movies and some reoccurring roles on a few tv shows. Eventually, while doing all that, he began getting into the production of various types of films. We had stayed in a somewhat distanced contact over the years thanks to social media. After a Facebook post that I put up regarding high school bullying a few months earlier, Scot and I had reconnected.

Sending him a message, I had what I considered a simple idea. Maybe an "infomercial" on PTSD and first responders. Nothing big, complex, or pricey. Immediately we ended up on the phone going back and forth about mental health, suicide, and the crisis with both. Scot shared some of his own personal experience, showing vulnerability and a drive to make a change. He asked about my own story, and how I had been writing about it the past five or six years. Giving him a CliffsNotes version of my life, he was in awe.

Scot tasked me with writing a three-page pitch on my life story in an effort to be able to "sell" it to a producer out in tinsel town. I set out on this project immediately. I was scared and nervous. Happy and proud all at the same time. Sitting on the cusp of bringing at least one lived perspective to the attention of many was daunting. I poured myself into my work. With the help of a friend, I created what we both felt was a jaw dropping summary of how I survived the life I had. Within a week Scot and I met with Cory, a producer who ran his own studio and hailed from the MTV days. His niche was interviews and creating gripping documentaries on the various, often not spoken about, parts of our society.

After a virtual meeting that lasted about 45 minutes, the three of us came to the agreement to produce a documentary centered around my life story. I was blown away that finally I was going to be able to take all the good, bad, and terrible parts of my life and put them together in a way that could potentially help millions.

My discipline stronger than ever, fueling a seemingly

unstoppable motivation and drive, I set out to make another big change in my life. Now 43 years old, I was beginning to feel the mileage I had tacked on in both physical and psychological ways. I had recently been diagnosed with five bulging discs in my spine. Two of which were in my neck, with the remaining three in my lower back right at my hip. Both knees had been all but destroyed from not only the job but being a big dog my whole life. My shoulders, more specifically my rotator cuffs, hurt almost as often as my back. Making all this worse was my weight skyrocketing to 300 pounds come Christmas. So, I decided to change all of it. Immediately after the New Year, I joined one of the local gyms, and set up a healthier meal plan.

My ability to constantly want to improve myself, my family and the world was at an all-time high. The progress I was making with getting back in shape further drove my determined mindset with battling the stigma. I used the physical discomfort I often felt at the gym as an outlet to some of the pain and anguish I had been holding onto for decades.

I threw myself into everything I did.

With 2022 now beginning, I was getting acclimated to a position I took at a startup business back in the fall. Life coaching was something I was unfamiliar with up to late October. The owner, reaching out through Facebook, felt I was a good fit for her recently established company. The wife of a first responder herself, she had started this coaching business in an attempt to bring another modality to the men and women of the industry. With what I had been doing publicly, she brought me on as a form of "street credit" in the hopes that my past experiences and respect on the job would bring in droves of first responders and their families. I thought this meant I was going to be speaking in front of people more, telling them my story, like I had gotten a taste for in recent months.

My position turned out to be one more of a salesman, which I am not. What started with the promise of doing speaking gigs resulted in me sitting behind a vendor booth at conferences and seminars. Even though I had been coached, was now a coach, and the director of the business, standing in front of someone trying to sell them this product, brought back too many memories from the life insurance fiasco.

I couldn't sell. I can teach and instruct, even tell complete strangers the horrors of my life. But I cannot sell. Every time I tried to do it; my heart wasn't into it. I would get nervous, easily intimidated. Often times I would begin to feel like an insecure teenager that had just walked out in front of the entire student body. Waiting to be laughed at. With where I was at this last year or so, I tried to look at this as a challenge. A challenge to embrace the uncomfortable and become comfortable with it. I was also focusing on what I felt was both me and the owners goal of changing the culture around mental health.

So, I pressed on.

Still pursuing the podcasts, conference speaking, and more and more writing opportunities, I poured myself into my work. I also poured myself into trying to heal more. What used to be a knee jerk reaction to run away from certain challenges became a conscious effort to face the obstacles of life. Sitting with this newfound strength I pondered more and more into what felt like foreign land up in my head. I was a Viking floating across an icy ocean in search of answers of what was out there. There was danger, but at the same time a thrill to discover and unearth what was always buried deep inside me.

My childhood having the nightmarish parts it did, formed my mental foundation. One that was built out of the most uneven field stones, each barely holding their form as the new floors of adolescence and eventually adulthood were built above. The abuse and neglect I felt as a child along with the lies and manipulation created an unstable spectrum of emotions. My fight or flight destroyed; I was like a deer in the headlights. Only that deer had been given steroids and cocaine and was at times rampaging out of control all while trying to dodge cars.

For decades I denied myself the feelings and emotions associated with being molested and raped. As I read more on DID, I was beginning to learn that I may not have been doing this consciously. The often misunderstood and misrepresented condition known as dissociative identity disorder, is forged in trauma. Essentially your brain creates what are called "alters". These "alters" are, psychologically, separate parts of you, formed from a traumatic event that exist under the impression that the event is still happening. The emotions, feelings, and perspectives of this "alters" are trapped in whatever age the trauma happened at. Sometimes numerous "alters" can be created from repeated exposure to the same type of trauma. This was very common for rape victims.

Now tapping into a full palette of emotions, some of which were still very young in age, I was truly beginning to find long-term healing. I was giving space to the younger voices in my head that had been crying out for a stage for a long time. I put aside the embarrassment that went with acknowledging hearing others in your head. As I took an honest look and listen to what was inside me, I grew stronger and more confident with every day.

My relationship with Tyler and Elizabeth had come to a standstill. After a very brief phone conversation shortly before Christmas, I heard nothing more from them. It had been years before that phone call that the three of us spoke, and now it seemed that more years would pass before we spoke again. For some reason, this possible outcome wasn't sending me into a debilitating tailspin. I owned my part in being a possible tyrant to my two older children. The yelling. The temper and fits of anger. As much as I never laid a hand on them, the terror I knew I caused, did damage that may have been worse. I promised myself, Riley would not live the same childhood.

I was still not experiencing much enjoyment with my position at the coaching business, but it was getting me to conferences in cities across the country. I looked at this as a win. I was also growing closer to the owner, building a friendship based on a common interest. As much as I really did not want to work the job I was with her, I also didn't want to give up on it more out of fear of losing the relationship I took a chance on establishing. My other uncertainty was whether or not my gut reaction was just these other parts of "me" acting up every time an uncomfortable situation arose.

Production on the documentary started mid-March. We did all the interviews and other b-roll filming in a weeks' time. I had selected over a dozen individuals from different parts of my life to be interviewed, Adele included. I spent the most amount of time in front of the camera as the main character. I was asked questions on not only the job, but my childhood, family dynamics, and true sexual identity. At first none of this seemed to phase me. I was doing what needed to be done. After a day of filming was over, however, I found myself having angry outbursts. Anger that was rooted in a younger time within a younger mind. After a fallout with Adele, fueled by blind rage, we realized I needed to pay more attention to what was happening inside of me. More specifically, I needed to look into what was happening when I told my story in a public way.

As odd as it sounds, there was a sense of betrayal deep inside me every time I spoke about my life. A betrayal that felt like I hadn't asked for permission to be saying to people what I was either on stage, on a podcast, and now in front of a camera for a movie. A permission rooted in the trauma itself which was causing a bit of a mind fuck when I gave it any attention.

Telling my story in whatever format had almost always provided a cathartic long-term effect. However, every time I did, there was an inner voice that was upset that these "other parts" weren't asked permission to do so. The unspoken and likely unknown part about being a motivational speaker and telling others the deepest, darkest parts of your life, is that you have to go back to some of these events in order to deliver the power necessary to capture your audience. Inadvertently, while going back in time in my head, these younger parts of me, were being shaken up and not attended to after. Making this worse was my lack of including them in the decision-making process. It wasn't that they didn't want me to tell my story. They just wanted to be asked first.

Revealing this to my newest therapist, who was trauma focused, I was told it made complete sense. My childhood was forged in awful things happening to me without my permission. My innocence taken from me without a say. Being touched while not wanting to be. Being forced into situations not being able to say no to as a kid, created parts that eventually turned the adult version of me into a people pleaser. Never saying no, and not ever asking myself if I wanted to do what was either offered or demanded of me, strengthened this mindset. One I was now trying to break cold turkey.

What started as a "crazy" concept of having a condition in which I had several different identities, turned into further healing. Through this acknowledgment of these other parts of me I was beginning to feel more whole. More at peace. Most importantly, I was feeling more empowered. I began sharing more feelings with not only my wife, but Riley. I gave myself to those I loved in ways I never had in the past.

Over the years, whenever an uncomfortable feeling or emotion would arise deep inside me, I would cast it aside as something I needed to avoid. Now stronger and more confident, I was facing these uncomfortable and at times awkward feelings and sensations head on. Come to find out, all they were was love, happiness, fear, and sadness. Granted I had felt love several times throughout my life, but now I was getting the opportunity to feel a whole-hearted version. It filled me with hope, compassion, and a level of empathy unmatched at any other point in my life. Embracing all of this, I grew even closer to my wife and youngest daughter. I began to value the other relationships I had and felt optimistic at what life had in store for me, which was a breath of fresh air.

As 2022 pressed on through the summer heading towards fall, I was getting more and more speaking gigs at conferences around New England and the country. I was even able to orchestrate the creation of one at the New Hampshire Fire Academy, a goal I had dreamed of for the last few years. I was asked to be part of two more documentaries on first responder PTSD. Along with that came the opportunity to be filmed for several training videos on post traumatic growth and how to heal after a life of trauma.

Through my 21 years as a firefighter and EMT, I always told people I was completely fulfilled with my job and all it entailed. Inside, however, there was a void. An empty space that wasn't being satisfied, and often left me questioning whether I was doing what I was truly meant for or not. Now tackling the stigma on mental health from various angles as often as I was, I knew I was where I was supposed to be.

That is, as an advocate.

My work at the coaching business was not as satisfying and there was even a question of whether or not me and the owner had the same goals anymore. Come late fall, I changed positions, still remaining in management but doing no more sales, in hopes of reigniting my drive to continue in the business. Once 2023 kicked off, I knew that wasn't going to happen. What I was focused on and where I felt I was needed the most didn't line up with that of the business. So, for the second time in six years, I decided to resign from a job that was making me unhappy and causing me unnecessary stress.

The difference this time was I wasn't upset at myself. I knew who I was more than I ever had before. I knew what I needed to do to feel fulfilled. I knew what I wanted to change in the world. I also knew that I was in control of what needed to be done to achieve all of those things.

Being fearless is an oxymoron in my mind. There is no way to be free of fear. The only way to be anything close to the meaning of this word is to face all your fears and control your reaction while doing so. Something I was finally beginning to do at 44 years of age on a consistent basis. My biggest fear is loss. Seems like a broad category and in some ways it is, loss had come in many different forms throughout my life. Most of them I had no say in. What I now realized was what I had a say I was my reactions to these situations. Due to the astronomical amount of trauma and loss I had experienced, when I was faced with loss, I reacted the same no matter what end of the spectrum it was on.

After stepping away from the coaching business and subsequently losing a friend along with a job, I sat with what I was feeling inside. I embraced it. All of it. The pain, anguish, sadness, and even temptation to go and get it all back. I realized most of what I had experienced as a child, as terrifying and awful as it was, created an unwanted comfort zone of reactionary feelings and sensations within me. This comfort zone is where I ended up growing to operate in no matter what the loss was. As uncomfortable as it was to live in the feelings of a loss, it seemed more comfortable than trying to face it and heal. Something I was beginning to put an end to come the summer of 2023.

I felt unstoppable and full of hope. I was still having some really bad days. Adele and I were still having some heated fights. The difference now was I was facing this shit and controlling my reaction in a way I never had. I was growing more comfortable with being, well, uncomfortable. This discomfort was the best thing for not only me, but those around me. I grew stronger and more whole each and every time I refused to react in a negative way.

With my devotion to my psychological well-being came with it a increase in my physical health. Come September, I had lost 70 pounds. My back no longer hurt every day. I didn't lose my breath when I rolled over in bed at night. Even my sleep had improved, though I've yet to get more than a solid 5 hours at a time. I had better self-esteem. I smiled more. I laughed more. I enjoyed more of the little things.

I was finally living a happier life.

When I left the job in 2017 I thought my days of helping people was over. Throughout the 21 years I had worked in small towns and big cities. Seen the best and worst of society. I always thought of helping people as a hands on practice. Something I needed to see happen right in front of me to believe it was actually happening. Instant gratification. With all I've done and experienced as an advocate, I know I've helped more people than I ever did on the job. Something I hold onto each and every day.

Come then end of September, the documentary was ready to be released. We were fortunate enough to get a distributor to take the film and spread it across so many streaming apps to reach as many people as possible. Before that happened, we were able to orchestrate a local premiere and screening. As a fitting tribute to my life story and several of the others in the film, we did this at the high school I graduated from in Townsend.

With over 150 people in attendance including most of the cast and crew, members of several of the surrounding fire departments, family, friends and even some political figures, we shared with the world for the first time First Responders in Crisis. When it was over, Scot, Corey and I took the stage to answer the audiences questions and to tell how this movie came to be. During the film, Adele had to walk out due to the power of hearing parts of our story on the big screen. As we were wrapping up the questions, the love of my life appeared in the doorway of the school theater in the back. Riley beside her, smiles across both their faces. Walking down to them and making sure Adele was ok, I knelt down next to my youngest daughter.

"Do you want to come on stage with daddy?" I asked, not needing to wait long for her response as her head was already nodding yes.

Walking hand in hand, Riley came right out on stage showing no fear in the face of countless strangers. As I stared in awe, I felt the warmest smile begin to grow on my face, as a familiar hand grabbed mine. Adele had joined us. The three of us stood looking out at an audience that seemed to be captivated by our appearance. After my wife shared a few words from the perspective of a spouse, Corey brought the night to a close. With that every single person in that theater came to their feet and applauded. Some were crying, some were forcing half sad smiles, while most were nodding in approval of what they had just witnessed.

I lived most of my life not caring if I woke up the next morning.

Now I live each day looking forward to what the next morning will bring. The lights and sirens may be gone, but the ability to touch another human life doesn't need to be. Sometimes, it just takes telling your story to give someone else the ability to survive theirs.

This book may be at its end, but my journey is just beginning.

This is Traumatic Strength.

RESOURCES

Boulder Crest Foundation
www.bouldercrest.org
FHE (Shatterproof program for First Responders/Veterans)
www.FHEHealth.com
Firefighter Behavioral Health Alliance (FBHA)
www.ffbha.org
First Responder Therapy Dogs
www.firstrespondertherapydogs.org
Forge/VFR Health
www.forgehealth.com
Harbor of Grace
www.harborofgracerecovery.com
McLean's Hospital (LEADER Program for First Responders/Veterans)
www.mcleanhospital.org/treatment/leader
National Alliance on Mental Illness (NAMI)
www.nami.org
Recovery Centers of America
www.recoverycentersofamerica.com

ABOUT THE AUTHOR

Keith Hanks is a retired Firefighter and EMT that dedicated 21 years of his life to the service of others. He serviced his community as a training officer, certified educator, and field training officer. Keith worked both inner-city EMS as well as municipal fire. Like many in the first responder community the job has its cost. From childhood trauma and sexual abuse, traumatic calls, the tragic passing of his first wife, Keith has faced many trials and tragedies that resulted in self-harm, substance abuse, lies and multiple suicide attempts. After decades of damage Keith began to put the pieces of his life back together.

Keith was diagnosed with Complex PTSD in 2015. The job, the service, his dedication caused this injury, and consequently his retirement. What PTS didn't change was the love and devotion to his community and to his fellow first responders. Keith has since dedicated his life to advocating for mental illness, substance and alcohol abuse recovery, and suicide awareness. Since starting this mission Keith built an international support group through Facebook for First Responders and Veterans for PTSI and other job-related mental health issues. Keith was asked to be a part of the Deconstructing Stigma Project and has a Billboard that hangs in the International Terminal at Logan Airport in Boston MA, along with the Manchester Regional Airport. In March 2022 he completed the filming of his 1st feature length documentary focusing on PTSD in the first responder community and has since been featured in two other related documentaries. Keith is a international speaker/podcast personality, and published author. He is a contributing author at Fire Engineering, Firefighter Nation, and The Volunteer Firefighter magazines/forums. He also wrote a featured chapter in the ongoing Amazon best-selling series Scars to Stars Volume 3.

Keith's transparency in his own life has led him to share his story through social media and many other platforms to reach the most people he can. He is known for saying that his life goal is to reduce suicide in the first responder community through education, support resources and to make it OK to reach out for help. He resides in New Hampshire with his wife and is the proud father to three incredible children.